THINKING BIG

Copyright © 2021 Jim Blanchard

Great Plains Publications
1173 Wolseley Avenue
Winnipeg, MB R3G 1H1
www.greatplains.mb.ca

Great Plains Publications gratefully acknowledges the financial support provided for its publishing program by the Government of Canada through the Canada Book Fund; the Canada Council for the Arts; the Province of Manitoba through the Book Publishing Tax Credit and the Book Publisher Marketing Assistance Program; and the Manitoba Arts Council.

Design & Typography by Relish New Brand Experience
Printed in Canada by Friesens

LIBRARY AND ARCHIVES CANADA CATALOGUING IN PUBLICATION

Title: Thinking big : a history of the Winnipeg business community to the Second
   World War / Jim Blanchard
Names: Blanchard, Jim, 1948- author.
Identifiers: Canadiana (print) 20210119381 | Canadiana (ebook) 20210119411 |
   ISBN 9781773370583 (softcover) | ISBN 9781773370590 (ebook)
Subjects: LCSH: Winnipeg (Man.)—Commerce—History. | LCSH: Winnipeg (Man.)
   —Economic conditions.
Classification: LCC HF3230.W55 B53 2021 | DDC 381.097127/43—dc23

ENVIRONMENTAL BENEFITS STATEMENT

Great Plains Publications saved the following resources by printing the pages of this book on chlorine free paper made with 100% post-consumer waste.

TREES	WATER	ENERGY	SOLID WASTE	GREENHOUSE GASES
7	590	3	25	3,220
FULLY GROWN	GALLONS	MILLION BTUs	POUNDS	POUNDS

Environmental impact estimates were made using the Environmental Paper Network Paper Calculator 4.0. For more information visit www.papercalculator.org.

Canadä

FSC
www.fsc.org
MIX
Paper from
responsible sources
FSC® C016245

Thinking
BIG

A HISTORY OF THE WINNIPEG BUSINESS COMMUNITY TO THE SECOND WORLD WAR

Jim Blanchard

GREAT PLAINS
PUBLICATIONS

CONTENTS

THE FUR TRADE YEARS

The land occupied by the modern City of Winnipeg was once covered by the massive Laurentide glacial ice sheet, which receded and advanced several times over a period lasting thousands of years. The ice sheet finally melted during a period of climate warming between 9,500 and 5,000 years ago, completely disappearing 7,500 years ago. The meltwater created Lake Agassiz. Where Winnipeg now stands was the bottom of a lake that at its greatest extent covered most of modern Manitoba and extended into Ontario and North Dakota.

When the lake began to recede from the Winnipeg area and southeastern Manitoba emerged from the water, birds, animals, and people moved into the area. Archaeological work at the Forks Historic Site has revealed clear evidence of human beings camped in the area 3,000 years ago.[1] Archaeological evidence shows that people were living in the western parts of what is now Manitoba for millennia before that date. The junction of two navigable rivers was a natural place to meet, trade, feast and negotiate agreements, but what we now call the Red and Assiniboine Rivers did not always meet at the modern forks. The Assiniboine once emptied into Lake Manitoba. About 4,000 years ago it began to flow through a channel that joined the Red at the mouth of the modern Seine River. The Assiniboine eventually changed course again and began to flow into the Red at the Forks.[2]

The 80,490 artifacts found in archaeological digs at the Forks tell us quite a bit about the people camping there. The large number of fish bones indicate that people were catching, eating, and perhaps preserving fish from the rivers. The various projectile points present at the site show that people from at least three different cultural groups were likely camping in the area. The flint that the arrowheads and tools found at the site were made of came from North Dakota, eastern, western, and southwestern Manitoba as well as the Lake Superior area. The artifacts confirm that Indigenous people from different areas came together at the Forks in order to trade with one another.

Some of the artifacts were made from Knife River flint, a highly valued stone from an area on the modern border between North and South Dakota. It was used to make strong and durable projectile points, knives, axes and hide scrapers. Flint was widely used because of its hardness and the fact that it could be shaped by skilled "flint knappers" to produce high quality tools and weapons. Knife River flint blades and arrowheads were desirable trade goods for people who did not live near a source of good quality flint.

In pre-contact Indigenous cultures, as in all cultures, trade was a way for different groups of people to obtain tools and materials they did not otherwise have access to. To many ancient North American peoples, trade also had an important role in diplomacy and was part of the formalities used to seal treaties and agreements. That trading sessions between different Indigenous groups and, later, Indigenous and Europeans were accompanied by ceremonies, music and dancing testified to the importance of the activity.

Writer Niigaan Sinclair has described the movements of the Indigenous people who met at the Forks in more recent times.

> From the north many Cree travelled seasonally on Lake Winnipeg and south along the Red River to meet and trade with relatives. ...

From the west the Lakota, Dakota and Nakota travelled east along the Assiniboine River and, while sometimes conflicting with the Anishinaabeg and Cree, hunted bison along a migratory path and ended up here too…From the south the Anishinaabeg travelled up the Red River and joined with other communities to help birth the Selkirk Treaty of 1817, officially welcoming Europeans and eventually the Selkirk Settlers.[3]

Recently, elders have resurrected the ancient Cree names for the forks of the rivers. The area south of the junction of the Assiniboine and the Red is called Niizhoziibean and the area north of the Forks has the name Musogote'wi.

The Rise of the Hudson's Bay Company

For the Indigenous people of what is now Canada, trade was an important part of intercultural relations, and when Europeans began to visit the east coast to fish, the local population naturally began to trade furs with them. In return, Indigenous people secured iron tools, weapons, and cooking vessels. When Jacques Cartier visited the Atlantic coast in 1534, the local Mi'kmaq people invited the French to trade. He wrote that they "showed a marvellously great pleasure in possessing and obtaining iron wares and other commodities." He described the ceremonial acts that accompanied the trading, including "dancing and going through many ceremonies."[4] No doubt Cartier also felt a "marvellously great pleasure" in acquiring the valuable furs the local people brought to trade.

The fur trade had many negative aspects for the Indigenous populations that participated in it. Those trading furs with the Europeans slowly abandoned their usual ways of living, their foods and economy. Diseases like smallpox, much more lethal to the Indigenous population than to Europeans, brought great loss of life. Trade goods like rum disrupted communities.

By the late 1600s the French settlers along the St. Lawrence River had developed the fur trade with the hunters and trappers farther west around the Great Lakes. French coureurs des bois moved trade goods in their birchbark canoes over vast distances between Montreal and the remote northwest and carried furs back to New France.

As part of their colonial strategy, the French crown established fur trading companies and gave them monopolies over the trade. In 1663, Louis XIV declared French Canada a royal colony and thereafter all furs were to be sold to a Royal Agent. Often only low-quality furs were offered for sale to the Crown. The better furs were smuggled to the south by traders and sold in the Dutch and English colonies where they brought better prices.[5]

In the late 1600s, two adventurous fur traders from French Canada, Pierre-Esprit Radisson and his brother-in-law Médard des Groseilliers, had an enormous influence on the development of the fur industry. Radisson was born in France and came to Quebec as a child. He was captured by a group of Iroquois and adopted by them. As a result, he learned the language and way of life of people who were the enemies of the French.

After a number of adventures, Radisson and Groseilliers, in 1659/60, embarked on a trip to the west along Lake Superior. They wintered with groups of Huron and Ottawa people and were present at a "Great Feast of the Dead" attended by eighteen different Indigenous groups. They gathered useful information about the country and the rich populations of beaver and other fur bearers between Lake Superior and Hudson Bay. They realized Hudson Bay's potential as a deep-water route into the heart of fur country. They traded for furs and brought them back to Quebec, where they were confiscated by Royal officials.

Undeterred, they made their way to London and made contact with King Charles II and his court. Radisson and Groseilliers were successful in convincing English investors, including some of the courtiers of Charles II, to become shareholders in an expedition to

Hudson Bay. Charles gave them a charter granting a monopoly of the fur trade and declared the shareholders the "true and absolute lords and proprietors of the land draining into Hudson Bay." And so in the 1670s the Hudson's Bay Company (HBC) was born and the English began trading with Indigenous people at posts along the shores of the Bay. Their ships carried trade goods from Britain on the trip to the Bay and furs on the voyage home. London was the site of a great fur market where the Company's furs were auctioned.

The Company made many shareholders rich, but their monopoly proved difficult to enforce. As early as 1672, an expedition came overland from Quebec to challenge Charles II's charter and claim the Company's territory for Louis XIV. In 1697 a French ship commanded by Pierre Le Moyne d'Iberville defeated three Hudson's Bay Company ships at the mouth of the Hayes River at York Factory. As a result of this victory, the French controlled access to the Hudson Bay fur trade until the Treaty of Utrecht in 1713, after which France abandoned its claim. Traders from New France continued to trade for furs farther south however, arguing that the actual borders of the Hudson's Bay Company land grant were not clearly defined.

In the 1720s Pierre la Verendrye, a French-Canadian soldier, landowner, and fur trader became commandant of the French fur trading posts in the Great Lakes area and began to push westward, opening new posts to establish the French presence in what is now Manitoba and Saskatchewan. He was also searching for a river route to the west coast of North America and onward to China.

In September 1738, La Verendrye visited the forks of the Red and Assiniboine rivers, invited by two Cree chiefs who were camping there with their people. He stayed two days with the Cree, encouraging them to bring their furs to French traders in the south instead of to the Hudson's Bay Company posts. He then continued on his westward journey, visiting with the Mandan in what is now North Dakota before pursuing his search for a route to the western ocean and China.

A simple log structure named Fort Rouge was erected at the Forks in 1738 by Mr. de Louvière, one of La Verendrye's party. Its location is not known, but it may have been on the high north bank of the Assiniboine where it flows into the Red. It was the first known structure erected by Europeans in what is now Winnipeg. So the first structure of the European settlement that was to become Winnipeg was a business building. The post was not heavily used, and it fell into disrepair. It was finally abandoned in 1749.

When the French regime in Canada ended with the Treaty of Paris in 1763, English and Scots traders from other parts of British North America quickly settled in Montreal and, sometimes with local French partners, challenged the Hudson's Bay Company for control of the fur trade in the West. As historian Michael Bliss has written, they made "the old French system their base for bolder, tougher competition than the French had ever attempted."[6]

The area around the Forks now became an important hub for the Montreal traders in spite of being on land to which the rival Hudson's Bay Company laid claim.

For a century, the HBC had limited their activities to their trading posts along the shores of Hudson Bay. The Indigenous trappers and traders brought furs, often over great distances, to the posts. In the early 1760s HBC men had begun to warn their superiors in England of the threat posed by competition from the Montreal traders who were aggressively moving deep into the Northwest. As early as 1778 for example, the North West Company's Peter Pond crossed the Athabasca River and entered the last great untouched fur region.

After 1774, the Governor and Committee of the Company in London, alarmed by the losses they were experiencing, decided to move inland. They began by building Cumberland House on the Saskatchewan River and other inland posts followed.

At the Forks, the North West Company's Fort Gibraltar was in operation from 1810 to 1816. The fort was built under the direction of John Willis, a "bourgeois" or official of the Company, by local Métis men,[7] on the north bank of the Assiniboine on the high ground above the junction of the rivers. It was a central post handling the movement of trade goods and furs and a "focal point of the pemmican industry, with food supplies being brought here, stockpiled and then transported to the smaller posts."[8] The Partner's house was described as being "comfortable."

The Struggle to Control the Fur Trade

In 1812 Selkirk settlers began to arrive in the Forks area, travelling from Britain in Hudson's Bay Company ships. First Nations people had grown beans and corn in the area near Lockport before the arrival of Europeans. The Selkirk settlers were the first Europeans who came to the area with the intention of farming.

They soon found themselves at the centre of the conflict between the rival fur trading companies. They settled on land granted to their sponsor Lord Selkirk by the Hudson's Bay Company. Their lots stretched back from the east bank of the Red River north from what we now know as the Point Douglas area. Two years later, Fort Douglas was built by the settlers and Hudson's Bay Company employees 2.5 kilometers downstream from the North West Company's Fort Gibraltar at the Forks.

The North West Company opposed settlement in the area, believing it threatened the fur trade and, by driving the bison away, traders' food supplies. They attempted to push the settlers out. In 1815, when North West Company employees destroyed Fort Douglas, many Selkirk settlers left Red River for York Factory or for eastern Canada. In the winter of 1815-16 some of the settlers returned and rebuilt the fort. In the spring, some Hudson's Bay Company men and settlers took control of Fort Gibraltar, pulled down the walls and buildings and took the materials to Fort Douglas, burning what they did not use. The situation worsened when Miles Macdonell, the governor of Selkirk's colony, issued the Pemmican Proclamation, banning the export of food from Red River. This confirmed the North West Company's fears about their food supplies. Then Macdonell ordered the North West Company to leave, a demand he could not possibly enforce.

The North West Company's agent, Duncan Cameron, addressed the local Métis hunters who provided the Company with pemmican, saying:

> Macdonell is now determined not only to seize our pemmican but to drive us out of the Assiniboia district and consequently out of the Northwest. Hostilities will no doubt begin early spring...You must assist me in driving away the colony. If they are not drove away, the consequence will be that they will prevent you from hunting. They will starve your families, and they will put their feet in the neck of those that attempt to resist them. You can easily see how they mean to finish by what they have begun already.[9]

The aggressive language on both sides served to inflame the situation.

On June 19, 1816, a series of incidents and clashes finally culminated in bloodshed at Seven Oaks near Fort Douglas, when 25 Hudson's Bay employees and settlers confronted 61 North West Company buffalo hunters. About 21 of Macdonell's group, including the governor himself, were killed, along with one Métis hunter. Each side claimed self-defence, and a Canadian inquiry commission concluded that the incident was part of a private war between two rival companies and condemned both sides.

The struggle over control of the lucrative fur trade of the Northwest was finally settled in 1821 with the merger of the two companies. At this time, the British House of Commons extended the Company's monopoly to the entire Northwest. Never again would competition among the business community in Winnipeg result in open bloody warfare.

■

After the merger, the whole vast territory was reorganized under the Company's North American governor, for many years George Simpson. He had a great deal of influence, but the Governor and Council in London were the ultimate authority in the Company.

During the 1820s, the Hudson's Bay Company presence in the area around the Forks grew as its servants began to retire to the Red River Settlement, joining the Selkirk Settlers and Métis buffalo hunters on the long narrow river lots along the riverbanks. In 1832, construction began on Upper Fort Garry on the banks of the Assiniboine River near the site of Fort Gibraltar. This post would become the Hudson's Bay Company headquarters in the Northwest, conferring upon what would become Winnipeg an increased importance. By 1853 the stone fort had grown to twice its original size.

In 1836 the family of Lord Selkirk sold control of the Selkirk colony back to the Hudson's Bay Company so that, in addition to operating its fur trade enterprise, the HBC now became responsible for administering the Red River settlement.

The monopoly of the Hudson's Bay Company was renewed for 20 years in 1838, but it was increasingly difficult to enforce in the face of continuing challenges from trappers who gathered furs that should have been sold to the company and instead took them to American fur buyers at Pembina south of the border. From time to time the Hudson's Bay governor, George Simpson, and the local administration of the HBC attempted to cut off this trade in furs.

Free Traders

There were, however, a group of "free traders," men who operated outside the HBC monopoly but with its tacit approval. They could import goods and trade with trappers on the understanding that they would sell their furs to the HBC and no one else. They provided various services to the Company, such as growing feed for animals, carrying freight in their own York boats, and operating dry good businesses, grist mills and other such enterprises. They were, for the most part, tolerated, and the HBC carried their trade goods from Britain and items like tallow for export and sale back to Britain in Company ships. They charged the free traders a tax for all goods leaving the colony.

Two of the early independent traders were Andrew McDermot and his son-in-law A.G.B. Bannatyne. They were both former employees of the Hudson's Bay Company and when they completed their terms of employment, they began to trade for furs on their own account. They also operated as general merchants, selling dry goods, groceries, and other merchandise that the Company might not carry to the inhabitants of Red River.

Andrew McDermot was born in Ireland, a member of an old Irish family. His people, in spite of a proud lineage, were not wealthy and so could not send him to Europe to study as wealthy Catholic families sometimes did. Instead, he learned what he could from the so-called "hedge schools," small illegal schools where Catholic youths got their education, the Catholic Church being banned by law from operating schools in Ireland at the time. McDermot was originally hired by the Hudson's Bay Company to be a "writer," or record keeper, and in 1812 he sailed from Ireland for York Factory aboard the ship carrying some of the first Selkirk Settlers to Red River. They taught him some Scots Gaelic on the voyage, and he got to know some of the people who would one day be his customers.

He worked in various parts of the HBC domain until his contract expired in 1824. He decided to settle near the forks of the Assiniboine and Red Rivers. He spent time with the Métis buffalo hunters centered around Pembina, learning about the hunt and the animals that were so central to the lives of plains people. McDermot was also a friend of Governor George Simpson, the two men having first met in 1821. Simpson encouraged him to become an independent trader and for some time the two men were on good terms. Later, when Simpson moved to Montreal, they drifted apart.

Andrew McDermot acquired his own York boats to bring goods south from York Factory. He won contracts for freighting supplies for the HBC and he supplied Fort Garry, within sight of his Emerald Lodge farm on the bank of the Red River, with feed for horses and firewood. He also imported cattle from the United States. He gained title to land that was part of the Selkirk estate and he also had lots in St. James Parish, St. Charles Parish and in St. Boniface. He built water mills on Sturgeon Creek and Rowley's Creek. He had a windmill on his farm where his house and store were also located. It was there that he and his wife, Sarah McNab, raised 15 children. Sarah had Scottish, Cree, and Ojibway ancestors and she helped her husband learn the Indigenous languages that he needed to do his job with the Company and to later run his own enterprises.

The McDermot children married into many of the other independent trading families at Red River. Their daughter Annie, for example, married A.G.B. Bannatyne. The Bannatynes lived just north of Emerald Lodge in the 1850s and 1860s.

John Inkster was another example of a former Hudson's Bay employee who became an independent merchant. Like many Company men, he was born in the Orkneys. He came to Rupertsland in 1819 to work as a stonemason for the Company and he married in 1826. His wife was the daughter of the Chief Factor William Sinclair.

Inkster left the Company's employ in 1823 or 1824 and began farming on land that belonged to his uncle. He was a freighter and a general merchant, selling local produce, pemmican, shot and powder and many other things of use in the colony. His business led him to make contacts from St. Paul all the way to York Factory. The Hudson's Bay Company carried some of his trade goods in company ships.

He was one of the partners in a steam-powered flour mill built in the colony in 1856. The mill operated until 1860 when it was destroyed by fire. He also taught school, served as a magistrate, and was the auditor of public accounts and a member of the Council of Assiniboia. His home, Seven Oaks House, built between 1851 and 1853, still stands and is a museum.

A.G.B. Bannatyne was born in the Orkneys in 1829. When he was 14, he entered the service of the Hudson's Bay Company, following in the footsteps of his great-grandfather, grandfather, and uncle, all of whom had been employees of the Company. He worked in Sault Ste. Marie and in Red River until 1851, when he left the Company shortly before the end of his term of employment. He had to get permission to leave early because junior clerks were not allowed to marry and he was leaving to marry Annie McDermot.

Bannatyne became a free trader, and from time to time this led to conflicts with the Company. In 1856, in Norway House, the local chief factor, George Barnston, charged him with illegal trading. The case was heard in the House of Commons in London, where the matter went against the Company. The charges against Bannatyne were dropped with the approval of the Company administration in London.

In 1858, at the age of 29, Andrew Bannatyne opened a dry goods business on Post Office Street, now Lombard Avenue, where, in addition to selling merchandise, he continued to trade furs. He would be in business in this area for close to 20 years. His first stock of trade goods from Britain arrived aboard an HBC ship and was carried south in the Company's York Boats. Ten years later, he formed a partnership with Alexander Begg, a native of Quebec. They opened a store on Main Street. Bannatyne was truly a transitional figure, beginning his business career in the shadow of the Company and carrying on to become one of the first Main Street merchant retailers and wholesalers after Confederation.

There were other so-called "free traders" in the area. William Drever, like Bannatyne and McDermot, had worked for the Hudson's Bay Company. Born in Orkney, he came to York Factory in 1821. In 1839 he arrived in Red River and worked in both Upper and Lower Fort Garry. He married and had a family of six children.

After retiring in 1851, he opened a dry goods store within sight of Fort Garry on the Main Road, as Main Street was then called, just south of the Portage Road. This led to conflict with his neighbour Henry McKenney because his store blocked McKenney's view of Fort Garry to the south. So in the midst of literally thousands of square miles of empty prairie we see the first squabble between neighbours brought on due to overcrowding. Drever stayed in business until 1872 when he became ill. He died in 1887 at the age of 84.

Robert Logan was another early merchant. He was born in 1773 in Jamaica, where his father was a planter. During a slave rebellion their plantation was destroyed and the family decided to move to Montreal. Robert completed his schooling there and became a fluent French speaker. He went to work for the North West Company in 1801, and from 1806 to 1814 he was stationed in Sault Ste. Marie. In 1814 he began working for the Hudson's Bay Company and continued until 1819 when he became an independent trader in Red River.

In 1822 Governor George Simpson wrote that Logan was "the best settler about the place...has a little spirit of enterprise ... with command of a little money." In 1821 he was living on the east side of the Red River on a farm of 214 acres he had purchased from the Selkirk estate.

In 1825 Logan was able to purchase the remains of Fort Douglas, the former North West Company Fort, 100 additional acres on the west bank of the Red River and a windmill, all for £400. He used his windmill to grind grain for the farmers in the area, earning the customary 10% of the flour produced as his payment. Logan became a wholesale merchant, supplying the Company fur brigades with supplies for their trips.

Logan was involved in public life in Red River. He was made a justice of the peace and a magistrate. He was a member of the Council of Assiniboia, and in the 1840s he was chair of the Board of Works. He was married twice and had a total of 16 children, many of whom became involved in business in Winnipeg. He built a fine house on what is now George Street and lined the street with trees to break the monotony of the open prairie. He may, therefore, be considered the father of the great urban forest that still shades Winnipeg. He died in 1866 at the age of 103, just before the entry of Manitoba into Confederation.

John Higgins was, like Andrew McDermot, a native of Ireland. He came to Red River in the early 1860s, and began making his living as a peddler, carrying his wares about in a Red River cart. A man in his fifties, he was quite a bit older than most of the merchants who established businesses in the early years, but by 1865 he had amassed enough capital to build a general store on Main Street. He had a number of partners over the years and in 1865 he went into partnership with W.H. Lyon. In 1873, with partner David Young, he built a three-storey brick building on Main Street to house their dry goods business. Alexander Begg called it a "handsome store…one of the finest buildings in Winnipeg."[10]

W.H. Lyon was an American who arrived in Red River from the United States in 1859 "with only a red shirt on his back" as he often said later. His appearance did not inspire much confidence and when he asked for credit in Andrew Bannatyne's store, the merchant was dubious about extending it. But Lyon's obituary said that by "pluck and perseverance and good business tact" he became a success. This particular phrase was often used to describe successful businesspeople at the time. Interestingly, it emphasizes hard work and tact over other virtues like good business judgement and skill or aggressive salesmanship. It may be that in the small community of Winnipeg, tact really was of paramount importance.

Lyon secured a loan from a Mr. Paul in St. Boniface and succeeded in "scraping together a little money by trading with the Indians."[11] As mentioned, he became a partner of John Higgins, and in 1869 he established his own business, renting space in one of Andrew McDermot's log buildings. He then built a wood-frame store at McDermot and Main from which he sold dry goods. He rented out the rooms on the second floor, joining the many other building owners who became landlords. Like other merchants, he made semi-annual trips to St. Paul to replenish his sales stock. These Winnipeg traders travelled to St. Paul in Red River carts, which were gradually being replaced with flat-bottom boats and river steamers that made the trip down river to Winnipeg.

In 1875 Lyon sold his dry goods stock to A.H. Bertrand and began to specialize in groceries. This was followed in 1879 by the decision to sell wholesale groceries. He sold his store on Main to R.J. Whitla for $19,000, an enormous sum, roughly the equivalent of $228,000 in modern money. He then began building a three-storey wholesale warehouse at McDermot and Albert. This structure was later incorporated into the Bate Building, which still stands on the same corner. In 1880 he became a partner in the wholesale grocery firm of Lyon, Mackenzie and Powis. W.H. Lyon was one of the founders of the Winnipeg Board of Trade and, in 1881, of the Winnipeg and Western Transportation Company that operated steamboats. In 1883 Lyon left Winnipeg after 24 years and went to live in Salt Lake City, where he died in 1897.

■

From time to time the Company changed its policy of non-intervention and attempted to enforce its monopoly on the fur trade, but there was realistically no way to do this, there being no permanent police or military forces in the colony. Nonetheless, the ability of the free traders to carry on their business was sometimes curtailed.

In the 1840s the Hudson's Bay Company governor, Alexander Christie, decided to enforce the Company's monopoly and set out to stop the free traders. Christie was concerned about the increasing contact with American traders from St. Paul and about Norman Kittson's fur trade post, where free traders and trappers could acquire trade goods from St. Paul and sell their furs for good prices. Kittson had set up a fur trade post at Pembina on the American side of the border in 1844 and was a major buyer of furs from Métis and other trappers from Red River, providing them with an alternative market. Kittson was born in Quebec in 1814 and had worked for the American Fur Trade Company in the United States. In 1843, at the age of just 29, he became a partner in the company. At first, he was their agent at Pembina and then he became an independent trader. In 1854 he moved to St. Paul and began a successful business career. He was elected mayor of the city in 1858-59 and soon became involved in the steamboat business.

Christie targeted free traders Andrew McDermot and his partner, James Sinclair, both former Company employees. He was convinced they were trading with the Americans. Christie cancelled their freighting contracts with the HBC and refused to carry their trade goods on Company ships. They fought back. Sinclair travelled to London carrying a petition complaining to the London Board of the Company about Christie's actions. Alexander Isbister, a Métis man born in the Northwest who had gone to London to live and practise law, helped Sinclair get the petition into the hands of Members of Parliament. But the British House took no action. Andrew McDermot, who had been a member of the Council of Assiniboia, the HBC-appointed governing body of the colony since 1839, eventually resigned in protest against Christie's actions.

In 1849, the Hudson's Bay Company efforts to protect its monopoly resulted in several Métis traders, including Guillaume Sayer, being charged with illegally selling furs to the Americans instead of the HBC. Most were released, but Sayer stood trial in the Company's small courthouse at Upper Fort Garry. On the day of the trial, May 17, 1849, around 300 Métis men surrounded the building. Louis Riel senior, Father Georges Belcourt, and James Sinclair were allowed in to support Sayer. Sinclair participated in the selection of the jury and managed to eliminate many potential jurors who he thought would not be sympathetic to his friend.

Sayer's defence was that he thought he had permission to trade furs. The jury found him guilty but recommended clemency. No sentence was passed by the court after the verdict was heard. The assembled Métis shouted "Vive la liberté" and "le commerce est libre" and fired their guns in the air to celebrate what they saw as a great victory.[12]

This failure to punish Sayer "effectively opened the trade of Southern Rupert's Land to many small-scale competitors."[13] A growing number of independent operators began to do business in Company territory and those that lived in the area that became Winnipeg laid the foundations of the city's retail and wholesale sectors. McDermot regained his freighting contracts and the use of the Company's ships. He again became a member of the Council, only to resign once more, claiming that his business affairs did not leave time for Council work.

∎

The free traders bridged the gap between an economy dominated by a chartered company, one that was in possession of a monopoly on trade, and a new economy based on the activities of a large number of independent entrepreneurs. Some, like A.G.B. Bannatyne, who were active before Confederation, continued to be prominent businessmen in the new city of Winnipeg. These men lived close together and had similar backgrounds and business interests. They were later active members of the Board of Trade through which they were able to influence the growth of Winnipeg by securing a railway bridge for the Canadian Pacific Railway (CPR) in the city as well as CPR yards and repair shops. They took on the mighty Hudson's Bay Company, and built, in pre-Confederation Red River, the foundations of the powerful business community of later years in Winnipeg.

St. Paul Connections

When the HBC headquarters moved to Upper Fort Garry, more and more shipping and travel began to move south through St. Paul instead of through York Factory on Hudson Bay. The first regular connections to St. Paul were made by the cart brigades in the 1840s and 1850s. The famous Red River cart was widely used in the Northwest, a vast region without roads or bridges, or blacksmiths or sources of iron parts. The two-wheeled carts were mentioned as early as 1800 in the diary of Alexander Henry the younger.

A partner in the North West Company, Henry was a widely travelled fur trader, explorer, and diarist. He described a cart with wheels made of slabs of wood three feet in diameter. Henry appears to have made improvements to the cart's design, substituting larger spoked wheels that were dished and had various diameters. Many other individual owners of the carts made small modifications over the years.

The Métis buffalo hunters of Red River took the two-wheeled carts along to transport supplies for their large buffalo hunts and to transport meat and hides home at the end of the hunt. The Hudson's Bay Company employed as many as 300 carts each year to carry furs and trade goods west from Red River to Edmonton. The carts were also used to carry furs, buffalo hides and other goods from Red River for sale in St. Paul, and to bring back trade goods on the return journey.

Each cart could carry from 270 to 360 kilograms of freight. They were made of local wood and held together by wooden pegs. The simple design and use of easily found woods made the carts excellent vehicles for long journeys through rough country. The wheels were sometimes wrapped with a rim of buffalo hide that had been wetted. As it dried it shrank and formed a tight fit. No grease was used on the wheels and axles because the dust would soon mix with the lubricant and stop the wheels from turning. As a result, the cart trains sent up a deafening racket as they moved over the prairie.

The first trains of freight carts went to St. Paul in the 1840s and consisted of only a few vehicles. The size of the cart trains grew over the years: in 1851, 102 carts travelled south; in 1858, 600 carts made the journey; and in 1869 there were 2,500 carts. The arrival of first the riverboat service and then the railway in 1878 largely replaced the cart trains, and by 1900 Red River carts were a quaint curiosity.

Working on the cart trains was an important source of employment in Red River. Métis men were often hired as expert teamsters. Some Métis entrepreneurs became independent freighters. James McKay was one of these men. He was born at Edmonton House in 1828, the son of a Scottish-born Hudson's Bay Company boatman and guide, and his wife, whose mother and perhaps father were Indigenous. The family moved to Red River when James was 12 and his father retired from the Company. James was educated in Red

River and his mother taught him several Indigenous languages; he was fluent in both Cree and Ojibwa.

James, or Jemmie as he was called, worked for the Hudson's Bay Company from 1853 to 1860, managing several small trading posts and acting as a guide and interpreter for Company officials like Sir George Simpson. He established his own business when he left the employ of the HBC. He worked as a trader, a freighter and organizer of cart trains to St. Paul, as well as a postmaster and supervisor of road construction. He was a memorable figure, in his later years weighing over 300 pounds and, although short, immensely strong. We have a description of McKay in 1859, by Martin Marble, a writer for *Harper's Magazine* who met him on the trail when McKay was leading a cart train from Red River to St. Paul:

> Presently we saw, galloping ahead of the train, a young smart. The rider, young McKay, who was captain of the train, sat his horse finely. His clear bronzed face was set off by a jaunty cap. He wore a checked flannel shirt, and each shoulder bore its fancy wampum bead belt, that suspended the powder horn and shot pouch. He had upon his feet moccasins worked with beads and quills, and carried in hand a short-handled riding-whip with a long, thick last of buffalo hide ...[14]

In 1859 James married Margaret Rowan, the daughter of a Hudson's Bay Company chief factor, and he built a beautiful house at Deer Lodge, where the Winnipeg hospital is now located. This house was the headquarters of his business and also a place where he and his wife often entertained.

He acted as a guide and translator for the Palliser Expedition during their journey from Fort Ellice to Fort Carlton. In the 1870s he travelled with the Treaty Commissioners who settled Treaties 1, 2, 3, 5, and 6 between 1871 and 1876, acting as both negotiator and interpreter. His knowledge of Indigenous languages and his understanding of Indigenous culture and expectations were important supports for the government negotiators.

He was appointed to the Council of Assiniboia in 1868 and served briefly as a Councillor in Riel's provisional government. He went to the United States to avoid having to choose between his Métis friends and the new Canadian regime.

After Confederation, Lieutenant Governor Archibald appointed him to the Legislative Council, similar to a senate, of the new province of Manitoba. He was a member until it was abolished in 1876, serving as Speaker for a time. He was also appointed to Archibald's executive council and sat on the Council of the Northwest Territories from 1873 to 1875. He was elected as the MLA for Lake Manitoba in 1877 and served as the provincial Minister of Agriculture until his death in 1879.

McKay encouraged the development of agriculture and immigration, being at the same time willing to help with the issues of the Métis and Indigenous people in his area. His tact and good judgement were badly needed and helped smooth the way during the transition from fur trade area to Canadian province.

■

American interest in the Red River colony continued to develop in the 1850s. St. Paul was incorporated as a city in 1854 and at the end of the decade, it became the capital of the new state of Minnesota. The ambitious new city was eager to develop the vast territory that would become its hinterland. In the minds of St. Paul merchants this included the Red River Colony.

The growth of the American transportation network strengthened the connection between St. Paul and Red River. In 1852 the railway reached the Mississippi at Rock Island, Illinois and steamboats were able to bring freight from the rail head upriver to St. Paul. This improvement in transportation led to a steady expansion of trade between Red River and St. Paul. By 1856 imports from St. Paul constituted nearly half of all goods brought to Red River and 4/5 of the furs shipped out of St. Paul came from the north.

George Simpson, Governor of the Hudson's Bay Company, became interested in using the St. Paul route to move the Company's freight into and out of the Northwest, replacing the expensive and arduous York boat route from York Factory down the rivers and Lake Winnipeg to Fort Garry. In 1857 Simpson's agent Ramsay Crooks negotiated an agreement with the American Treasury Department that allowed Company freight to pass, sealed, bonded and duty free, from New York through US territory and St. Paul and on to Fort Garry.

The next year, a test shipment of 40 tons of freight was sent from London to New York and then to St. Paul by train and steamboat and by Red River cart train to Fort Garry. St. Paul commission agents J.C. and H.C. Burbank supervised the shipment. A second shipment, of 150 tons, was sent in 1859 from London via Montreal to St. Paul. It was calculated that this method was 35 to 40% cheaper than sending goods through York Factory. Simpson suggested carts be used to take the shipment to Breckenridge on the Red River and that a steamer be launched on the Red to take the goods the rest of the way to Fort Garry.

The St. Paul Chamber of Commerce, responding to Simpson and interested in spreading their city's trade into the Northwest, offered a $2000 prize to hotel owner Anson Northup to build a steamboat to sail on the Red River north to Fort Garry. During the winter of 1858-1859, Northup hauled the machinery from his own boat, the *North Star*, from the Mississippi across country to Lafayette on the Red River. The boiler alone weighed five and one-half tons. It took 17 teams of horses, 13 yokes of oxen and 30 men to move the equipment.

The new boat's hull was built beside the Red River in Lafayette and the steamer was completed and launched with the name *Anson Northup*. The builder took his $2000 prize and captained the boat on its first trip. His ambition was to monopolize freighting on the river and charge high rates. This was to become a common ambition for steamboat operators on the Red, but the river was full of sandbars which made the trip a hard struggle. In June 1859, the *Anson Northup* arrived in Fort Garry, making it the first steamboat to make the journey to Red River. This opening of river traffic from the south put the American annexationists in a stronger position.

The *Anson Northup* proved hard to handle—she had a way of heading unexpectedly for the riverbank. The wheelhouse was on the hurricane deck, the coolest place on board. The second deck had four enclosed staterooms and a large cabin with 24 single berths separated by curtains. Because the chimneys passed through this cabin, it was stiflingly hot.

Simpson refused to pay *Northup's* high rates and began instead to use flat boats to ship goods downriver. Northup's business failed and he lost the boat. Simpson quietly suggested that the St. Paul firm J.C. Burbank and Company operate the *Anson Northup* with the HBC as a silent partner. This would avoid the law that prohibited foreigners from owning boats operating in the US waters. Burbank and Company signed a contract to carry 500 tons of freight annually for the Hudson's Bay Company from St. Paul to Fort Garry. Freight went at first from St. Paul where the railway now ended, then by cart to Georgetown on the Red River, and then by boat to Fort Garry. Georgetown was a Hudson's Bay Company post built by Simpson. It had dormitories, a sawmill and gristmill, and warehouses serving the company's freighting activities.

Trips to Red River were intermittent because of low water and the animosity of the local Indigenous people, who wanted compensation for the boat's use of the river and the excessive consumption of scarce firewood that they argued was theirs. The boat's splashing paddlewheel also disturbed the fish in the river.

In the winter of 1861-1862 the boat, now called *Pioneer*, was tied up for the season at Cook's Creek, below Fort Garry. When the water level dropped suddenly, the lines securing the vessel to the riverbank tightened and pulled the boat sideways. It rolled over and slowly sank in nine feet of water, never to sail again.

The Burbanks replaced the *Anson Northup* with the *International*, built at Georgetown for a cost of $20,000. It was 137 feet long and 26 feet wide and proved too big to maneuver easily in the narrow upstream reaches of the Red River. (The Red is 500 to 1000 feet wide in Winnipeg.) The *International* first arrived at Fort Garry on May 26, 1862. It was out of service for most of the year because of low water and worry about the opposition of the local Indigenous people. People in Red River were also unhappy, complaining that all the profits from the shipment of freight were flowing to the Burbanks.

After the establishment of Manitoba in 1870, the freight business picked up. There was now more certainty about what would happen in the area and businessmen predicted Confederation would mean there would be an influx of immigrants needing a way to get to Manitoba.

In 1872 the Northern Pacific Railway reached Moorhead on the Red River, so it was no longer necessary to use carts to bring goods overland from St. Paul. In St. Paul, interest in the Red River colony continued and a group of businessmen including James J. Hill and Theodore Griggs formed a company that put a new steamer, the *Selkirk*, on the river to compete with the *International*. They then eliminated competition from the *International* altogether by securing a change in the US regulations so that unbonded carriers were blocked from hauling freight from the US to Canada. The *Selkirk* happened to be the only bonded steamship available. With the *International* out of the way, Hill and Griggs raised the rate for carrying a hundred pounds of goods from $2.80 to $4.00. Hill and Griggs had a third partner in their company: Norman Kittson.

In 1858-1859 Norman Kittson had begun operating a steamboat that brought people and freight to Red River. Governor Simpson thought highly of Kittson, and in 1862 he appointed him the Hudson Bay Company's shipping agent at St. Paul and Georgetown, Minnesota. In this role Kittson "coordinated the importing of trade goods from England, and the exporting of furs between Red River, Georgetown and St. Paul by Red River cart and on the Company's steamboat *International.*"[15] Red River carts continued to be used because there were often difficulties navigating the Red with its shallows and sandbars.

Kittson abandoned the HBC in 1872 and joined Hill and Griggs to establish the Red River Transportation Company, investing $75,000 in the new venture. The new company proceeded to add eight new boats to their fleet and successfully dominated transport on the Red River. Red River Transportation continued to charge high rates. The Winnipeg Board of Trade complained that $750,000 was paid to the company by 1873 for moving 40 million pounds of freight.

A Winnipeg company, the Merchant's International Steamship Line, was formed in 1874 to offer some competition, but because it was foreign owned, it was blocked from operating in US waters. The company, therefore, took in some St. Paul board members. The Merchant's International placed two boats on the river, the *Manitoba* and the *Minnesota*, and freight rates dropped. In 1875 the Red River Transportation Company moved to once more eliminate competition. In June, the *Manitoba* was rammed amidships by the *International* and sank. The Merchant's line sued Red River Transportation for $50,000 and the *Manitoba* was raised and repaired. By fall of the same year, however, both the *Manitoba* and the *Minnesota* were seized because the Merchant's Line was bankrupt. Freight rates immediately went back up. It is thought that the American shareholders of the Merchant's line made overtures to Kittson, who took over the company, paying the American shareholders in Red River shares. The Canadian shareholders got nothing. In the spring of 1876, the Merchant's line was sued by its creditors, who received 75 cents on the dollar in the final settlement.

The steamboat business had been profitable for the St. Paul owners. The *Selkirk*, one of the Red River company's freighters, paid for itself on its first trip and on a subsequent trip this boat cleared a $30,000 profit. Freight rates fluctuated over the years from a high of $5 per hundred pounds to a low of $2 in 1875, when the Merchant's Line offered competition for a short time. Passenger rates varied depending on the boat and whether people were travelling first or second class. In 1860 it cost $35 to travel from St. Paul to Fort Garry. In 1872 a first-class ticket cost $22 and second class was $17. The high rates were a topic in Ontario newspapers and may have discouraged some potential settlers from coming to Manitoba. They were used as an argument in favour of the CPR which, of course, would also be attacked for charging sky-high rates.

The St. Paul, Minneapolis, and Manitoba Railway, linking Emerson to St. Boniface was in the last phases of construction in 1878. Steamboats carried equipment and supplies for the railway builders. The *Selkirk* alone carried a total of 14,000 tons of steel rails, enough to build 16 miles of track. The steam engine Countess of Dufferin was brought to Winnipeg in a flatboat towed by steamer. The last spike on the railway was driven December 3, 1878. With the beginning of rail service there was no longer a need for riverboats on the Red, although some boats did continue to operate for a time on the river and on rivers farther to the west.

In 1878, the year the railway reached Winnipeg, the Winnipeg and Western Transportation Company was founded. It was yet another Winnipeg organization that attempted to gain control of some of the riverboat business being monopolized by Red River Transportation. The interim directors named at the beginning of the company's life were Winnipeggers W.H. Lyon, the successful wholesale merchant; lawyer Sedley Blanchard; and E.V. Holcombe, a steamboat captain from St. Paul. Two Montrealers, John Turnbull, a merchant, and Charles Black, an accountant, were listed. Turnbull was involved in business enterprises with George Stephen, one of the founders of the CPR, and may have been involved in raising the capital for the business. A.G.B. Bannatyne and James Ashdown were also board members of the company.

The company began life hauling freight between Winnipeg and western points on the Assiniboine like Brandon and Fort Ellice that were not yet served by the CPR. Even after the railway reached Brandon in 1882, there was still work for the steamboats carrying freight to Fort Ellice and country into which the railway had not yet penetrated. Later in the 1880s Western Transportation moved its operations to the Saskatchewan River, carrying freight and passengers from Grand Rapids on Lake Winnipeg up the river to Prince Albert, Battleford and Edmonton. Many of the captains employed, like Captain John B. Davis of Rock Island, Illinois, were men who had years of experience on the Mississippi. By the 1890s the railway had been extended to all the territory served by the company and in 1898 advertisements appeared in the papers offering three of its river steamers for sale. The *Marquis*, the *Northwestern* and the *Northcote* were all grounded at different locations on the banks of the North Saskatchewan, sad monuments to an industry whose time on prairie rivers was past.

Prelude to Confederation

Interest in the Red River settlement had grown in Upper Canada during the 1850s. The establishment of free trade in Great Britain in the 1840s opened a vast new market for imported wheat. Therefore, Upper Canadians began to claim that the Northwest country held by the Hudson Bay Company was Canada's by right of "discovery and settlement," correctly predicting that the area would become a great producer of wheat for export. Some Canadian politicians, including Sir John A. Macdonald, were in the early stages of thinking about uniting all of British North America, including the northwest.

A group of Upper Canadians, which included John McLean, newspaper editor George Brown, William Dawson and his brothers Aeneas and Simeon, Captain Kennedy, and William McDougal, began lobbying for the annexation of the Northwest to Upper Canada. In 1857, the British House of Commons, aware that the Americans were settling the territories directly to the south, initiated an inquiry into the Red River district.

In the same year, two scientific expeditions made their way into the northwest to take a closer look. One of the expeditions, led by John Palliser, set out to explore the country along the border with the United States, through the mountains to the Pacific coast. It was sponsored by the British Royal Geographical Society and paid for with a £5,000 grant from the Colonial Office. The British government assigned Palliser the additional tasks of examining the old North West Company canoe route from the Great Lakes to Lake Winnipeg as well as the country south of the Saskatchewan River. Palliser and his colleagues travelled to the west by way of New York, the Great Lakes and by canoe to Lake Winnipeg. They were in the West from 1857 to 1860 and produced three reports describing such things as the mineral wealth, potential for farming and settlement, the weather, the inhabitants, and the astronomy of the area.

A Canadian expedition led by George Gladman in 1857 and 1858 travelled west from Toronto. The engineer Simeon Dawson and Henry Youle Hind, a chemist and geologist from University of Toronto, accompanied him, along with a party of 40 others. Simeon Dawson surveyed a route for a road from Lake of the Woods to Red River on this trip. While the Dawson Road would not be built for some time, it encouraged the idea that the Northwest was not as difficult to reach as had been thought.

The Canadians also made their way through the Great Lakes by steamer and then by canoe to Red River. They explored a number of western river valleys and their resulting reports joined those of Palliser in presenting a vast amount of new information about the Northwest to the outside world. Like Palliser, the Canadians were interested in establishing whether the country could support settlers and agriculture.

Many of the things these scientific groups "discovered" and wrote about in their reports had been known by Indigenous people for thousands of years and by Hudson Bay Company employees for a century or more. The Hudson Bay Company, for whom settlers were a nuisance that interfered with the smooth working of their industry, had given out very little information and typically portrayed their vast fur trade empire as being uninhabitable and unsuited for agriculture. The publications of these expeditions served to encourage Upper Canadians to see the Northwest as a potentially rich colony to be exploited and populated by settlers from the east.

■

In the 1850s Red River also began to attract more attention from its southern neighbour. In 1851 two Americans, W. Lesley Bond and Alexander Ramsay, the governor of Minnesota Territory, visited Red River. Ramsay was impressed with the small prosperous-looking farms that lined the riverbanks and with the abundant crops of grain produced in the area. For the next two decades, Ramsay was a promoter of the idea of annexing Red River to the US. In the years before the Northwest became part of Canada in 1870, a number of other Americans crossed the border and took up residence in what would be the Winnipeg area. As historian J.M. Bumsted has written, the local population followed the well-known American pattern: "Soon an American population would creep north of the border, demanding the rights of Americans, and Manifest Destiny would claim more British territory."[16]

One of these Americans was actually born in Canada. Henry McKenney arrived in Red River on the steamboat *Anson Northup* on its first trip from the south in 1859. McKenney was born in Amherstburg, Ontario, across the river from Detroit, and had briefly operated a general store with his brother in Minnesota. Shortly after his arrival, McKenney purchased a log building from Andrew McDermot and converted part of it into the Royal Hotel, the first hotel in what would become Winnipeg. He soon opened a general store on the premises and began exchanging trade goods for furs and pemmican. The next year he sold the hotel to "Dutch George" Emmerling, another American, and then went into business under the name McKenney and Company. He moved to a strategic location just south of the hotel he had owned on the Main Road. He opened a general store on a lot that he calculated would one day be the junction of the Main Road, later Main Street, and the Portage la Prairie Road, later Portage Avenue. The lot was in a corner of a much larger river lot belonging to Andrew McDermot. McKenney paid McDermot £110 for the lot, £60 in cash with a promise to pay the rest in five years at 6% interest. When McKenney left Winnipeg for good in 1870 he still owed McDermot the £50 and interest.[17]

Old hands criticized his choice of location because it was in a low spot that often flooded in the spring. They joked that the building looked like Noah's Ark and that was appropriate because come spring it might well float away. But he had the last laugh when the location he chose did in fact become the northwest corner of Portage and Main, although he did not stay in Winnipeg long enough to benefit from his good judgement. Property in the area began to increase in value once his store opened.

McKenney almost immediately acquired a neighbour to the south with whom he feuded for some time. William Drever, one of the retired Hudson's Bay Company men who had gone into business on his own, built a large building south of McKenney's store on a narrow river lot.

The two store owners feuded over many things, but their main concern was whether the trail to the west, later Portage Avenue, would pass on the south side of Drever's building or between the two rival stores. The latter option would place McKenney on the future intersection of the two roads, where he had planned to be. Because of such friction over properties, the Council of Assiniboia began to pay attention to surveying the streets to ensure that none of the stores beginning to rise in the area would end up in the middle of a thoroughfare. This, however, is exactly what happened to Drever. The route of the Portage trail was established to run through his building.

To accommodate him, Portage Avenue was narrowed and surveyed at a width of 66 feet rather than 132 feet, the width of Main Street. Drever's property was bypassed, but in 1883 the City decided that Portage Avenue should assume its full 132-foot width. The Board of Trade became involved by passing a motion supporting a petition by ratepayers calling for the immediate demolition of a cluster of dilapidated buildings blocking Portage at its corner with Main Street. The petition said that the buildings "besides being an eyesore to the citizens are also detrimental to building progress in that quarter and a source of danger as regards fire." The property, by then owned by H.S. Donaldson, was sold to the city for $35,000; the buildings were demolished, and Portage and Main assumed its final dimensions.

McKenney also built a sawmill on the shore of Lake Winnipeg on the Manigatogan River, but it was not a success, partly because the boat he chose to haul lumber back to Winnipeg had too deep a draft to successfully navigate the Red.

McKenney held some official posts. On 8 June 1861, he had been appointed petty magistrate of the Middle District of Assiniboia. His interest in the law was manifested in his near constant litigation, bringing cases before the Quarterly Court of Assiniboia no less than 30 times between 1860 and 1869. In 1868 he became Sheriff of Assiniboia and Governor of the Gaol. This was an appointment that continued under Riel's Provisional Government.

In 1870, when it became clear that Red River would not be annexed to the United States as he had hoped, McKenney left the country. Two of his sons continued to operate his Winnipeg store, which was demolished in 1887. He held public office as sheriff of Pembina in North Dakota, and he set up a sawmill there that was more successful than his attempt on Lake Winnipeg. Between 1874 and 1877 he lived in Winnipeg again before returning for good to the US, where he is thought to have died around 1886.

BECOMING THE FIFTH PROVINCE

In 1870, with the passage of the Manitoba Act, the Red River settlement and all of the other lands previously held by the Hudson Bay Company officially became part of the Dominion of Canada. Huge changes took place to prepare the Northwest, including Manitoba, for its transition. There had been many opinions about what should happen to Rupertsland. Some people wanted to see it annexed to the United States and there was a group that wanted it to become a crown colony. The British Colonial Secretary, Edward Cardwell, did not favor that idea, but felt that continued rule by the Hudson Bay Company blocked progress and left the area vulnerable to American annexation. He asked the government of Upper Canada if it would be willing to take over administration of the area.

At the 1864 Quebec Conference, one of the meetings that eventually resulted in Canadian Confederation, the possibility of acquiring both Rupert's Land and British Columbia, thus extending the proposed new country from sea to sea, was on the agenda. Delegates from Upper Canada strongly favored this expansion of the proposed new country by means of the largest land acquisition in Canadian history.

In 1868 the British parliament passed the Rupert's Land Act, transferring all the Hudson Bay Company lands to the new Dominion of Canada, leaving the terms to be worked out later. The Company received £300,000, a block of land adjoining each of their posts (a total of 50,000 acres) and 1/20th of the land in the fertile belt. In return it surrendered its 200-year-old charter to Canada, gave up its monopoly trading rights, and abandoned its legal jurisdiction over the 3.8 milllion square kilometers. The Company maintained the right to carry on its business in the area. The deed of surrender stated that the rule of Canadian law would extend to the fertile belt, that is the land bounded by the Rockies in the west, the US border to the south and the North Saskatchewan River in the north, and Lake Winnipeg and Lake of the Woods in the east. Never in history had a country acquired such vast territories in such a seemingly painless manner. But, as would soon become clear, not everyone was in favor of the change or the way it was being managed.

Louis Riel and the Red River Resistance

In fact, the government that took over jurisdiction of the Red River colony portion of the Hudson Bay Company's territory was not, as planned, the Canadian government at all but a provisional government headed by Métis leader Louis Riel, a 25-year-old without previous political experience who belonged to a family of community leaders. Riel emerged out of the turmoil created by the transfer as a champion of Métis interests and to some extent the interests of the broader community of Red River. The issue, as he saw it, was that the transfer to Canada had been arranged without consulting the local residents. The French and English Métis constituted the largest population group in 1870 in Manitoba.

The prospective lieutenant governor of the Northwest, William MacDougal, provided Riel with a way to begin the consultation when, in fall of 1869, he sent Colonel Stoughton Dennis, a surveyor and militia officer, to Red River to begin the massive job of surveying the Northwest. Dennis was aware that land along the Red and Assiniboine had already been divided into river lots of the sort used in Quebec. He made it clear he did not intend to survey any river lots using the square township method that would soon be applied in the rest of the Northwest. He began his work by running the principal meridian north from the 49th parallel and then extending baselines east and west of it. The eastern baseline ran through the St. Vital farm of the prominent Métis farmer Andre Nault. This motivated Louis Riel and a small group of his supporters to stop the survey on October 11, 1869. Riel put his foot on the surveyor's chain, a powerful symbolic act to express his resistance to the way in which the transfer was being handled.

Five days later, he and his supporters formed a Métis National Committee, the first step in a carefully managed assumption of power. Riel was the secretary of this group and John Bruce, a Métis carpenter and sometime lawyer from St. Norbert, was the president. At the end of October, Governor MacDougal arrived at the border of his new domain, but on November 2 he was denied entry by a company of Métis under the command of Ambroise Lepine, who informed him that the lieutenant governor was not welcome to assume his new position until there had been a proper negotiation between Canada and the people of Red River.

On the same day, 70 miles north, Riel peacefully occupied upper Fort Garry, establishing control of the most important strategic location in the colony. Now he began the process of broadening his base of support by inviting the English parishes to join with the Métis in a convention to discuss the situation. Riel proposed the establishment of a provisional government to carry out negotiations with Canada. He did not have complete support for this proposal among the residents of the colony, whether English, French, or Métis, nor did they all support the List of Rights that he had drawn up as the basis of the area's entry into Confederation. But Riel pressed on.

December 1, 1869, the day that Canada legally acquired the Northwest, passed without being acknowledged or celebrated, and a week later the Métis National Committee declared the establishment of the provisional government, of which Riel was elected president.

Under Riel, the Red River settlement elected its first representative legislature with members from each parish. Riel's cabinet proceeded to assume many of the administrative responsibilities previously handled by the Council of Assiniboia. Riel had the support not only of much of the Métis population but also some of the Selkirk settlers, as well as, in the early days of the government, some sympathy from the prime minister. Riel's actions alerted John A. Macdonald that he had blundered in concentrating on the mechanics of the transfer from the Hudson Bay Company while not bothering to talk to the representatives of the main population groups in Red River, the largest being the Métis. He now proceeded to attempt to rectify the situation and sent a delegation to meet with him.

Meanwhile, there was a relatively small group of residents in Red River who were anxious for the union with Canada to proceed. They did not recognize Riel's leadership, and some wanted to overthrow his government by force.

One of the most prominent of these was John Christian Schultz. Dr. John Schultz, Henry McKenney's stepbrother, came to Red River first in 1860 to visit McKenney but returned to Ontario to continue studying medicine. He studied at Queen's College in Kingston and Victoria College in Coburg but did not earn a medical degree. He nevertheless advertised his services as a physician and surgeon when he settled in Red River in 1861. He did practice medicine but may not have found it very lucrative. At one point he advertised he would treat people for free if they could not pay. Schultz also worked with McKenney, managing the Royal Hotel, and became more focused on business and buying land than medicine. He soon owned several rental properties on Main Street. He continued his partnership with McKenney in a store that sold dry goods and bought furs.

The partnership between McKenney and John Schultz ended in an 1868 quarrel over money. They disagreed over who was responsible to pay debts owed by their partnership and McKenney, in his role as sheriff, resolved the issue by throwing his half brother in jail. A group of Schultz's friends, led by his wife Agnes, proceeded to help him break out.

Schultz was a big man who could act in a threatening manner in order to get what he wanted. He became the leader of the small group of Canadian immigrants in Red River. In 1865 he bought control of the *Nor'Wester*, the colony's English newspaper. He used the paper to argue that the colony should become part of the Dominion of Canada and that the Hudson Bay Company should give up its control over the Northwest. His behavior and personality made him unpopular with his neighbors in Red River and with politicians in Ottawa. When Louis Riel began his campaign to negotiate the entry of the colony into Confederation, Schultz opposed him at every step.

In early December 1869, Schultz gathered a group of supporters, including Charles Mair, in one of the buildings he owned. They were intended to be an armed force to oppose the Provisional Government; instead, they were arrested and locked up in Fort Garry by Riel.

On December 27, delegates from Ottawa arrived to meet with Riel and his government. Donald Smith had been sent as John A. Macdonald's official Commissioner. Charles de Salaberry, a militia officer and the member of an old Quebec family and Abbé Thibault, a missionary who had worked in what is now Alberta for 35 years, also arrived. They were emissaries of Macdonald's French colleagues, George-Etienne Cartier and Hector Langevin. Riel chose not to recognize the two French delegates and the initial meeting with Smith did not accomplish very much. Donald Smith decided to bypass negotiations and hold a public meeting at which he told the crowd some of what the Canadian government was willing to offer.

Riel then proceeded to strengthen his position and regain control of the situation by proposing a convention made up of equal numbers of French and English representatives. This group approved his List of Rights, a statement of concessions that he said must be made before the colony would join Confederation. Smith then suggested that a delegation should be sent to Ottawa to negotiate face to face. Riel welcomed this idea.

The convention approved the idea of an elected assembly to represent the parishes of Red River with 12 English members and 12 French members. This body became the first democratically elected Legislature of Manitoba. During its short life, the provisional government began to assume some of the responsibilities of the old Council of Assiniboia.

While this was happening, many of Riel's prisoners, including Schultz, escaped from Fort Garry and Riel paroled the rest. Many of them began to organize an armed resistance to Riel. In the process, a Métis man, Nobert Parisien and a young Red River resident, John Sutherland, were killed, and members of Schultz's group, including Colonel Boulton and Thomas Scott, were re-arrested and imprisoned by Riel. Colonel Boulton was condemned to death for plotting to overthrow the provisional government and escaped that fate only because Donald Smith intervened on his behalf.

Thomas Scott was similarly condemned, and this time Riel was unmoved by Smith. Scott was an Orangeman, rabidly anti-Catholic and anti-French, who continuously attacked Riel verbally and on at least one occasion struck the Métis leader. On March 4, 1870, convicted of trying to overthrow the government, he was executed by firing squad.

John Schultz and Charles Mair, who had fled to Ontario, carried on an effective campaign there during the spring, appealing to anti-French and anti-Catholic prejudice to undermine Riel's government. Schultz's speeches and newspaper pieces helped turn Scott into a martyr for conservative Orangemen.

After the union with Canada and the arrival of Canadian militia in Winnipeg, Schultz continued his attacks on Riel. His contempt for the man was evident during his political career as well. Schultz was elected to the Manitoba Legislature in the 1870s and he became the MP for Selkirk constituency, serving from 1871 to 1882. During his time in Parliament, he seconded the motion made in the House of Commons by Mackenzie Bowell that Riel not be allowed to take his seat after his election in Provencher riding in 1874. Then, when Prime Minister Alexander Mackenzie made a motion to exile Riel for five years, Schultz supported that as well.

An interesting thing about John Schultz is that as time went by, he became a defender of the Métis and of the Indigenous people in Manitoba. He spoke out about the failure to provide the Métis with the land promised in the Manitoba Act and more than once he called for an improvement in the payments being made to Indigenous people covered by the seven prairie treaties.

After his defeat as an MP, he was appointed to the Senate in 1882. In 1888 he was made lieutenant governor of Manitoba by John A. Macdonald, who wanted him to try and prevent Premier Greenway from abolishing the use of French as an official language and removing the educational rights of the French population guaranteed in the Manitoba Act of 1870. Schultz attempted to convince Greenway to abandon these measures, but he was not successful. His final years were marred by sickness. His time as lieutenant governor came to an end in 1895 and he died soon after.

Schultz was, before all else, a businessman. He acquired a good deal of property in Winnipeg and in 1884 his holdings were assessed at $66,900.[18] He was the president of the Northwest Trading Company and a director of the Great North Western Telegraph Company. When Lady Schultz died in 1929, her will contained bequests that provided $400,000 for religious, charitable and hospital organizations, as her husband had wished.

■

Though the prime minister's support for Riel cooled after the execution of Scott, Macdonald and Riel did negotiate through intermediaries and some concessions were made in response to the list of rights

Riel's government had drawn up. The concessions were embodied in the Manitoba Act of 1870. These included Red River entering Confederation as a full-fledged province.

Three men were chosen by the provisional government to travel to Ottawa and negotiate the terms of the colony's entrance into confederation. They were Abbé Noël Joseph Ritchot, Alfred Henry Scott, and John Black. Both Scott and Black had been elected as delegates to the Convention in January. Black was a representative of the English population and had become chair of the Convention. A former chief trader of the Hudson Bay Company, he had served as the recorder or judge in the colony and a member of the Council of Assiniboia. Scott represented Winnipeg and he may have been an American. He had worked as a clerk and a bartender during his time in Red River. Abbé Ritchot was a supporter of the Métis cause and had worked beside Riel in the early days of Riel's campaign for Métis rights.

The three men left Red River on March 23rd and 24th, after the execution of Thomas Scott. When they arrived in Ottawa, Ritchot was arrested on a private warrant for complicity in the death of Scott. He was soon released for lack of evidence. They began to negotiate with Sir John A. Macdonald and George-Etienne Cartier at Cartier's home on April 25. Abbé Ritchot was an effective negotiator and was able to get approval for a number of the points in the List of Rights. The most important were that the colony was to enter Confederation as a province of Canada with bilingual and bicultural institutions and 1.4 million acres were to be reserved for the Métis. Ritchot left Ottawa with the impression that the land claims of the Métis and others would be settled quickly. He also had been given the impression that a general amnesty would be granted to everyone involved in the resistance. Yet by August, as the military expedition led by Garnet Wolseley approached Red River, Louis Riel fled the region, while Ambroise Lepine was sentenced to death for his role in Scott's execution. Macdonald failed to spare Riel from execution fifteen years later, a decision that cost him a good deal of political support.

The agreement reached during the negotiations with Macdonald became the basis of the Manitoba Act, introduced in the House on May 4, and passed and given Royal Assent on May 12, just a week later. On July 15, Manitoba officially became the fifth province of the Dominion of Canada.

Treaties

In order to establish the new Canadian Northwest, it was first necessary to deal with the claims of the original peoples who had inhabited the west for at least 12,000 years. The Métis, the products of the many marriages between Indigenous and French and English people involved in the fur trade, also had claims to settle. The Dominion government, eager to begin developing the new territory by filling the west with tens of thousands of farmers from eastern Canada and overseas, moved to resolve these claims.

The Manitoba Act contained three important sections dealing with the land of the new province. Section 30 made it clear that ungranted and waste lands would be "vested in the crown and administered by the Government of Canada." This retention of land was not what had been done in the east where natural resources were in the hands of the provinces. The land was of central importance for the government of Canada because it was with land that the company building the transcontinental railway would be paid, in part, for their work. All railroads received huge tracts of saleable land along their routes and the CPR was granted alternate sections within 24 miles of the rail line as part of the Canadian government's support for the company.

Land had already been used as part of the compensation paid to the Hudson's Bay Company, and in the federal government's treaties with the Indigenous people, grants of land in the form of reserves were included in the list of concessions made in return for the surrender of Indigenous title to the country.

For the Métis, grants of land were made to acknowledge their past occupation and use of land in the areas where their communities existed. Section 31 of the Manitoba Act set aside 1.4 million acres of land "for the benefit of the families of half-breed residents." Lots and tracts of land were to be divided "among the children of the half breed heads of families residing in the province at the time of the transfer."

Section 32 went on to say that the Crown would confirm by grant, among other categories, land "held in peaceable possession" at the time of the transfer. This was taken to mean that river lots that the Métis and other Red River residents had been living on without holding title to them would now be theirs. The original Manitoba, called the postage stamp province, consisted of 8.9 million acres. As much as a sixth of this land was set aside for the Métis alone.

After the arrival of European fur traders, Indigenous people had played a central role in the development and operation of the Canadian fur trade. They shared with the fur traders their knowledge of country and the animals and they provided the furs. Without the collaboration of knowledgeable Indigenous guides and translators there could have been no fur trade.

Indigenous people suffered a good deal from contact with Europeans, dying in vast numbers from European diseases and government policies that destroyed both lives and livelihoods. The early years of Winnipeg saw Indigenous communities and cultures struggling to survive in the midst of an horrific storm of tragic events. In the early 1870s one of the periodic smallpox epidemics swept over the West, leaving enormous numbers of Indigenous people dead or disfigured in its wake. At the same time, what had seemed the endless bounty provided by the great bison herds came to an end due to disease, drought, westward expansion of settlement, commercialization and industrialization of hunting, and the introduction of domestic animals from eastern Canada. Later, the advent of the residential school system caused enormous harm to Indigenous children and their families.

Between the summer of 1871 and the fall of 1877 seven different treaties were signed between the federal government and the leaders of Cree, Ojibwa, Chippewa, Blackfoot, Blood, Piegan, Sarcee, and Stoney communities on the prairies. The government saw the treaty process as one in which the Indigenous people surrendered their title to the lands of the Northwest in exchange for reserves, annual payments, and other promises. The treaties would thus open the Northwest for exploitation by settlers and business interests.

The viewpoint of the Indigenous negotiators was different. They saw the treaties as important because they were a way for their people to share the land with the European settler and ensure their own survival. Their opening position was often ambitious, in one case asking for an area half the size of Manitoba for their reserve. There was a good deal of discontent over the fact that the Hudson Bay Company had sold the land and the Indigenous population had not received a share of the payment. The treaty negotiations did not always go smoothly. In the case of Treaty 6, the treaty was not finally settled until 1899.

The government had decided in the summer of 1873 to make treaties only as the territory was required for settlement or other purposes. It was prepared to do no more that summer than to give general assurances to the Saskatchewan First Nations people that their rights would be respected. This promise did not satisfy Indigenous leaders. A letter written in March 1873 by Charles Bell to Alexander Morris, the lieutenant governor of Manitoba and a treaty negotiator, detailed some of the problems facing the Indigenous population. Bell was a Winnipegger who was trading for furs in the Northwest at the time and would in the years ahead become a prominent member of the business community. The letter "warned that the Cree were getting restless as the traders had told them each year that a treaty would be made, but it was never done." He said that the Cree now thought that there would be no treaty but that settlers would come and occupy their country. Bell also said "There will certainly be trouble with the Plains Cree if word is not sent early to inform them of treaties to be made with them in the coming summer." Bell also wrote that starvation was a real danger because the buffalo were under pressure from the increasing number of hunters.[19]

Winnipeg is included in the territory of Treaty 1, signed at Lower Fort Garry on August 3, 1871 between the government and the Swampy Cree and Ojibwa leadership. That the treaties were a bad bargain for Indigenous people is now commonly accepted. As well, it has been established that not all provisions of the treaties were honored. For many years litigation and negotiations have been underway to correct these shortcomings. Some progress has been made and additional grants of land and money payments have been made to some groups, but much remains to be done.

Métis Land

In the 1870s, land was distributed by using scrip, certificates giving the holder the right to claim either dollar amounts or specific numbers of acres of land. In what was not Manitoba's finest hour, a long sorry list of measures were taken to make it easy for speculators to acquire scrip and land intended for Métis children. One of the most egregious examples of bad behaviour was the case of Chief Justice Edmund Burke Wood. He drafted the Infants' Estate Act, which outlined how cases in which the parents of Métis children who asked to sell the land granted to their offspring were to be handled. The infant—the term was applied to anyone under 25—was to be interviewed by the Chief Justice to make sure the circumstances of the sale were fair. In the late 1870's Woods passed many hundreds of sales without ever looking at the documentation or seeing the Métis children involved. The requests were submitted on identical printed forms filled out by the purchaser, sometimes in batches of 25, and were approved in bulk. They were often signed with an "x" by the parents and the child in the presence of no one but a government commissioner and a speculator who purchased the scrip on the spot.

Judge Woods' sons were involved in the buying of Métis land and money scrip. They worked with Arthur Wellington Ross, a Winnipeg real estate promoter who was heavily involved in buying and selling scrip. Ross came to Winnipeg from his native Ontario in 1877 and was called to the Manitoba bar in the following year. He was elected to the Legislative Assembly in 1878 and again in 1879, and he was the federal MP for Selkirk for three terms. At the height of the Winnipeg real estate boom in 1881 and 1882, Ross owned a large number of properties in the city, not to mention most of the suburb of Fort Rouge, where he built a large mansion on Roslyn Road. Ross purchased Métis scrip and then exchanged it for land. He employed men, two of whom were J.P. Wood, the son of Chief Justice Wood, and Napoleon Bonneau, to purchase scrip from Métis people. Wood, Bonneau, and other speculators would be present at sittings of the commission that gave scrip to eligible Métis. They were in position to offer cash for the scrip on the spot, often for less than face value. Faced with the extremely complex process of exchanging the scrip for an actual grant of land, many people simply sold it.

During the great real estate boom of 1881-1882 land acquired in return for scrip was often on the auction block. Many Winnipeg businessmen bought and sold Métis scrip. By 1882 Alloway and Champion's private bank had increased its capital to some $175,000. About the same time, the firm became an agent for the CPR's lands. To its work as a real estate agency, it later added payments for pre-emptions of federal lands and transactions for the Canada North-West Land Company. Most of their dealings in land, however, were done indirectly through the purchase and resale of land- and money-scrip, military bounty warrants, and tax sale certificates. The acquisition of Métis scrip was greatly facilitated by William Alloway's brother Charles Valentine, who would become a junior partner in the firm in 1885. Charles was one of the scrip buyers who travelled with the government commissioners, offering to pay cash for scrip as soon as it was given to the Métis recipients.

Augustus Nanton, another prominent businessman, had also traded in scrip, explaining that he had always paid a fair price for it. In this Nanton was pointing to one of the disreputable aspects of the trade in scrip, namely that speculators often bought it for far less than face value.

There were, of course, Métis people who were involved in business and were perfectly capable of negotiating the paperwork necessary to secure their grants of land, but they were in the minority.

The treaties and the stipulations for awarding scrip to the Métis people were considered by Canada to have cleared away the impediments of Indigenous title to the land of the Northwest so that the process of settlement could begin.

In recent years, there has been extensive litigation over the promises made to the Métis in the Manitoba Act by the governments of the day. A great deal of research has been done by academics like Professor Douglas Sprague and Professor Thomas Flanagan, who have acted as expert witnesses, studying the issue in great depth, and clashing over how the Métis were treated. In 2013, the Supreme Court of Canada finally ruled that the federal and provincial governments had failed to follow through on promises made to the Métis people in Section 31. This decision forms the basis of negotiations going on at the time of writing to compensate Métis people for their treatment 140 years ago.

WINNIPEG BUSINESS COMMUNITY
The Early Years, 1870–1880s

The following photo is often reproduced. It shows what we now call Main Street and Portage Avenue early in the 1870's. In the Archives Canada dataset, a short note is attached to it: "These settlers travelled from Brussels Ontario to the Palestine district near Gladstone Manitoba."[20] Brussels is a small town north of London, Ontario and the Palestine district is east of Gladstone. The people in this grainy photo are therefore among some of the first in a huge influx of settlers who came through Winnipeg on their way to establish farms on the prairie.

There are four horse-drawn wagons stopped at different angles. About 20 people, mostly men, are standing around the wagons, talking or just waiting to begin their journey to Gladstone. Perhaps they have just arrived from Ontario after a long journey by train and river boat.

Portage and Main, c. 1871 LIBRARY AND ARCHIVES CANADA/MISCELLANEOUS COLLECTION/A051938

There are a handful of clapboard buildings in the photo, arranged at different angles and not as though they are aligned with a street. Some of these were businesses, like the Garrett Hotel in the center of the frame. The sun is shining, and in the distance the empty horizon cuts straight as a knife edge across the bottom of the sky. Comparing the position of the Garett Hotel with its location shown on early maps, we can deduce that the camera is pointed east toward the Red River and the roads in the foreground really are Portage and Main.

This is a view of part of the unincorporated village of Winnipeg, population less than 100. A year later that figure would be 271. The picture does not show the Hudson Bay Company's stone fort, Upper Fort Garry, out of the frame to the right, a short distance to the south. It was a much more imposing and important edifice than the wooden buildings in the picture. There, for many years, the Company's Canadian headquarters had hummed busily away, managing the corporation's vast fur business. In 1870, the operations of this large and venerable old corporation overshadowed the business transacted by the few retail merchants whose establishments were a short distance to the north of the Fort along the Main Road, soon to be Main Street.

The Rise of the Wheat Economy

Winnipeg's growth could be attributed, in part, to the growing market for agricultural products. In 1812, the year the first Selkirk settlers arrived in Red River, Selkirk Settlement Governor Miles Macdonell cleared a plot of land so that winter wheat could be planted. The experiment failed because Manitoba's climate was too cold for this variety, planted in the fall and harvested in early summer, to survive through the winter. The settlers then tried spring wheat and in the fall of 1815, they harvested their first crop. They continued to grow wheat on their river lots. For 10 of the first 55 years of wheat growing the crop was a failure: grasshoppers ruined their crops in 1818, 1819, 1857,1858, 1864, 1867 and 1868 and seeding was delayed by floods in 1826, 1852 and 1861. In 1868 the crop was completely destroyed and the colony was forced to ask for charity in England, Canada, and the US. Famine was avoided when £7,500 were donated to buy flour and grain, which was hauled in on sleds from St. Paul.

The soil along the rivers was fertile, enriched by regular floods over the centuries. Never having been farmed on a large scale, the land was not depleted, and good crops were harvested in most years. Manuring the fields was not part of Red River agriculture because it was not necessary.[21] By the 1830s the settlement was producing surpluses of wheat. Unfortunately, there was no market to absorb the surplus. The Hudson's Bay Company bought some grain, but the amounts of wheat and flour they purchased from each farmer were small. The pemmican that was produced for the Company by Métis families in Red River was of more use because, unlike flour, it was easily transported in canoes and York boats and could be stored for long periods without going bad.

After a visit to the colony in 1851, Governor Ramsay of Minnesota reported that the settlers were producing good crops but with such a small market their surpluses were large and they were "smothering in their own fat." Standing in the way of export was the problem of transportation. In order to ship grain out it would have to be bagged and carried by Red River cart or, later, by steamboat to St. Paul.

In addition to the Selkirk Settlers, some of the land along the two rivers was occupied by Métis farmers. Many were descended from employees of the North West and Hudson's Bay Companies, made redundant by the merging of the two organizations. Some were simply retired from the service. The Métis population at Red River grew, and by 1850 there were 6,000 Métis in the area; at the time of Confederation in 1870 their numbers had doubled to 12,000, or 80% of the total population.

The Métis farms, and all Red River farms for that matter, were mixed farms with vegetable plots growing potatoes, cabbage, and carrots as well as wheat and some oats and barley. The diet of many was supplemented with fish and bison meat harvested during the large bison hunts that took place every summer. Using the local knowledge of their Indigenous ancestors, Métis farm families also gathered wild berries, mushrooms and various wild vegetables.

Wheat grown by farmers in North America falls into two broad categories: hard red spring wheat and white winter wheat. Winter wheat is grown in warmer climates, like those in the middle and southern United States. The hard red spring wheats are grown farther north and do well in the cooler dry climate in the Canadian northwest. They are planted in the spring and harvested in the fall. One advantage they have over white wheats is that they have higher gluten content and so produce larger, heavier loaves of bread. Hard red wheats are often mixed with white wheats to add "strength" to the flour, that is, to produce the larger loaves demanded by the baking industry.

Manitoba and the Northwest were ideal locations to grow hard red wheats, but the stone grinding mills in use in the early 1800's crushed the hard wheats, mixing particles of the outer layers of bran into the flour. The result was a course flour and bread that was dark in color.

The Métis farmers in Red River grew a variety of spring wheat called Prairie du Chien. It seems to have been first grown in Wisconsin around present-day La Crosse. Red Fife wheat, a hard red spring wheat, was brought to Ontario from Russia through Glasgow. Farmers in the Red River began to grow it around 1868.

In the 1870s two things happened to improve the prospects of wheat farmers in the Canadian northwest. The first was that with the incorporation of the Northwest into Canada, farmer immigrants and new settlers began to arrive from Ontario and Quebec. This new population constituted both a local market for farm products and an army of new producers to grow wheat. The construction of the CPR made wheat exports on a large scale from Manitoba and the Northwest possible.

Secondly, the milling industry underwent revolutionary changes at this time. Grist mills equipped with grinding stones were slowly replaced by new flour mill machinery and techniques. The new mills used large corrugated steel rollers to scrape wheat kernels apart. Particles of bran and the course outer layers were removed with fans and sieves leaving pure white flour that produced the white bread that was in demand.

The use of steel rollers to grind material was not new. Roller mills had been used in India to grind sugar in the past. It was in Hungary that the modern roller mill techniques for grinding wheat had been perfected. In the 1870s flour mills were being converted across Canada and the United States.

In Winnipeg, in 1881, the Ogilvie company built a large flour mill in Point Douglas beside the new CPR main line. The mill used a combination of stone grinding and the new steel roller mill equipment to produce a pure white flour. George V. Hastings, whose mother was a member of the Ogilvie family, worked on the construction of the mill and eventually became the manager. He had already been involved in the construction of several steel roller mills in Ontario and the US. He stayed in Winnipeg for the rest of his life. He was later one of the shareholders of the Lake of the Woods Milling Company. A project of the CPR, Lake of the Woods operated a large flourmill, built in 1887 at Keewatin beside the main rail line.

In Minneapolis, the most important American milling centre, mills were converted in the 1870s. In 1878 the Washburn A mill, the largest flour mill in the United States, was demolished by a huge dust explosion. Grain dust is extremely volatile and explodes more easily than gunpowder. When the Washburn mill was rebuilt, the grinding stones were replaced with steel rollers

An article in the *Manitoba Free Press* of January 2, 1875 reviewed the changes taking place. The new type of flour mill, said the *Free Press*, was making white winter wheat less desirable, and the more southerly states where it was grown were now losing immigrants to northern areas like Minnesota where the hard red wheats flourished. The red spring wheats now commanded a 50-cent bounty such as in the past had been paid for white wheat.

For those wishing to attract settlers to Manitoba, the changes in milling technology and the emphasis on different varieties of wheat were selling points. On January 23, 1873 the *Free Press* reprinted an article from the *New York Independent* touting Manitoba as "one of the finest wheat-growing countries in the world" with black alluvial soil to a depth of two to four feet. "Some of the fields in the Red River Valley" rhapsodized the *Independent*, "produced 40 successive crops of wheat without fallow or manure, with yields as high as 50 to 60 bushels to the acre, even under the farming of natives." This sort of endorsement, insulting as it was to the locals, undoubtedly motivated some prospective homesteaders to move to Manitoba.

However, what was not known in January was that 1875 would be a year of one of Red River's periodic grasshopper infestations and the insects ate the wheat plants as they sprouted. The size of the crop was reduced to about a quarter of a normal year's yield. The government distributed free seed wheat to farmers who had lost their crops.

Nevertheless, there was fast and widespread development of Red Spring Wheat as a crop in Manitoba and the Northwest. Specifically, Red Fife wheat was promoted as the variety to grow. In 1882 the millers of Winnipeg were encouraging farmers to plant Red Fife and nothing else. The Provincial Agricultural Society echoed this message and William Van Horne, general manager of the CPR announced that "in order to assist farmers in procuring pure Red Fife for seed it will be conveyed free of charge over the CPR."[22] The following year the Department of Agriculture announced that Red Fife would be allowed into Canada for seed purposes without tariff. The papers carried a stream of articles about Red Fife's advantages. In January 1884, the *Free Press* published an article stating that a barrel of Red Fife flour would produce between 25 and 40 more pounds of bread than the same amount of white wheat flour. The writer did admit that Red Fife drew more nutrients out of the soil and so yields would begin to decline fairly soon if land was not periodically left fallow, a practice that not all farmers believed in.

White wheat did not have the same effect on the soil, but it was much more susceptible to smut, a kind of fungal infection that could destroy a crop. The treatment for smut was to "pickle" or soak the seed grain in a solution of bluestone, also called copper sulfate. The smut fungus consumed the starch in the grain kernels, destroying the value of the wheat. Red Fife had the advantage of being resistant to smut.

Seed companies advertised that they had stocks of Red Fife for seed. In Winnipeg in 1883, Brown, Oldfield and Co. informed farmers that they had imported a shipment of Red Fife three years before and contracted with farmers in different regions of Manitoba to grow the wheat for them. They argued that "the extra price offered by millers and the offer of free freight by the CPR is an inducement to farmers to supply themselves with seed so they can sow this valuable hard wheat." The Winnipeg millers McMillan Brothers had Red Fife seed wheat for sale in the spring. This campaign to encourage the planting of Red Fife was motivated by the necessity of providing the West with a good quality, desirable product to export. The success of the settlers, the railway, the millers, and Winnipeg itself depended upon it.

During the 1870s, as more and more Manitoba wheat was exported, its quality was recognized and in 1876 R.C. Steele of Steele Briggs

Seed Company came west to purchase 5,000 bushels of Manitoba wheat to improve the quality of Ontario seed wheat. He was only able to find 857 bushels in Winnipeg. This was shipped to Minnesota by riverboat before the river froze for the year. It was added to 4,000 bushels of spring wheat from Minneapolis and sent by train to Duluth and then by boat to Sarnia and on to Toronto.

In 1878, when the rail link between Winnipeg and St. Paul was completed, wheat began to move by train. In that year 1.1 million bushels were produced in Manitoba and much of the surplus was sent to Minneapolis, where it was purchased by the milling industry.

In that same year, wheat was first shipped by rail for export to Britain. Thompson Brothers of Brandon shipped 1000 bushels of number 1 hard wheat in sacks to food importers Barclay and Brand of Glasgow. It took just 21 days to make the trip. In 1883 the CPR line from Winnipeg to the Lakehead was complete and shipments of wheat by that route began. The opening of this line spurred the growth of the grain elevator system. In 1884 the first two of many terminal elevators were completed by the CPR so that large quantities of wheat could be stored at Fort William and Port Arthur before shipping in lake boats to the east. Steam-powered barges carrying up to 10,000 bushels were also used to transport grain through the Great Lakes system. Once the lake froze at Port Arthur in early December, wheat could be sent directly to Montreal by rail or simply stored until spring.

Manitoba's crop grew from 1 million bushels in 1880 to 16 million in 1890. Between 1890 and 1900 the number of acres under crops doubled, and in 1901 Manitoba production had increased to 50 million bushels. The size of the crop fluctuated greatly due to such factors as diseases and weather but the growth continued year after year. The quality of the western Canadian export crop began to be noticed in Britain and in 1892, for the first time, the price of Manitoba wheat was quoted separately in the Liverpool grain market.

A Changing HBC

The 1860s had brought many fundamental changes to the Hudson's Bay Company. It was still by far the largest business enterprise in Winnipeg and the West but by 1870 it was a very different entity than the Company had organized 200 years before. In 1863, the International Financial Society bought a controlling interest in the HBC. Most of the new shareholders were less interested in the fur trade than in speculating with the Company's vast land holdings. The owners of the Society "included prominently in its membership representatives of the Glyn and Baring Brothers banking houses who were deeply involved in the Grand Trunk Railway"[23] and others who understood the role of the railway in the economic development of the West. Their plans were modified somewhat after the absorption of the Company's territory in the northwest by Canada. If the Northwest was to be filled with settlers, the Company's sales shops, formerly devoted to trade goods for the fur trade, would now begin to supply the new farm population.

The new Hudson's Bay directors, especially Sir William Watkin, a British railway promoter who was president of the Grand Trunk Railway, were concerned about the railway's survival and believed it could be guaranteed by the construction of an extensive railway network in the Northwest. Among other things, this would greatly increase the value of the Hudson's Bay Company's vast land holdings. Company shares were offered on the open market and the likelihood of rich returns from land sales was prominent in the marketing prospectus. As part of the agreement with the HBC at the time it surrendered its territory, it received 1/20 of all the land in the fertile belt. This was calculated to be equal to two sections in every fifth township and one and three-quarter sections in all the other townships. They received land surrounding all their trading posts. In Winnipeg, this so-called "Hudson Bay Reserve," the 500 acres around Upper Fort Gary, was marketed as an exclusive neighbourhood and a number of luxury homes were built along Broadway and the streets running south to the river.

From 1870 to 1879 Donald Smith served the HBC as company commissioner, chief commissioner, and land commissioner. He was also a Conservative MP and well placed to make sure that any new legislation was drafted in a way that benefited the HBC. He also secured contracts for the Company to pay out treaty money, manage payrolls for the North-West Mounted Police and provide supplies for relief shipments to prairie Indigenous groups. The Company became one of the main providers of relief supplies, a major item in the federal budget in the 1880s and 1890s after the collapse of the bison herds left Indigenous people without their primary source of food. The government spent as much as $500,000 a year on relief in the early 1880s, declining to between $150,000 to $200,000 by the mid 1890s.[24]

The 1870s were also the years when Donald Smith was beginning to partner in ventures with his cousin George Stephen in Montreal, eventually going into the railway business. In general, says one writer, Smith "became the conduit through whom Montreal Financiers made investments in Manitoba."[25] Finally, having been criticized for not paying enough attention to Hudson's Bay matters, Smith resigned from his position with the HBC, saying his personal affairs required his attention. He did not, however, give up his shares, eventually becoming the largest investor. He also made sure his own offices were located in the Hudson's Bay Company buildings in Montreal and Winnipeg. He clearly did not intend to give up his connection.

Had Smith involved the HBC in his railway ventures, which led to his being a major shareholder in the CPR, the Bay might again have become a dominant corporation in western Canada. Some modern scholars are critical of the inaction of the Company during the 1870s and 1880s. Michael Bliss writes: "The Company had opportunity upon opportunity to develop profitable new business and muffed almost all of them." Another writer concludes: "Instead of dominating or even monopolizing trade commerce and transportation in western Canada, the company ceded the territory to others."[26]

The Company's three areas were the fur trade, land sales, and the sales shops where food, tools, cloth, and a wide range of goods could be sold. In the 1870s and 1880s the HBC had a large inventory of land to sell. In July 1872, 91 lots were sold in the Hudson Bay Reserve in Winnipeg for $76,300. But they had been sold too soon: the sales could not be completed because the federal government had not issued patents for the land. By the time this had been done in 1873, a depression had set in and all but a few of the buyers backed away. Only $6,000 was realized.

The Company policy, inspired by Donald Smith, was one of holding on to land, waiting for conditions to improve and prices to rise. It was assumed that land sales would be sluggish as long as the federal government was giving away homesteads. During the remainder of the 1870s, 290 lots were sold but 58 buyers withdrew from the sales and the total income was $116,662 instead of the expected $198,929. In an effort to make the Company put lots up for sale, the provincial government instituted a school tax on land of 1 cent per acre for resident owners and 5 cents for non-residents.

In 1879 a new Land Commissioner, C.W. Brydges, was hired. He was a railway manager who had worked for several British and Canadian railways. He was ambitious for the Hudson's Bay Company and among other things, very willing to sell lots even though he was criticized for not waiting for a better price. Between his arrival in 1879 and 1881, over 42,000 acres were sold throughout the Northwest for $239,000. In the 12 months that followed, at the height of the Winnipeg real estate boom, another half-million acres were sold for $2,780,142.

Unfortunately for Brydges, the boom collapsed in the spring of 1882 and 60% of the buyers, mostly speculators, defaulted. Sales in the following year amounted to only 7000 acres.

Donald Smith and his allies in the Hudson's Bay Company used this situation as a pretext to attack Brydges, who worried Smith was trying to have him fired. At a shareholders meeting in November 1883,

Smith engineered a takeover of the company and was elected gover-
nor. Brydges and Smith continued to feud, engaging in conflicts that
Smith usually won because of his control of the Company. In 1889
Brydges died of a heart attack.

Land sales continued to be slow until around 1900 when an influx
of new settlers created increased demand. Smith nevertheless continued
a policy of delaying land sales in anticipation of higher prices later. As
a result, in 1913 when the boom of the previous decade collapsed and
land prices fell, the HBC still had a sizeable inventory of unsold acreage.

■

The other two businesses of the Company, the fur trade and retail
sales, also underwent major changes in the decades after 1870. The
sales shops at Hudson's Bay trading posts were the origin of the retail
business conducted by the Company, but following Manitoba's entry
into Confederation, the Company realized it would be sharing the
area near the forks of the rivers with stores and warehouses dealing
in an ever-greater variety of trade goods and it prepared to compete
with the new merchants operating further north along Main Road.

It began by taking down part of the stone wall on the east side of
Fort Garry to open the front entrance of the Fort's retail store to the
street. Some sources say that the stone wall actually collapsed, and
this is possible because the Fort was generally in very bad condition.
To the condition of the buildings was added the fact that they were
no longer suited to the requirements of the company's new roles as
retailer and real estate developer.

The fort was also in the way. C.J. Brydges, the Hudson Bay
Company's land commissioner, had received permission from the
Company's board in London to build an iron bridge across the
Assiniboine River at the end of the 1870s. The bridge was aligned
with the south gate of the fort and with Main Street beyond. But the
walls and buildings of Fort Garry blocked the straight path from the
foot of the bridge on the riverbank and Main Street.

For these reasons, the decision to demolish the Fort was taken during 1880.[27] A few of the buildings inside the walls were moved east along the riverbank to the location of the Company's flour mill and warehouse. The governor's residence, which until its demolition in 1888 served as the home of the new provincial lieutenant governor, and the stone gate that still stands near the corner of Main Street and Broadway were all that remained of the Fort. In October 1881, the magnificent new three-storey brick Hudson Bay store on Main Street and York Avenue opened for business. Some of the stone used in the new store came from the walls of the Fort. At first the retail store only occupied the front portion of the building; the rest of the space was used as a warehouse for furs and merchandise for the store. The store would eventually develop into a department store that sold every-thing—groceries, dry goods, liquor and much else. The Company offices, including those of the land and fur trade departments, were located in the store for some years, moving across Main Street to the new Hudson's Bay House in 1912.[28]

During the decade before these immense changes were made to the Hudson's Bay property, enormous changes were also being made along the Main Road 1.5 to 2 kilometers north of the Fort. Here, where the pre-Confederation free traders had built their stores and houses, what would become the heart of the future city's business district began to take shape on the flat prairie. But in contrast to the HBC era, the development was not masterminded by corpora-tion managers who had to ask permission from a board in London. Instead, ambitious individuals started businesses in locations along Main Street, believing that Winnipeg would soon become a substan-tial city. Working alone or with a partner, these people converted what was a disorganized cluster of frame buildings in the early 1870s into, by the end of the 1880s, a handsome business street lined with brick and stone buildings like those in any small Ontario city.

Early Entrepreneurs

The population of Winnipeg grew steadily from 241 in 1871, to 5,031 in 1874, 5,521 in 1876, 7,995 in 1881 and 26,529 in 1891. As the populations of the Northwest and Winnipeg grew, the city's retail and wholesale merchants prospered. At the beginning of the period, however, the Winnipeg business community grew faster than its market. After 1870, the newspapers carried growing numbers of advertisements for all types of retail stores, operated by individuals or partnerships. The outside world took note of their numbers. In 1887, for example, Dun, Wiman and Company, the Canadian branch of the Dun credit reporting agency, cautioned lenders that there were a larger per capita number of businessmen in Manitoba and the Northwest than in Ontario: one trader for every 50 people, or 8 times the ratio in Ontario. This reflected the large numbers who had come west to open businesses, banking on a population explosion of new settlers.

But the anticipated growth in population was slow in coming and the numbers of businesses declined. The newspapers often carried announcements of going-out-of-business sales as stores came and went along Main Street. As David Burley wrote of these early entrepreneurs, "the vast majority of businessmen gave up on their adopted city. Either the collapse of the western land boom in 1882 and recession that started in the same year forced them out...or their achievements did not match their dreams."[29] Their departures resulted in a ratio of businesses to potential customers closer to the norm in Ontario towns.

There was a solid core of survivors. Some of the members of this early business community were people who had already been free traders in the area before Confederation. John Higgins was one of the early businessmen who continued to operate his Main Street store after 1867. Higgins usually had a partner. Alexander Begg wrote: "It may be that Higgins, getting on in years, depended on his various partners to help carry the load of running a retail store." One such person was David Young, who had gone to work as a clerk for Higgins in 1870 and became a successful merchant in his own right.

David Young was born in Scotland near Glasgow in 1848. As a ten-year-old orphan, he immigrated to Upper Canada to live with his uncle. He ran away from his uncle's home and worked in Toronto as an errand boy in a grocery store. He was a sailor on the Great Lakes for a time and then joined the American Union Army. After his discharge, he worked in a number of cities along the Mississippi as a clerk in dry goods stores.

In 1870 he was back in Canada and came to Red River with the Wolseley expedition as a member of the Ontario Rifles. When his term was up, he stayed in Manitoba and went to work for John Higgins. Young, because he was experienced, was a valuable employee. In 1875 Young became a full partner at the age of 27. Alexander Begg wrote that: "Mr. Young, by tact, perseverance and energy had built up the business of Mr. Higgins from the time he entered as a clerk. He had continued to infuse new life into the business of that gentleman. The firm has had several changes in co-partnership since that time, but Mr. Higgins and Mr. Young still stick together."[30] They were involved in more than the retail business of their store, and on at least one occasion the two men acted as executors, winding up the affairs of a business that had gone bankrupt. They were very successful, and when they both retired in 1880, they each had personal fortunes of about $250,000.

Young was involved in local sports. He was president of the Dufferin Park Association, a coordinating body that maintained an athletic field where Young played lacrosse. It was funded by the city's most important athletic clubs.

He was an early member of the Board of Trade and served on the Board's council in 1879. He was active in the city's successful lobbying to ensure that the CPR main line passed through Winnipeg. He was the secretary-treasurer of the Manitoba Southwest Colonization Railway. He was active in local politics, working for Alexander Morris during his campaign against Donald Smith in the 1878 federal election.

In 1881 Young began to have health problems and he decided to spend a part of each year in Florida, where he owned a nursery and an orange grove. He moved to Florida permanently in 1885 and passed away in 1887 at the early age of 37.

A.G.B. Bannatyne also continued in business after Confederation. He formed a partnership with Alexander Begg, an Ontarian who had come to Red River in the late 1860s. The partners continued to trade for furs in their store. In the 1870s furs and buffalo robes continued to be carried in cart trains to St. Paul for sale, and the proceeds used to purchase merchandise for the store. Riverboats, and after 1878, the railway, reduced the use of the Red River cart trains for freighting. While they continued to carry on the old trade in furs in his store, this aspect of the business decreased in importance. In 1868 Bannatyne and Begg had arranged for the first riverboat cargo of the year to unload at the dock at the foot of Post Office Street, now Lombard Avenue, where they had built a receiving warehouse in a location much closer to their business than the Hudson Bay Company warehouse and landing near Fort Garry.

The transformation of the western economy was symbolized by the fact that by the end of the 1870s, Bannatyne was also paying market prices to local farmers for wheat and barley.

In August of 1870, Wolseley's troops entered Winnipeg and their arrival was godsend for everyone's business. Bannatyne and Begg's store on Main Street was crowded with new customers with money to spend. C.N. Bell, then a young man who had come west with the Wolseley expedition, was hired to be their warehouse clerk. Bell would have a long career in Winnipeg as the secretary of both the Grain Exchange and the Board of Trade, among other jobs.

Andrew Bannatyne had been sympathetic to Louis Riel, and he joined Riel's government as postmaster, a job he would continue to hold after the union with Canada. He was also a member of Riel's elected assembly. Riel did briefly imprison him in Fort Garry, but Bannatyne was released after a short time and the two men parted on good terms.

Bannatyne's wife, Annie, was the Métis daughter of Andrew McDermot. She was a strong-willed woman, as she demonstrated when she expressed her feelings toward Charles Mair, one of the Canadian allies of John Schultz. Annie slapped and hit him several times with a riding whip over some disparaging comments about "half-breeds" in an article he had written.

Later in the 1870s, Bannatyne campaigned unsuccessfully for Riel to be pardoned and allowed to take his seat in the House of Commons. He lobbied, also unsuccessfully, to have Ambroise Lepine, serving a two-year sentence for the execution of Thomas Scott, pardoned and released from prison.

This connection with Riel did not disqualify Bannatyne from leadership roles in the new province. He established himself as one of the leaders of the small but growing business community. He helped found the Board of Trade. Because he had arguably the best house in the village, the first session of the Legislative Assembly, in 1870, took place in his home, which stood a short distance east of Main Street.

In 1872 he was made a member of the Council of the Northwest Territories and he ran for parliament twice, in 1874, when he was defeated and in 1875, when he was elected to represent the riding of Provencher in Ottawa. He did not run again in 1878 and retired from politics.

In 1879 Bannatyne was still in his store at 292 Main Street. He described his business as wholesale and retail groceries, provisions wines and liquors. He advertised in the *Tribune* of April 21, 1879 that he had just received a carload of pork and a carload of coal oil. In addition to lard in pails he had a "choice lot of butter" for sale. Two carloads of whiskey were "expected any day."

A few days later, on May 7, he announced that he had just received 500 barrels of oatmeal, 50 sacks of cornmeal, one carload of mess pork—salt pork cut in pieces and sealed in barrels—and 10,000 pounds of plain ham. He also had salt, lard in 3- and 5-pound cans, syrup in 5-gallon kegs, currants, raisins, prunes, and dried apples. This time a carload of smoked bacon was "expected any day".

Items like sacks of cornmeal and barrels of oatmeal and salt pork would come under the heading of "provisions" and were the sort of bulk items that cooks feeding crews working on railway construction or cutting timber would buy. Cans of lard and dried fruits would be considered "groceries" and would likely be purchased by local families. As the CPR rail line made its way from the head of the Great Lakes to Winnipeg and then out across the prairie, supplies for the cook houses would come almost exclusively from Winnipeg.

Bannatyne's entry into the wholesale business was a step many Winnipeg retailers took. Finding the local market within the city to be too small to be profitable, they expanded, searching for customers across the vast northwest.

Bannatyne speculated in real estate in the later 1870s and during the boom of 1881-1882 he made a great deal of money. However, he held on to some properties too long and lost heavily when prices collapsed in the spring of 1882. He was still a wealthy man, living in a large Scottish Baronial style house on the riverbank in Armstrong's Point. He became ill and in 1889 he died while on a vacation in St. Paul.

Main Street began to take shape as an established road in May 1871, when it was surveyed. The street was 32 feet wide with a generous 16-foot strip on each side for sidewalks. Since Winnipeg was being erected on a sea of Red River mud, sidewalks were in demand. Post Office Street was surveyed at the same time.

Bannatyne and some of the other former free traders were already established on Main Street in 1870, but they were soon joined by newcomers. James Ashdown moved into a new Main Street store in 1871. Alex McMicken opened the first bank in the community in 1873. It was taken over by the Ontario Bank. W.T. Alloway, who had been operating a veterinary practice, opened a tobacco shop on Main in 1873. He too would open a private bank in the years ahead. Both the Merchants Bank and the Bank of Montreal opened branches in Winnipeg in the 1870s. With the arrival of banks and their ability to lend capital, businesses were able to grow.

In this view of Main street in the early 1880s, George Ashdown Hardware, Davis House, Symonds Furrier, Cable Hotel, J. Lister Outfitter, Rossin House, the Blue Store, and the first City Hall are visible. CITY OF WINNIPEG ARCHIVES

The business section on Main continued to grow steadily throughout the 1870s. Many local people built buildings that were rented to others or sold as a speculation. The Bishop of Montreal wrote of Winnipeg "every lawyer in the city to say nothing of most of the merchants were all more or less large land owners, and also dickered in land."[31] William Hespeler, who had acted as the agent of the Canadian government in getting Russian Mennonite immigrants to come to Manitoba, settled in Winnipeg in the 1870s. He built a building on Main and rented the main floor to the Dominion immigration department. John Schultz built several buildings which he rented or sold. Alexander Morris, the Lieutenant Governor of Manitoba, bought 25 acres of land in 1873 from the estate of William Drever, one of the early free traders. He paid $25,000 for it and by 1880 it had increased in value by a factor of 10. He divided part of the property into lots which he auctioned off for $13,000. He built a frame building at Portage and Main which was rented to businesses.

Both Andrew Bannatyne and John Higgins built new three-storey brick buildings on Main Street. By 1874 there were no less than 40 retail stores of various kinds in the city. Not all these businesses survived, there being, as we have seen, too many stores competing for the business of a relatively small population.

Some people had very quick success. J.W. Winnett, for example, started a second-hand furniture and picture framing business in a shanty on the prairie outside Winnipeg in 1873. He moved to a small building on Main, and by 1875 he was renting a fine establishment for his growing business.

The people coming to the city to set up businesses or find work were an international group. In 1875 Begg wrote that one could see Englishmen, Irishmen and Scots on the streets, as well as Icelanders, Yankees and Métis, French Canadians, Black people, Mennonites, Norwegians, and Welshmen. How he was able to identify the origins of all the people is not explained.

The businessmen of Winnipeg began to campaign to have their city incorporated so that it could become the established heart of the developing community. They were nervous that the Hudson Bay Company would beat them to the punch and establish a city centre and business district on their land south of Portage Avenue, consigning Winnipeg to the role of northern suburb. Improvements like sidewalks, streets and surveys could proceed more quickly once incorporation was accomplished. There was resistance to incorporation from the Hudson's Bay Company, the largest landowner and potentially largest taxpayer. They were justified in worrying; their tax bill in 1875 was $595,312. Andrew Bannatyne paid $84,275 that year and his father-in-law Andrew McDermot owed $78,876.

The Company also wanted their property, the Hudson Bay Reserve, to be the centre of any new community, and they vied with Winnipeg to be the location for government buildings like the post office, the land titles office, and customs house which would draw traffic to their areas. In the end incorporation happened, and the post office

General Post Office, 1927   CITY OF WINNIPEG ARCHIVES

was built in Winnipeg, on the corner of Main Street and McDermot, opening for business in August 1876. The other two buildings went up on Main Street within the area owned by the Company.

■

Upper Fort Garry and, before it, Fort Gibraltar were distribution centers for the large fur trade companies. The location of the forts at the junction of the Red and Assiniboine Rivers meant that they were at the hub of the same vast network of rivers and lakes that had made the Forks a natural meeting place for Indigenous people for millennia. The network connected the company forts to trading posts where the fur trade was carried on. From this junction trade goods, pemmican and other supplies were sent out and furs were gathered for export.

During the nineteenth century, as the Hudson's Bay Company's monopoly on trade slowly loosened, the free traders and Métis businessmen who managed the cart trains carrying goods to St. Paul also settled near the junction of the rivers, adding another aspect to the distribution business.

The city began taking on the role of wholesaler to the Northwest during the 1870s. After Confederation, the new city of Winnipeg carried on in the role of center of a provisioning and wholesale trade serving the North-West Mounted Police, trading posts, missions and the growing population of new settlers now living and working in the Northwest and the new province of Manitoba. Wholesale was attractive to Winnipeg merchants as a way to expand their pool of customers. W.H. Lyon sold his retail grocery business in 1877 and became the first wholesale grocer in the Northwest, with customers as far away as the Rocky Mountains.[32]

James Ashdown was one of the most successful of those who added a wholesale company to their original retail store. Ashdown came to Winnipeg in 1868 at the end of June, having walked most of the way from Kansas where he had been working on a construction project. Born in London, England, Ashdown immigrated to Upper Canada as a boy with his family. In 1862, when he was 18, he apprenticed with a tinsmith. After he arrived in Winnipeg, he took on several different jobs to earn a living and in 1869 he signed on with the survey crew of John Stoughton Dennis, who had been sent to Red River to survey the area. His was the survey halted by Louis Riel.

Ashdown went to jail in Fort Garry for a time because he had associated himself with John Schultz. Once Riel's government was replaced with that of the province of Manitoba, Ashdown began his business career. With his savings and a loan of $1,000 from Colonel Dennis, Ashdown set up a tinsmith business and, on 14 September

1868, purchased the hardware store of George Moser, making him the owner of one of the only Winnipeg-based hardware companies.

In 1870 Ashdown bought the location on Main Street where his business would be located. In 1873, Ashdown had added a wholesale department to his hardware business and in 1876 an example of the orders Ashdown's received was one for 3,500 tin pails, 1,500 half-pint cups, 1,800 pint cups, 1,800 round pans, 1,500 oval pans, and 400 teapots.[33]

By the mid 1870s, Ashdown had established a retail and wholesale business selling farm equipment, tools, and all sorts of settlers' supplies, from water pails to wood stoves. Despite there being many other firms selling most of the same items, James Ashdown was one of the few early business owners who survived to become the head of a large corporation with warehouses and stores all across the prairies.

The first store was a log building that was erected in 1875, and in 1881 he added a warehouse to the rear of the store on the corner of Bannatyne and Albert. In 1890 Ashdown had a tin sheet metal manufacturing business and he employed between 40 and 50 workers to handle the orders received. His salary bill was $25,000 a year.

He imported and sold equipment for grain elevators, many of which were being built at the time. This equipment included scales, belts and buckets used to move grain, metal siding and shingles. The firm also sold a wide variety of general hardware items including bolts and nuts, nails, iron, steel, paint and glass, rifles, and sporting goods.

Ashdown's Main Street store and warehouse were completely destroyed in a huge fire in 1904. The store was rebuilt as a two-storey building in a matter of weeks and Ashdown's business continued to grow and occupy more and more space on Main and east along Bannatyne.

Another early wholesaler in Winnipeg was William Forbes Alloway. He came to the west as a private with the Wolseley expedition. In 1871 he was discharged from the militia and settled in Winnipeg, working as a veterinarian. A year later he began working for James McKay in his freighting business and was soon a partner in the company. In 1876 Alloway started his own forwarding and shipping business, carrying freight and mail to the construction crews of the CPR and to the North-West Mounted Police establishments across the west. In 1880 he established, with his partner Henry Champion, the private bank that they would operate for over 40 years.

Another Winnipeg dry goods wholesale began life in the 1860s as the F.E. Kew general trading company. Alexander Begg said that all the furs shipped from the northwest other than by the Hudson Bay Company were handled by Kew. He maintained trading posts in many locations, including some of the Catholic missions. He had been trading furs in the Northwest for a time when he entered into partnership with D.M. Stobart, an English coal merchant, in 1872. They purchased, in 1874, all of Bannatyne's stock of dry goods and rented his store. They began to operate a retail and wholesale dry goods business, as well as buying furs. Imports in 1873 were $918,336 and in 1874 $1,797,033. In the spring of 1874, their sales in Winnipeg and the Northwest were £30,000. In 1876 the partners shipped $45,000 worth of furs to England along with 205 bales of buffalo robes. Stobart bought F.E. Kew out in that same year and Kew retired from the firm.

Arthur Eden became a partner and the business became known as Stobart and Eden. In 1878 Stobart and Eden moved into a new brick building that they erected on Main Street for $20,000. Begg says it was "a monument of the growing thrift and enterprise of our city, spoke volumes of the march of progress which had so practically and earnestly set in. It was 100 feet by 33 feet and 3 stories high. There was a basement the whole length of the building. It was native white brick with galvanized iron cornices and window caps, massive supporting cast iron columns and pilasters and a magnificent plate glass front… It presented to the gaze of our citizens an appearance typical of Chicago or other large cities."[34]

In 1880 Stobart's son Frederick came to Winnipeg to look after his father's trading posts but, with the growing influx of settlers arriving in the west, he decided to concentrate solely on a wholesale dry goods business. In 1883 Eden retired and the firm became Stobart and Sons. Frederick William Stobart managed the firm and lived in Winnipeg until 1905, when he returned to England. After operating in several locations, Stobart built a large brick warehouse that still stands at McDermot and Arthur. The company employed a number of travellers and had branches in Prince Albert and trading posts in other places in the Northwest.

On 28 June 1899, F.W. Stobart incorporated the business as Stobart, Sons & Company, with the majority of stock held by Stobart and his brothers. He became involved as an investor and board member in a number of other Winnipeg businesses. These included the Canadian Fire Insurance Company, the Edinburgh Life Insurance Company of Scotland, the Canada Life Assurance Company, and the Northern Bank and the Northern Trust Company. He was president of the Winnipeg Board of Trade (1893) and the Manitoba Club (1903), and a founding member, in 1905, of the St. Charles Country Club. He died in England in 1935.

Establishing a Board of Trade

After an earlier attempt in March 1873 was not successful, the business community in Winnipeg founded a Board of Trade in January 1879. The first president was Andrew Bannatyne, and the secretary was Thomas Howard, who had come west with the Wolseley Expedition. He had stayed and became a member of the Legislature, cabinet minister, and public servant before moving to Victoria. The two men represented the old and the new in the city, working together to improve conditions for business and build the city up.[35] On March 28, 1879, at a meeting in the City Council chamber, the Board began organizational work. The committee that had been assigned the task of drawing up bylaws recommended adoption of the bylaws of the Montreal Board of Trade with "some necessary alterations." A printed copy was mailed to all members so that the document could be discussed at a later meeting. It was a measure of their aspirations that they chose to use the bylaws of the Board of Trade of Canada's greatest metropolis.

In the years ahead the Board typically discussed an issue, then passed a motion which was sent the City Council where a Board member would address it and answer questions. There was usually quite a lot of overlap between the membership of Council and the Board of Trade and so it was relatively easy to secure changes or improvements in regulations or bylaws using this method. As the Board became better organized and better funded it was often able to produce reports and studies to help Council understand issues.

The Board soon began the work of lobbying on behalf of the city, their main focus from this point on. The Board acted on dozens of issues that affected the Winnipeg business community. We'll look at a few examples here.

On April 5, 1880, a special meeting of the Board addressed complaints about freight handling by the CPR in St. Boniface. The amount of freight arriving at the station from the south was continuously increasing. The existing warehouse was not big enough and freight was piling up outside. Related to this issue was the practice of the customs officers holding cars for inspection and causing delays at the border.

The *Free Press* editor said that the complaints regarding "the unsatisfactory working of the Pembina division of the CPR are fully justified by the facts."[36] The paper criticized the new Conservative government for reducing everyone's wages. The engineers on the line had threatened to quit and the Minister of Railways, according to the *Free Press*, said to go ahead because they could be replaced for lower wages. The CPR and its policies would continue to be the target of many complaints from the Board and westerners in general for years to come.

In March 1882, the Board looked at the issue of fire damage and fire insurance. President Mulholland "announced the object of the meeting was to consider the question of better protection of the City against fire. He said it was desirable for the Board to co-operate with the City Council in establishing an adequate system." Fire insurance was an issue because Eastern underwriters set the rates for Winnipeg higher than for other cities. Two Board members, A. McKeand and J. Turner, were assigned to recruit two insurance companies to set up shop in Winnipeg with a guarantee that they "will not enter the existing "fire insurance ring" that was keeping rates for fire insurance "unwarrantably high."

In January of 1883 at the Board's Annual Meeting the secretary, L.M. Lewis, talked about the improvements in fire protection completed in 1882. A paid fire brigade had been hired and new fire halls built. In the summer ahead, hydrants would be placed on the streets. The City had also extended its fire limits, that is areas of the city in which only brick or stone buildings could be erected, in order to reduce the chance of fire spreading. Arthur Eden, who had been chairing a Board committee on the topic of fire prevention, presented the group's report and recommendations. They said that buildings on Main Street should be of brick or stone construction and that brick veneer buildings should be limited to two stories with a metal roof. The report was received, and the committee was instructed to continue working on the matter in consultation with the City Council and the insurance underwriters.

Board member Arnett thought that the Board, by expressing its opinion, would strengthen the hands of the Council. Lewis Arnett had brought his family to Winnipeg in late 1879. He became one of the pioneer merchants of the city, establishing Arnett's Golden Lion which, a year later, was the largest dry goods and carpet store in Winnipeg. He later moved to Brandon, passing away in 1891.

A number of aldermen were present at the meeting. The future close relationship between the Board of Trade and the City Council was being established at meetings like this one. The aldermen stated that there was a fire bylaw and a paid fire inspector, but he did not have the necessary powers to enforce the law. The city officials said they would strengthen the Inspector's hand.

■

The discussion turned to the problem of unsafe buildings being erected in the city. Lumber and bricks were arriving by train every day and the summer would see many additional buildings erected, often by unskilled workmen. The shortage of trained carpenters and bricklayers led to their work being done by whatever men could be found. This issue was closely connected with the introduction of craft unions to the city because skilled workers would often bring their unions with them and this was not popular with some members of the business community.

At this meeting, the Secretary said that the phenomenal growth of the city meant that the Board's role had become of greater moment and it had a greater responsibility to be involved in the city's development. C.J. Brydges, who was the land commissioner of the Hudson's Bay Company, became vice president at this meeting. He said the Board needed to claim a more prominent place. One way of doing this was to increase the number of members from 75 to 100. He also suggested they hire a salaried secretary to handle the increasing correspondence. This was voted on and approved along with a salary of $500 a year.

The Board turned its attention to petitioning the federal government to dredge the Red River to improve navigation to Lake Winnipeg. Special mention was made of the need for locks and dredging at St. Andrew's rapids so that boats could move safely up and down the river.

A constant worry in Winnipeg was maintaining and increasing the flow of new immigrants, and a motion was passed at the meeting that the City provide immigrant reception sheds to make new arrivals more comfortable and give them a positive first impression of the city.

The interest in building local railways both in southern Manitoba and north to Hudson Bay was one manifestation of western frustration with the CPR monopoly, which prevented the construction of competing lines south of the CP main line. There was a strong belief on the prairies that competing lines would force the CPR to lower their rates. The railway and Sir John A. Macdonald were still struggling at the time to secure funding to complete the transcontinental and did not want local Manitoba rail lines that might link with the Northern Pacific across the American border and drain away business. It was certainly the intention of J.J. Hill of the Northern Pacific to do just that.

When Premier Norquay, on July 2, 1887, chartered the Red River Valley Railway, Macdonald, in an angry letter to Manitoba Lieutenant Governor Aikins, said that the population at Winnipeg "must be taught a lesson." He instructed Aikins to send the statutes establishing the new railway to him at "the first convenient opportunity." The charter was disallowed by the federal government two weeks after its passage. Aikins complained that it was reckless of the Manitoba government to build the Red River Valley Railway, running down the west side of the Red River when the CPR line already ran down the east side, "when there is not business enough for the existing lines."[37]

The monopoly clause was finally cancelled in March 1888 when Macdonald and CPR president George Stevens decided that it was doing more harm than good to the railway. The Thomas Greenway government that succeeded Norquay's did make connections with the Northern Pacific but it did not result in a drop in freight rates because the two competing railways colluded to keep rates high.

In the late 1880s new settlers were not choosing to come to the Canadian northwest in large numbers, many choosing instead to take homesteads in the US. The Macdonald government, the railway, and the Winnipeg Board of Trade, along with many others, tried to correct the problem. The Board turned its attention to the many acres of vacant lands held by speculators that surrounded Winnipeg and which seemed to many to be a desirable area for new settlers.

In February 1886, the Board passed a resolution on this matter directed to the City Council stating that since the province was sparsely populated and many more could be accommodated than were presently living in Manitoba, and since the policies of the CPR and the federal government led immigrants to bypass Winnipeg and settle in the Northwest Territories, the City of Winnipeg should take certain actions. First, offices should be established in the east to dispense information about the good quality lands available around Winnipeg then a program should be inaugurated to drain the marshy land around the city and to build wagon roads linking Winnipeg with farming areas. The non-resident owners of land would be encouraged to sell. By these and other means, the Board argued that the population could be increased fourfold.

In response to a letter of enquiry in November 1886, James Steen, the secretary of the Board, wrote that they were gathering information about the owners of vacant lands, as well as which lands were for sale and at what prices. A committee was appointed, and they received offers of upwards of one million acres within 25 miles of Winnipeg. Some of the prices were quite high, probably because the land had been purchased during the boom of 1881-1882 at inflated prices.

Most land, however, was quoted in the range of $6.00 an acre. The Board's report on the matter said that, in fact, "farms for thousands of settlers are obtainable at prices of from $2.00 to $5.00 an acre." These prices were lower than those being asked for land offered by colonization companies in more remote areas. This information was circulated to combat the idea that land close to the city was very expensive. In spite of efforts to attract newcomers, it was to be another decade before immigration picked up speed.

End of the Land Boom

The telegraph arrived in Winnipeg in 1871, but what interested people most was ensuring that when a railway was built to link Manitoba with eastern Canada, it would pass through the city. There were many public meetings, much lobbying and bargaining, and by the end of the 1870s Winnipeg was linked to the US rail network by a line that terminated in St. Boniface and the City had successfully gotten an agreement that the Canadian Pacific Railway's main line would cross the Red River at Winnipeg.

As the 1870s came to an end, the long-awaited rail connection to the outside world was completed. In January of 1878, Thomas Nixon, a manager for the Canadian Pacific Railway until his death in 1904, issued a call for tenders for 165,000 ties for the branch line that would link Emerson and St. Boniface. A month later he called for bids for the grading, bridging and track laying on the line. The station for this line was to be in St. Boniface and a steam ferry would carry passengers and freight across from the end of Provencher Avenue to the Winnipeg side of the Red.

In the federal election of September 1878, Sir John Macdonald's Conservatives were returned to office after an absence of four years. His government reversed the policy of the preceding Liberal administration that had decided that the CPR main line would cross the Red River at Selkirk. The Conservatives promised that the crossing would be made at Winnipeg and the main line would run through the city.

The business community of Winnipeg had been lobbying to secure the bridge for several years and there would be more meetings and debate before it was finally settled that the city would pay for the bridge that crossed the river at the eastern end of Point Douglas. On August 26, 1881, the first train crossed the Red River over the new bridge.

It had been widely known that Winnipeg would be the crossing point for many months by the time this train crossed the river. The frenzied sale of lots in the business district along Main Street had begun in 1880. In that year $1.25 million was invested in real estate in the city.[38]

In the spring of 1881 "crowds of men began to arrive in the city to work on the railway and construction materials were piling up in preparation for the line that would soon be heading west toward Brandon."[39]

News of the beginning of construction was carried in eastern Canadian papers and excitement increased. It began to seem that all of Ontario was making the trip to Winnipeg to invest or look for work. Charles Bell described how, in many eastern towns and cities, companies were formed by several investors each contributing a few hundred dollars. Then one member would set out for the West with a letter of credit for the full amount and instructions to buy lots and sell them at a profit.[40]

In some cases, several such groups pooled their resources and purchased a river lot stretching back two miles from a 40-foot front on the river. Then a plan would be drawn up showing one or two parks and a grid of streets and lots. A lithograph of the plan would be made and distributed. Members of the syndicate would spend time in the various auction rooms in the city praising the lots available in the plan. Ads would be placed in the newspapers and then an auctioneer would be hired. Once a few sales were made, the owners would sell the remaining property for a lump sum and divide their profits.

Since it was possible to buy on margin—to pay only a percentage of the advertised price in order to gain possession—properties changed hands often and each time lots sold, the price went up. Bell gives the example of a man who went to the Hudson's Bay Company land office and bought two Company lots valued at $700 each. He was required to pay only 1/5 of the price, or $280. While he was leaving the land office, another man stopped him and offered to buy the lots. The owner asked for $400 and on being paid that amount ownership and the obligation to pay the balance owing were transferred. The original purchaser made a $120 profit in a matter of a few minutes.

Prices rose in April, May, and June. In April, land along Sherbrook Street, the western boundary of the city, was selling for $650 an acre. Streets running into Main saw price rises. On Market Street east of

Main, lots were selling for $130 per front foot and a lot on Rorie Street sold for $50 a foot. Randy Rostecki notes that with high prices the new owners were obliged to build substantial buildings on these lots in order to realize a profit on their investment. Frame houses were demolished and replaced with larger commercial buildings.[41]

In September 1881, the excitement seemed to be dying down when an auction of Hudson's Bay Company lots resulted in some very high prices being paid and the frenzied buying and selling began again. About this time Andrew Bannatyne sold 250 square feet of land at the corner of Rorie and Bannatyne for $25,000. He then sold the site of his original Main Street store at the corner of Lombard for $20,000. Needless to say, these were amazing prices for lots that fairly recently had been prairie.

In October 1881 people began to state that the boom was over, all the land suitable for business establishments having been sold. Once the land near the centre of the city was tied up in this way, speculators without much money were forced to enter the market by buying "outside" properties in the suburbs or on the open prairie. Malleson Farm, one mile north of the city, was bought and auctioned by Joseph Wolf for a profit of $9,000.

As the CPR line moved west, smaller land booms occurred in towns that sprang up along the way. Many were "paper towns," laid out on plans but never actually built. Not so with Brandon. There the arrival of the CPR was as beneficial as it had been in Winnipeg. On June 21, 1881, the *Winnipeg Times* ran a story describing how in the six weeks since the CPR crossed the Assiniboine River at Brandon the place had grown substantially with buildings of all sorts going up, including close to 100 houses. Homesteaders were pouring into the surrounding country in every direction.

As 1881 progressed, more and more people began to advise caution, saying that the boom was nearing an end. Robert Riley, working for Hamilton clothing manufacturer W.E. Sanford in Manitoba, was concerned about the amount of money his employer had invested in Manitoba real estate. He later wrote that he was unimpressed by some of Sanford's partners, men he had known in Ontario. The lawyer J.A.M. Aikins and the miller Daniel McMillan were trustworthy board members in the real estate syndicate, who had each invested $1000. But Sanford had also gone into various real estate investments with others in the heated atmosphere of the 1881-1882 boom. At the centre of all the deals was C.P. Brown, called by Riley "the King bee of them all." Brown was a provincial cabinet minister and the MLA for Westbourne. He already had a reputation for patronage deals and questionable practices and by the end of the 1880s his reputation was so bad he was no longer able to get elected.

Riley wrote that he was "sure a reaction was coming; the thing had gone too crazy" and he was anxious to get his employer out of at least some of the investments. He asked the partners to buy Sanford out and some eventually did although they were reluctant to pay.

The spring of 1882 brought a disastrous flood that played an important part in ending the excitement. Riley later wrote:

> We had snow and water such as I have never seen since. That was the year in which the Louise Bridge was washed out: in that year, the new city hall collapsed; it was the year in which we were rowing flat boats on the ditches and creeks for miles out on the prairie from main Street, and over the new graded street known as Notre Dame. There was a stream rushing across Main Street, where the Union Bank now stands, that would run a grist mill.[42]

The floods of the spring brought the great boom to a close.

Many people lost money when the land values dropped, and the same banks and speculators who had rushed to participate in the land casino were now critical of Winnipeg and Winnipeggers, blaming the City for their losses. A lot of speculators packed their bags and headed for the next boom town. Winnipeg, however, enjoyed some benefits because of the boom. The population had risen quickly, and a good deal of construction had taken place in the city. Some of the

Easterners who had come during the boom stayed and became contributors to the growth of the city in the decades ahead.

Competition for the CPR

Once the CPR main line and repair shops had been successfully located in Winnipeg, the business community and the growing farm community became concerned about the issue of CPR freight rates being too high. Everyone's favorite remedy was the construction of other railways that would offer competition and force rates down. Sir John A. Macdonald and the CPR argued that rates in Canada were lower than the charges across the border in the US. Macdonald defended the railway he had struggled to found, considering it to be essential for the successful creation of the Dominion of Canada. The railway was far from being profitable in the 1880s and he was not interested in lowering rates. The CPR's agreement with the government included a 20-year monopoly clause, barring the construction of any non-CPR rail lines south or southwest of the company's main line. This was intended to block American competition that would result if local railways crossed the border and made a connection with the Northern Pacific or Great Northern lines in the US. The monopoly clause was intended to give the Canadian road a chance to prosper and pay its debts, but it was considered by Westerners to be just another example of how their longed-for railway was oppressing them.

In the 1870s and 1880s there were attempts by the Manitoba government to charter local railways and Macdonald used the power of the federal government to disallow them all. One of the Manitoba lines was never disallowed, although it received very little support from the Dominion government. The Hudson Bay Route was intended to connect Winnipeg to the shores of Hudson Bay by following the rivers and lakes of the province and the Northwest Territories. It was the route that, for many years, the Hudson's Bay Company had used to move furs, trade goods, supplies and people south from the Bay to Upper Fort Garry by canoe and later York Boat. The idea of building a rail line more or less along this same route began to gain support in the 1870s. The Winnipeg business community supported the idea, and it was a Winnipegger, Hugh Sutherland, a Winnipeg lumberman and railway promoter, who would actually make a start on the project, although he was not the man to complete it.

Over the years, the Hudson Bay Route's many proponents have argued that it is a shorter route to Britain from western Canada than the path from Thunder Bay through eastern Canada to Montreal, Halifax and St. John and then by sea from there. The Hudson Bay Route is a distance of 5,238 kilometers as opposed to about 7,196 kilometers through the Great Lakes and the St. Lawrence. Western farmers were told they would enjoy savings in the cost of shipping grain to Britain. A second argument that was much more important in the nineteenth century than later was that it ran exclusively through Canadian territory, far from the US border and the competition from American railroads.

Colonel J.S. Dennis, the Dominion Surveyor General, wrote to Sir John Macdonald about immigration. Immigrants who landed at Port Nelson on the shores of Hudson Bay, said Dennis "may be placed on land at Prince Albert on the Saskatchewan more cheaply and within a few hours short of the time they could be set down at London, Ontario."[43] Robert Bell, an officer of the Canadian Geological Survey travelled extensively in the north on various expeditions. He became a strong supporter of the Hudson's Bay route. In the summers of 1875 and 1877 he explored James Bay, in 1878 he surveyed the northern shore of Lake Winnipeg, and the next year he mapped the Nelson and the Hayes rivers. In 1880 he surveyed the Churchill River and then sailed from Churchill to England in a steamer. Bell concluded the route could be a cheap and direct highway for immigrants.

In 1878 Henry Youle Hind testified before a House of Commons committee on immigration saying that the Bay route was an ideal way to bring settlers from Europe to the west.[44]

In the provincial election of 1878 Conservative John Norquay included mention of the Hudson Bay Railway in his platform. He made a general pledge to give local railways, including the Hudson Bay road, provincial aid, and to move the northern boundary of the province so the entire Hudson Bay route would be within Manitoba.

Norquay and his colleague Joseph Royal went to Ottawa to press for these changes, but Macdonald put them off, claiming he was too busy to attend to them. He saw the proposed Hudson Bay line as one more threat to the CPR and so he never acted on Norquay's requests. He did, however, move the northern boundary, but not far enough to give the province access to the shore of the Bay.

Between 1877 and 1880 two railway companies came into existence. The Nelson Valley Railway and Transportation Company was backed by a group of wealthy Montreal businessmen. With a head office in Montreal, its charter authorized the company to build a railway from the north end of Lake Winnipeg to the Churchill River. The other company, the Winnipeg and Hudson's Bay Railway, was promoted by Hugh Sutherland. Sutherland's associate, MP William Bannerman, introduced the bill to incorporate the railway and they then had the right to build a line from Winnipeg to Port Nelson at the mouth of the Nelson River and to issue $2 million in common stock.

Sutherland was a Liberal who had, during Alexander Mackenzie's government, held the post of Superintendent of Public Works. With the fall of the Mackenzie regime, he lost this job, and the collapse of the real estate boom in Winnipeg put an end to Sutherland's extensive lumber business. His railway promotions were likewise not very successful, both because of John A. Macdonald's opposition and the fact that 1881 saw the beginning of a depression that would last until 1894. The price of wheat began a long decline from $1.25 a bushel in 1881 to 51 cents in 1894. The number of homesteads taken up in 1884 was half the 1881 figure. Given these conditions, British investors were not anxious to put money into Canadian railway projects. The start of the Northwest Rebellion in 1885 only made matters worse.[45]

Finding it difficult to secure financial backing, the two Hudson Bay railways began to discuss amalgamation. This happened in April 1884. With the CPR almost complete, Macdonald encouraged the merger and Parliament voted to grant $70,000 for an expedition to explore Hudson Strait. Macdonald granted support in the form of 6,400 acres per mile within the province of Manitoba and 12,800 acres per mile for the line in the Northwest Territories. Secured by this land grant, the Province issued $1 million in bonds. The new railway was called the Winnipeg and Hudson Bay Railway, with Hugh Sutherland as the president.

Sutherland set out to raise additional funds in England, but he was no more successful than he had been before the amalgamation. When he approached John A. Macdonald for support, the prime minister told him that the fact that he had been unsuccessful in raising money indicated that he should probably wait until economic conditions improved. But Hugh Sutherland did not give up.

At the beginning of 1884 the project had a good deal of support. The Winnipeg Board of Trade expressed approval for the railway and for a survey of Hudson Strait at their annual meeting in January. Then in February the Board passed a resolution of support and another encouraging the federal government to move the northern boundary of Manitoba north to the 60th parallel, where it is currently located. This would not be done until 1912. Also in January 1884 there was a convention in Grand Forks, to which the Board of Trade sent their Secretary, that brought together Americans interested in the idea of a railway to the Bay. The Manitoba and North West Farmer's Union, a political organization formed in 1884, also supported the construction of a northern railway in their platform. In March the Manitoba Legislature supported a cautious motion to set up a committee to investigate the establishment of a system of communication between Manitoba and Hudson Bay.

At this time, C.N. Bell—a Winnipegger who would soon become the secretary of the Board of Trade—published a pamphlet, containing detailed information that the Board had requested. Using American government information and books about the Bay, Bell was able to report on tides, hours of light, length of the ice-free period each year, temperatures, ice conditions and winds encountered while navigating the Hudson Strait. He commented that documents by Hudson's Bay Company officials were sometimes not very useful, given the Company's desire to keep such information secret.

In 1885, the Northwest Rebellion had the effect of slowing railway developments and discouraging investors but by 1886 Sutherland was on the move once again. The Province agreed to issue $1 million in bonds, secured by the land grant that had been promised. He then used this money to contract with the West Cumberland Iron and Steel Company for steel rails and other equipment. The bonds, however, would not be available until the railway was completed. So he gave the West Cumberland company bonds as security until the provincial bonds were issued. He did this without the permission of his board of directors, who later would demand that he repudiate his action.

He then engaged two experienced railway contractors, Donald Mann and Herbert Holt, to begin building the road. Donald Mann would be the partner of William Mackenzie in building the Canadian Northern Railway a few years later and Holt became one of the wealthiest businessmen in Montreal.

During the provincial and federal elections of 1891, the Conservatives gained seats by making strong statements of support for the Hudson Bay Route. In Manitoba, Thomas Greenway, having lost some seats over the issue, introduced legislation that provided a $1.5 million payment when the railway was finally complete, stipulating that construction had to be finished in five years. In Ottawa, Macdonald supported an annual government transport contract worth $80,000 provided Sutherland agreed to go into partnership with his contractors. In spring 1891 the contractors Ross, Herbert Holt, Donald Mann and William McKenzie became partners in the Winnipeg and Hudson Bay Railway.

Economic conditions remained dire, however. The price of wheat continued to fall and the numbers of new immigrants also declined. Two of Sutherland's new partners, Ross and Herbert Holt, withdrew from the company. In the 1890s Mackenzie and Mann incorporated Sutherland's railway into their own enterprise and in 1899 the Winnipeg and Great Northern, as it was by then known, was amalgamated officially with their Lake Manitoba Railway and Canal Company under the name Canadian Northern Railway.

Sutherland continued his efforts to promote the Hudson Bay route for a time, but he gave up his dream and became an executive of Canadian Northern and spent the rest of his life occupying various posts in Mackenzie and Mann's organization. He remained a respected member of the Winnipeg business elite, living on Roslyn Road, a familiar figure riding his pure-bred saddle horses every morning in the neighbourhood. When Canadian Northern went bankrupt in 1919, he moved to England, where he died in 1926, shortly before construction on the final phase of the Hudson Bay line resumed.

Wilfrid Laurier, when he became prime minister in 1896, included the Hudson Bay Railway in his platform, having realized its popularity in the west. During the 1908 federal election both the Conservatives and Liberals supported the construction of the road. In 1911, before the election of that year, Laurier made a request for tenders to resume work on the northern railway. The Winnipeg contractor J.D. McArthur won the job. Laurier was defeated but the Conservative government of Robert Borden backed the project. From 1912 to 1917 work progressed on the line and track was laid with the objective of making the terminus at Port Nelson at the mouth of the Nelson River. Working conditions were extremely poor on this project. McArthur and his sub-contractors managed the work very badly. Confusion over how many workers were needed resulted in large numbers of penniless men travelling to the North only to live in abject poverty in The Pas after being turned down for work on the line. For those who did get jobs, the food was not of good quality and some men contracted scurvy. In 1917 work was stopped because the massive requirements for financing the war meant money for railways was very scarce.

When peace came there was disagreement about whether to finish the project or not. Finally, in 1925 a motion was passed in the House of Commons to restart the work. In 1926 the short-lived Meighen government included money in their budget to commence work. McKenzie King formed a government in 1926 and made the decision to complete the line in order to maintain the support of the Progressive Party in the Commons. Charles Dunning, the former premier of Saskatchewan and a supporter of the Hudson Bay line, was appointed Minister of Railways. The decision was now made to build the line to Churchill instead of Port Nelson, the harbor at Churchill being better. The survey of the line and the decisions about its location were made in 1927, and in 1928 the CNR began the task of repairing the line that had not been maintained for 10 years and then completing the track to Churchill. Much of the line was laid on top of muskeg in very wet conditions. The Hudson Bay Railway reached Churchill in March 1929 and the last spike was driven. Work on a terminal elevator began, and the first shipment of grain from Churchill sailed out into the Bay in September 1931. The rail line had taken half a century to complete. During that time shelf after shelf of committee reports, proposals and plans were produced by the various promoters of the line. The railroad was perhaps the most studied of any business in the history of Winnipeg and Manitoba.

AFTER THE BOOM

Winnipeg at the Turn of the Century

Many writers have painted the real estate boom and its collapse as a catastrophe for Winnipeg. Historian Randy Rostecki, however, differs. In his MA thesis, "The Growth of Winnipeg, 1870-1886," undoubtedly one of the best analyses of the boom, he writes that the months of the real estate madness drew thousands of new citizens to the city, many of whom stayed, permanently pushing the city's population into the range of a real city. The building that had taken place during 1881 and 1882 expanded the area of Winnipeg and established many of the services that any city must have. One effect of the real estate madness was to attract a number of young men from Ontario who would stay in Winnipeg for the rest of their lives and play an important role in the city.

Augustus Nanton came to Winnipeg in the early 1880s at the same time as a number of other young men from Ontario. Unlike the homesteaders who were beginning to claim their lands in Manitoba

Portage Avenue, c. 1907   CITY OF WINNIPEG ARCHIVES

or the waves of immigrants who came beginning in the 1890s, these
men came not as farmers, but as the representatives of firms head-
quartered in the east in Toronto or Montreal or some of the smaller
cities like Hamilton. They intended to be in on the ground floor, to
provide the capital, equipment, and supplies that the settlers needed.
Nanton, like many of these new arrivals, came from a wealthy background. His father had been a law partner of Alexander Galt, one of
the fathers of Confederation. Galt's son and nephew also arrived in
Winnipeg at this time, founding a wholesale grocery business and
creating the Blue Ribbon food brand that still exists today.

Nanton's mother was the daughter of William Jarvis, who was the
sheriff of Toronto and whose estate, Rosedale, later became the site of
the exclusive Toronto district of the same name. Augustus Nanton's
father died in his early forties from the effects of alcoholism, leaving
his family destitute. His wife was obliged to operate a private girls'
school in order to support herself and her children.

Augustus was educated at Upper Canada College but at the age
of 14 he went to work to help his mother. He paid for his brother
to attend the Royal Military College and took care of his mother's

debts. He worked first for Henry Pellat's brokerage firm and then for the firm of Osler and Hammond. In 1883, while still in his twenties, he was sent by this firm to reconnoiter in the West. He arrived immediately after the collapse of the great western land boom that followed the announcement that the CPR main line would be built through Winnipeg.

Many investors who had seen a chance to make quick money through speculation during the land boom had suffered losses when land prices collapsed in 1882. After that experience, many Easterners were unwilling to risk their funds in the West. Osler and Hammond, however, was interested in the longer term. Making a first tour of the West, Nanton, who would become a partner in the firm, travelled as far as he could on the CPR and then explored on horseback and by buggy, often sleeping under the open sky. He would be responsible for investing other people's money in the development of the Prairies and so he needed a good knowledge of the land and its character.

Nanton concluded that the West had enormous potential and should not be written off. His balanced, intelligent reports back to Toronto earned him the role of the firm's western representative and he moved permanently to Winnipeg in 1884 to establish a branch there.

As a young bachelor he lived in a house nicknamed the "Shanty" on Roslyn Road. W.T. Kirby of Oldfield Kirby and Gardner; lawyer G.W. Allan; lawyer Heber Archibald; and W.R. Allan of Allan, Killam and McKay, a Winnipeg insurance brokerage, all lived in the house as well when they were young. The *Tribune*, in W.R. Allan's obituary, recorded that "The Shanty was a great center of social activity in the old days, and the great room which served as living and dining room during the daytime was the scene of many a merry dance when night fell."[46] This shared experience created close bonds among the men, all of whom would be prominent in the city in the years ahead.

Nanton was successful in bringing Scottish, English, and eastern Canadian capital to the West and offering sound conservative advice on its use. He made many people rich and became rich himself by investing in mortgages and other loans to farmers.

He also gave money away, supporting charities in his adopted city and, during the Great War, donating enormous amounts of money—some sources say half his assets—and time to such causes as the Patriotic Fund, established to support the wives and families of soldiers who had gone overseas. He headed several prairie campaigns for the sale of Victory Bonds, a huge undertaking that raised millions for the war effort. He also took a personal responsibility for people that taxed his time and energy. One story typical of that time was how Nanton got up in the night to drive the pregnant wife of a soldier serving in France to the hospital because she had no one else to help her. By the 1920s he was on many national corporate boards, including those of the CPR and the Hudson's Bay Company and of Winnipeg concerns such as the Winnipeg Electric Company. His business interests connected Winnipeg to enterprises all across the country.

In 1924, when the death of his partner Edmund Osler left the position vacant, he moved to Toronto to become president of the Dominion Bank. When they left Winnipeg the Nantons were honoured with several dinners at which there was much talk about his many accomplishments and contributions to the city.

Nanton was still exhausted from his war work and he seemed unwell, giving only short responses at the official events. He settled into the work in Toronto but soon he became seriously ill with Bright's Disease—a kidney disease that would today be called nephritis. There was no cure and he died in Toronto on April 24, 1925 at the relatively early age of 65. Nanton was buried four days later in Winnipeg, in St. John's churchyard, after a funeral service in St. Luke's Church, where he had been a parishioner.

His funeral attracted enormous crowds an indication of his stature in Winnipeg. His body was brought to St. Luke's church at 10 o'clock in the morning and from then until the funeral started at 2:30, a constant stream of people passed by the casket. Robert Fletcher, the deputy minister of education, played the organ in the church, which was completely filled. A large overflow crowd stood in the streets outside. There were so many wreaths from businesses and from private individuals that they occupied the entire front of the church.

The pallbearers were friends and business associates who had worked with him over the previous 40 years: Hugh John Macdonald, the former premier and son of John A Macdonald; W.T. Kirby, a partner in Kirby Oldfield and Gardner; T.L. Peters; F.L. Patton, an old friend of Nanton and an official of the Dominion Bank; George W. Allan, a lawyer; H.F. Osler, son of the firm's founder and Nanton's partner; P.L. Naismith of Calgary; and T.R. Deacon, owner of Manitoba Bridge and Iron Works.

After the funeral service, the casket was taken to St. John's Cathedral. Many stores closed while the procession passed, and the streetcars stopped for five minutes. About 600 employees of the Winnipeg Street Railway, of which Nanton had been president, lined Nassau Street between River Avenue and Roslyn Road.

There was a sense that with the death of Nanton and many of his contemporaries, like James Ashdown, James Aikins and William Alloway during the 1920s, old Winnipeg was also dying. People began to replace Nanton in his many positions. In Toronto, Albert Austin became president of the Dominion Bank. Hugh Osler, Nanton's partner, became president of Osler Hammond and Nanton. Lawyer G.W. Allan became chair of the Canadian Committee of the Hudson's Bay Company. Andrew McLimont took Nanton's place as president of Winnipeg Electric and its various subsidiaries.

According to his will and the accompanying documents, the value of Nanton's estate at the time of his death was $1,053,610.00. Using a calculation based on inflation over the years that figure would have purchasing power equivalent to $16,043,707 today.[47] Because he had not yet established his change of residence with the Manitoba taxation department at the time of his death, his estate was taxed by Manitoba and Ontario and the federal government, and the total death duties were close to $200,000.

His estate was a reflection of his business interests. He had shares in many Winnipeg firms in addition to his own. The largest investments were in Great-West Life ($118,000), Winnipeg Electric ($13,000), Manitoba Cartage ($26,500), Manitoba Cold Storage ($11,000) and Crescent Creameries ($20,000). He also owned shares in Northern Trust, Northern Mortgage, and the Canadian Fire Insurance Company, Winnipeg firms that many members of the elite invested in. He participated in the management of some firms. He could be said to have been one of the founders of Great-West Life and served on the board. He was also on the board of Winnipeg Electric Company and had been the president for some years. Loaning mortgage money was an important part of Osler, Hammond and Nanton's business, and at the time of his death Nanton personally held 51 mortgages on farmland.

After making various bequests to relatives and employees, he stated that he wanted the bulk of his estate to be put into a trust to provide income for his wife, who would provide for their children until they reached the age of 25, when they would begin to receive the income from their part of the trust. At 30 the boys would get the capital. The daughters would continue to get only the income, and if they married, the trust ensured that the income would be their own property and not their husbands'.

Half of Nanton's estate consisted of $500,000 in shares in Osler Hammond and Nanton. He directed in his will that this investment should be sold five years after his death, but that if any of his sons was able to become a partner, $250,000 ($3 million in current dollars) should be left invested for him. His son Edward did become a partner and eventually president of the firm.

Nanton was generous to the servants who had worked for him for decades. He had purchased a house for his chauffeur, Charles Wright, when he retired and paid for his gardener, Charles Beavis, to return home to England when he stopped working for the Nantons. These men also received a small monthly pension from the estate.

Lady Nanton continued to live in Kilmorie, the Nantons' home on Roslyn Road, until 1935 when, in order to reduce her $3,200 tax bill, she had the house demolished. She lived in a smaller house on the property until her death in 1942.

Robert Riley is another example of a young man who came to Manitoba from Ontario as the agent of a large investor in the new province. His early career gives us a picture of how Ontarians with money to invest quickly entered the Manitoba economy. Later Riley evolved from the role of agent and became a leader in the Winnipeg business community as he established his own businesses and championed his city and province.

Riley was born in Yorkshire in 1851, the son of a ship owner and publisher. He went to the St. Thomas Charterhouse School in London and in 1873, after trying two different clerical positions in London, he decided to take a job accompanying a group of children travelling to Canada. The children were orphans and they were on their way to a Methodist Children's Home in Hamilton where they would stay until they were placed on a farm. There they could work, earn wages, and have an opportunity to go to school.

William Eli Sanford, a prominent Methodist, was on the committee for the children's home. Sanford was an orphan himself but one with wealthy relatives who helped him start in business. In the 1860s he had become a highly successful clothing manufacturer and by 1871 his firm was the largest in Hamilton, with 450 workers and yearly sales of $35,000. After 1879, when the Macdonald government placed high tariffs on many manufactured items, including British clothing, Sanford's business expanded greatly, and he opened retail stores and agencies in Ontario cities, Winnipeg, and Victoria.

Robert Riley decided to stay in Canada and began looking for a job. He worked at various things and eventually went to work for William Sanford managing the lands and projects Sanford had invested in in Manitoba.

In the spring of 1883, Riley brought his wife and children to Winnipeg from his farm in the Hamilton area. The family lived on the corner of Furby and Wolseley for a number of years until they moved into the "Gates" a short distance away on East Gate. The house was expanded twice over the years.

For a few years in the 1880s, Riley operated a stock farm on some of the 52,000 acres of land Sanford acquired in the Wesbourne area. Starting with 70 brood mares and 400 cows with calves, Riley made a good deal of money for his employer. It was not long before the farm had 1000 head of cattle and 200 horses. Sanford would charter a special train to bring buyers up from Winnipeg for his annual horse sales.

In 1889 Sanford reorganized his business into a joint stock company. Riley bought shares and became one of the directors. He did this in spite of the fact that he did not like merchandising and found it more interesting to buy and sell cattle, grain, horses or any sort of farm produce. He found the retail business to be a "great drudgery." He paid cash for his shares and, on Sanford's invitation, invested his dividends up to a limit of 49% of the company. When Riley asked if he could increase his holdings by $25,000, Sanford refused. Robert Riley asked Sanford to buy him out and he did. Riley then left the employ of the man he had worked for close to two decades and began working for himself as an investor and the founder of insurance companies.

His philosophy of investing is found in his memoirs. When he first came to Winnipeg, he had sold his farm near Hamilton and

> I was able to realize in all about $3400. I made up my mind that I would live on what I could earn and that the $3400 I would keep turning over and put by as a fund for the education of my family or the protection of my wife and myself in old age. I kept track of that original $3400 until by continually turning it over whenever I got a chance and taking a profit it assumed the very respectable proportions of $88,000, a good illustration of what can be done by compounding interest and turning your profits into capital.[48]

■

James Aikins was born in Peel County west of Toronto in 1851.[49] His father, James Cox Aikins, was a farmer who went into politics and served as a cabinet minister in two of John A. Macdonald's governments and ended his career as the lieutenant governor of Manitoba in the 1880s. The family was not well off when James was born and at 14, he began to help his mother manage the farm while his father was involved in politics.

James was educated at local schools and then at Upper Canada College and University of Toronto. A devout Methodist, he taught Sunday school and participated in bible study classes. He earned an MA in 1876 and articled in Toronto law firms.

He first came to Winnipeg in 1878 to visit his brother, who had been living in the city for some time. After passing the bar exam, he returned to Winnipeg and founded a law firm that over the years represented many important clients, including the federal Department of Justice, the Manitoba government, and the Canadian Pacific Railway.

His first office was in a Main Street building and consisted of a 10-foot by 10-foot room with a kitchen table and a few chairs. Soon after his arrival, in partnership with his brother and his father, he began making mortgage loans with money entrusted to him by friends in the east. During the land boom of 1881 and 1882 there was heavy demand for mortgage money as well as legal services and Akins' business must have been brisk. Of course, many mortgage lenders were never paid back by investors caught in the collapse of prices in 1882.

Aikins, with his brother and father, was involved in speculations during the boom. He owned the Brunswick Hotel at Rupert and Main, and he had extensive real estate holdings over the years, including the building now known as the Bate Building at McDermot and Albert Street. He bought the Somerset Block on Portage Avenue and Donald Street for $250,000. The firm had offices there for 50 years.

James Aikins would eventually hold many corporate directorships, including with the Imperial Bank, Northern Trusts, Canadian

Indemnity, and he was president of General Assets Ltd., an investment trust.

As a lawyer, Aikins was involved as the solicitor for many of the new businesses springing up in the city at the time and the board meetings of many new firms were held in his office. He and his partners were busy litigators, appearing in court frequently. In 1881 Aikins moved to more spacious quarters in the McKay Block. His brother, Somerset, moved his real estate office into the same building and the YMCA, of which Aikins was a founding member, was also located there. At this time, he was engaged by the CPR as their solicitor, and he opened a separate office in the McKay Block to house his work for the railway. He would eventually have an office in the CPR office building adjoining the station on Higgins Avenue. He held the position of solicitor until 1911 when he went into politics.

As solicitor he was involved in the company's land sales, which were considerable in the 1880s. By February 1882, the CPR had sold 85,000 acres of the land granted to it by the government for $7.50 per acre for a total of $637,500. Aikins was also busy negotiating for and representing the company in court. There was plenty of other work for the 29-year-old lawyer and his partners. Winnipeg's population grew from 6,000 in 1879 to 12,000 in 1880 and 20,000 in 1881.

When the land boom collapsed in spring 1882, many local businesses and individuals saw the value of the land they had purchased drop and their loans were called by the banks. Suddenly the city was oversupplied with lawyers, there being at least 200 practising in Winnipeg. Aikins' offices were destroyed by a fire in April 1882. When the Imperial Bank built a new building in the city, Aikins rented the second floor. He acted as the Bank's lawyer for many years. When his father became lieutenant governor of Manitoba in 1883, James moved into Government House. In 1884 the members of the firm were involved in 34 court cases. By 1885 Aikins had seven lawyers and eight articling students to share the workload. James Aikins was junior Crown Council at the appeal of Riel's conviction for treason. The appeal was denied.

At this time, the CPR was becoming firmly established and the corporation's financial problems beginning to recede. In August 1885 Winnipeg was linked to Montreal by rail and in summer of 1886, regular trans-continental service between Montreal and Vancouver began.

Aikins served on many Royal Commissions and was the Conservative MP for Brandon from 1911 until 1915. He led the Manitoba Conservative Party in the disastrous 1915 election when, as a result of the Legislature scandal, the party was reduced to four seats. He served on the boards of Wesley College, the University of Manitoba, and the Canadian Club of Winnipeg. He was a founder and first president of the present Canadian Bar Association from 1914 to 1927 and served as honorary colonel for two Manitoba militia regiments. He was lieutenant governor of Manitoba from 1916 to 1926.

When he died on March 1, 1929, Sir James' estate was valued at $1.7 million ($24,668,085 in 2020 buying power). He had investments in stocks and bonds worth $1.6 million. His money was held in an investment trust together with the money of other investors as a managed fund. He did not have a lot of property, although he held $36,000 in mortgages. A yearly income of $7,000 ($101,000 in 2020 buying power), was to be paid to his wife and when she passed away in 1931 this income went to his son, Harold Aikins, who was a partner in the law firm his father founded. He left various amounts of money to his daughters and to the United Church, the Canadian Bar Association, the YMCA, the Children's Hospital, and Wesley College, among other beneficiaries. He also left his son $100,000 in cash, his library, his shotgun, his watches and paintings, and some Venetian vases and bowls. Aikins, by leaving the bulk of his estate to his son, increased the likelihood that his law firm would survive. The law firm bearing Akins' name continues to serve the Winnipeg today.

Albert Austin was another Toronto man who came to Winnipeg in the 1880s. He founded the city's first street railway, but he was unsuccessful in competing with William Mackenzie's streetcar company and returned to the east after selling out to Mackenzie.

The Lumber Business

Until the early 1870s most structures in Winnipeg were either log or stone. As immigrants began to arrive and the city grew, the demand for lumber increased. In Winnipeg and other western communities one of the first businesses was a sawmill. Most of the quality timber along the rivers and lakes was cut by the turn of the century, leaving trees that were good only for the pulp and paper industry. Better wood for the sash and door and molding trade all came from south of the border. The railroads consumed vast amounts of wood for ties and trestle bridges. Winnipeg was the largest community and so lumber mills and sash and door factories set up in the growing city. As the railroad network grew, timber was hauled in from greater and greater distances. Previously, logs were cut and floated down the rivers and lakes of the area in vast booms.

Winnipeg was home to a number of the larger lumber firms, though they often had branches in smaller communities. Alexander Brown and Thomas Rutherford came to Winnipeg from Ontario in the early 1870s and began building houses for themselves and for sale in Point Douglas. They opened a small lumber mill in 1872 and later built a larger operation in Point Douglas. The company still exists under that name in Point Douglas as a wholesaler, but it now belongs to a larger corporation. It stayed in the Brown and Rutherford families until the 1950s.

In 1872 Brown and Rutherford imported timber from Minnesota. The wood was floated in huge log booms down the Red River to the city. In 1880 a Crown Timber Office was opened in Winnipeg and local firms applied for timber limits, areas of forest where they exclusively could harvest the trees. Brown and Rutherford had a timber limit on Moose Island, north of Hecla Island on Lake Winnipeg. Cutting timber there and bringing it to Winnipeg by water was cheaper than bringing it from Minnesota.

In the early 1880s the lumber business was the largest industry in Winnipeg because of the building boom. By 1882 lumber brought

$2 million to the city. Winnipeg-based companies took on a wholesale function for dealers in small centres. Sash and door manufacturing expanded for a lot of companies. With the end of the building boom, lumber slipped to fifth place after provisioning, milling, groceries, and dry goods.

One of the pioneer lumber merchants was Theodore Burrows, the son of the engineer who built the Rideau Canal. He came to Winnipeg from Ottawa in 1875, intending to work as a surveyor. He spent a short time as a student in a law office and then went to work for his uncle A.W. Burrows, the first land agent in Winnipeg. T.A. Burrows began in the lumber business in 1878 at Fort Alexander with a sawmill. He eventually sold out to his partner. He was involved in building a road to the Dauphin area where, realizing it would probably be the next big area for homesteading, he settled and became a booster for the town and for the construction of a railway into the district. Like many others, he accumulated timber limits. His holdings expanded and he became part owner of other lumber companies. He was elected as a Liberal MLA for Dauphin three times during the 1890s and spent time in the Legislature promoting the idea of a railway from Winnipeg northwest to Dauphin. When the Canadian Northern built the railway line, he worked from 1897 to 1904 as the railroad's land commissioner. He was well connected, being Clifford Sifton's brother-in-law, and this certainly provided the kind of information that would have helped his business career. In 1900 he and his family moved to Winnipeg where he lived until his death in 1929. He was a Liberal MP from 1904 to 1908 and in the last years of his life he was the lieutenant governor of Manitoba.

Another early lumber merchant was Daniel E. Sprague. He came to Manitoba from Ontario in 1872 and went into the lumber business with a partner, W.J. Macaulay. After working for Stobart, Eden and Company from 1877 to 1881, in 1882 he built a lumber mill and started the Sprague Lumber Company. This company was incorporated in 1903 with various members of his family as the officers. The company profited from the huge building boom over the following 10 years and Sprague served on the boards of the General Hospital, the Masons, and the St. Charles Country Club. He died in Ottawa in 1924 and was buried in Winnipeg.

D.C. Cameron was another Ontario native who was in the lumber business. He started in business in Kenora, called Rat Portage at the time. When, in 1900, the Manitoba and South Eastern Railway was built linking Winnipeg with Lake of the Woods, it was much easier for Cameron to move timber from Minnesota to Winnipeg, where he built a huge lumber mill in Norwood, just south of the St. Boniface Hospital. Cameron owned many timber limits all over the West and when the 1895 to 1913 boom took place, he was well placed to profit from it. He had retail lumber yards in many small towns selling building plans and the lumber with which to build houses and barns.

Cameron was also involved in Liberal politics and, like Burrows after him, he was lieutenant governor of Manitoba. He was in office when the scandal over the Legislative buildings blew up and caused the end of the Rodmond Roblin government in 1915.

Cameron died in the early 1920s and his wife and his sons moved to Vancouver to participate in the building boom there. In spite of all the money they had made in the prewar boom, Cameron was not a wealthy man when he passed away.

J.D. McArthur was another lumber man in Winnipeg. He had worked as a contractor during the building of the CPR and, like many such men, he was later involved in a variety of businesses. In 1901 he arrived in the area that would become Lac du Bonnet and built a brick yard and sawmill in anticipation of the growth of the town. He also had a lumber yard in Winnipeg on Higgins Avenue close to the CPR.

In 1918 he bought a mill site and timber limits near Fort Alexander. There was a thick growth of small trees on much of the land and this was ideal for processing into pulp for paper making. He intended to be the developer of the pulp mill which was built at Fort Alexander by the Manitoba Pulp and Paper Company, but he lost out to competitors and passed away in 1925. After his death his nephew, Alex McIntosh, began supplying the mill with wood from the district.

The lumber business was lucrative in the first 50 years of Winnipeg's history, when there was still a substantial amount of useful timber within reach of the city. But after the First World War most of the wood useful for lumber had been cut, and only wood suitable for pulp and paper remained. There would not be another building boom until after the Second World War

Wholesalers and Retailers

By 1890 there were between 70 and 80 wholesale firms in the city with total sales of over $15 million. The capital these firms had invested in the city was estimated to be between 6 and 8 million dollars. On December 20, 1890 the *Winnipeg Free Press* published a special issue about the wholesale business that gives us a snapshot of the complex and substantial industry that had grown up during the previous 20 years.

The territory served by Winnipeg wholesalers in 1890 stretched from the head of the lakes to the west coast and from the fur trade posts in the north to the US boundary. The city, with no real competition on the prairies, was a rail hub provided with warehouse space and experienced importers and jobbers able to respond to the needs of merchants in smaller communities further west. Massive warehouses, many of which survive, were built and enlarged to accommodate the burgeoning wholesale businesses.

Many of the wholesale companies in Winnipeg were the western branches of Ontario and Quebec firms, but locally owned businesses were growing and well able to compete. In 1890 the West was still in depression, waiting for the anticipated influx of settlers that had still not materialized.

Winnipeg merchants had been providing groceries and provisions since the 1860s and in 1890 there were many wholesale firms dealing in a wide variety of goods. McKenzie and Powis grocery wholesale

had been founded in 1868 by W.H. Lyon, one of the earliest traders. In 1890, Lyon had only recently sold his share in the business
and retired to Colorado. His partners were Kenneth McKenzie, the
son of William McKenzie who would build the Canadian Northern
Railway, and Edmond Powis. These two men had been partners in
Montreal in a tea importing business. In 1890 the firm owned the
building on McDermot and King later known as the Bate Building.
They employed three travellers and five other staff.

Turner and McKeand had been operating in Winnipeg since
1872. It was the local branch of the Hamilton firm James Turner
and Company. By 1890, McKeand, who had commanded the 90th
Winnipeg Rifles during the fighting in Saskatchewan in 1885, had
died, and Turner was carrying on with a warehouse located on
Bannatyne Avenue.

James Kirkwood and C.M. Rubridge had a warehouse on King
Street. They imported Chinese and Japanese teas and they were the
Winnipeg representatives for Pure Gold Baking Powder and the prod-
ucts of the Brantford Confectionary and Biscuit Works.

W.F. Henderson and Manlius Bull opened a commission house
business in 1882 on Bannatyne. Bull had been in the grocery business in Ontario before coming west. After a short time, he left the
partnership with Henderson and established the Royal Crown Soap
manufacturing company with a plant on King Street. Royal Crown
was fabulously successful, at one time supplying all the soap used by
the Canadian Northern Railway. There were branches in Calgary
and Vancouver. In 1910 Lever Brothers bought the company but
Manlius Bull stayed on as the Canadian director. Like many business owners, Bull invested in other companies and served on their
boards. At the time of his death in 1929, he was president of the Home
Investment and Savings Association, president of the City Provincial
Loan Company, president of the Standard Trusts Company, a director of the Great-West Life Assurance Company, and a director of the
Union Bank, by then a part of the Royal Bank of Canada.

Main Street looking north, 1910   CITY OF WINNIPEG ARCHIVES

The cousins George and John Galt established their grocery wholesale in 1882. Like others, they were attracted to Winnipeg by the extraordinary land boom which convinced many Easterners that the city and the Northwest had a bright future. Although the boom collapsed and growth slowed, the Galts remained in the city and enjoyed great success.

John Galt was the son and George the nephew of Alexander Galt, a father of Confederation and sometime member of John A. Macdonald's cabinet. Alexander Galt, amongst other businesses, had been involved in railway development in eastern Canada. By the 1880s he and his family were engaged in the development of irrigation, railway and coal mining projects in Alberta. The two Winnipeg Galts had started their careers in business in the East. George Galt had experience in the grocery trade when he came to Winnipeg and John had worked in the Bank of Montreal. Eventually their business was one of the largest grocery wholesales in Canada. In their warehouse at 103 Princess and Bannatyne, which is still standing, they carried a large stock, importing tea from China, fruit from the Mediterranean, wines and liquors and the varied products of their company, Blue Ribbon. They had staff and branches in Vancouver and Calgary and a team of travellers who rode the CPR to points between Port Arthur and the Pacific coast. Both men were involved in a range of activities in Winnipeg.

Another grocery wholesale merchant, Alexander Macdonald, had come to Winnipeg in 1871 and established a grocery wholesale company. By 1890, he had branches in Vancouver, Nelson BC, and Fort William. The headquarters of the firm were in Winnipeg. Like the Galts, he was involved in many Winnipeg companies, serving as the president of Great-West Life for many years and as a director of Northern Mortgage and Northern Trust and president of White Star Manufacturing, which made vinegar and other foods. Macdonald also served the city as an alderman and as mayor.

In 1884 George Frankfurter opened his dry goods store on Main Street near Logan Avenue. Like many of his fellow businessmen, he had come to Winnipeg by a circuitous route. Born in Germany in a village near Hamburg, Frankfurter emigrated to New York in the 1860s and worked as a clerk. In 1874 he moved to Detroit and worked as a foreman in a cigar factory. He married there. His wife was a native of Montreal. They moved to Omaha and then back to Detroit, where George operated his own cigar factory. Finally, in 1880, they moved to Winnipeg, attracted like many others by the news of its boom. George operated a dry goods store called the Fair. After 20 years he established a wholesale business.

When George and his family arrived in the city there were about 21 other Jewish families living there. One family, the three Coblenz brothers, had come in the 1870s. Edmond was the first to come in 1877 and his brothers Aachel and Adolphe, with his wife Sarah and his two children, came in 1878. Edmond worked for a short time in a dry goods store in Winnipeg and then moved to Sainte-Anne-des-Chênes where he opened his own store. The Coblenz brothers were natives of Alsace and spoke French.

Aachel worked for Stobart and Eden and then in R.J. Whitla's store on Main Street. The youngest brother, Adolphe, went to work in the Blue Store, a general store on Main Street owned by Noah Chevrier. After several years in Winnipeg, Adolphe and his wife Sarah moved to Emerson, where they operated the Golden Hotel. Eventually they owned dry goods stores in several small Manitoba towns.[50]

While most early Jewish arrivals in Winnipeg were from Germany, in the early 1880s there began an influx of Russian Jews, forced to leave home because a rash of pogroms followed the the assassination of Czar Alexander II, an event for which they were scapegoated. These early refugees were followed by thousands more Jewish people from the Russian Empire over the next decades

The Paulins Company was founded in Winnipeg by the Chambers brothers in 1871. In 1883 it became the property of W.A. Paulins and J.H. Chambers. A staff of 20 to 30 workers produced over 100 varieties of biscuits sold to retail stores across the west.

The fruit wholesalers Rublee and Riddell began as a branch of the Montreal firm of Vipond and McBride in 1882. In 1886 Rublee and Riddell purchased the business. In 1889 its turnover was $200,000 and it employed several travellers.

The firm of Porter and Ronald, established in 1881 at 33 Main Street, sold crockery and glassware. They employed two travelling salesmen. Every year their stock was replenished during a trip to Europe.

Irish-born Robert Jones Whitla came to Winnipeg in 1878 from Arnprior, Ontario where he had operated a clothing business. When he arrived in Winnipeg, he purchased the building that had formerly housed R.L. Lyons' retail store on Main Street. This was one of the first large real estate transactions of the boom. Whitla ran a retail clothing store for a time and during the boom, when the city was packed with people, he was grossing over $250,000 a year.

He decided to go into the wholesale business and sold the Main Street location. He built a five-storey warehouse on the southwest corner of McDermot and Albert in 1883. The building is still in existence and at one time was the home of the *Winnipeg Telegram* newspaper. The firm had several departments specializing in items like carpets, home furnishings and small wares.

In the same year, he took D.K. Elliot, who had worked for him for many years in Ontario and Winnipeg, as a partner. Every year, one of the partners would go to Britain and Europe to buy stock. In 1890 Whitla spent three months in Britain, returning in December.

In 1899 Whitla built his biggest warehouse on the corner of McDermot and King. The building is still in use. It originally had five storeys and two more were added in 1904. In 1900 he built a retail store at 460 Main Street. The building is three storeys and still exists. It was connected to the Imperial Dry Goods store directly behind it on Albert Street. In 1906 it was purchased by the Royal Bank. Whitla was one of the first wholesale merchants to begin manufacturing clothing and was involved in many aspects of Winnipeg life until his death in 1905. He was president of the Board of Trade and he served in the 90th Regiment as a captain during the fighting in Saskatchewan in 1885.

W.E. Sanford established a branch of his extensive clothing business in Winnipeg in 1882. Sanford was a major Hamilton clothing manufacturer and the warehouse in Winnipeg was a distributing center. At first R.T. Riley managed the business. He had worked for Sanford in various capacities in Ontario, as we have seen. He would soon begin an extremely successful career as the owner of a number of insurance companies.

The city was also home to a number of hardware and farm machinery distributors. Most of these represented established eastern firms or, in the case of farm machinery, American manufacturers.

There were two locally owned breweries in 1890. Edward Drewery owned the Redwood Brewery. Born in London, Drewery's father had been a brewer in Wales. The family immigrated to Minnesota in 1857 and established a brewery. In 1874 Edward moved to Pembina on the Canadian border and leased a brewery there, buying it in 1876. The next year he moved to Winnipeg and leased a brewery which had been opened in 1874 by Herchmer and Botkin. In 1881 he bought the brewery and invested between $60,000 and $70,000, the equivalent of $800,000 in today's dollars. In 1890 the Redwood Brewery was one of the largest in Canada, with 50,000 square feet of space in its buildings. With the brewery buildings, Drewery also bought Redwood House, a luxurious home on Redwood and Main built by William Inkster in 1857.

F.W. Drewery, Edward's brother, was a partner in the business. The brewery shipped beer and other products, like ginger ale, to all parts of Manitoba and the Northwest. Another brewery, The Empire, had been established in 1888 on Ross Avenue in Fort Rouge. The president was William Clougher and the vice president was Thomas Hannah. Empire had branches in Kamloops, Banff, Calgary and Lethbridge. Its original capital was $10,000 and it produced lager, porter and ale.

For wholesale businesses, railway freight rates were a central concern. In 1886 the new Board of Trade became involved in the issue of freight rates. On February 23, James Ashdown visited the City Council to read a resolution that the Board of Trade had adopted. In it they argued that CPR freight rates discriminated against Winnipeg's wholesale and forwarding businesses, diverting business to Montreal and points in the east. Under the prevailing rate structure, freight sent from Montreal through to Regina was charged $2.27 per hundredweight. If items were sent from Montreal to Winnipeg, the charge was $1.60, and Winnipeg to Regina, $1.19, for a total shipping cost of $2.69, 42 cents more than the direct-through charge. Winnipeg wholesale firms who ordered shipments from Montreal and then broke them down into smaller lots to ship to their customers further west were at a real disadvantage.

So that Winnipeg could compete, the Winnipeg Board of Trade was asking that the cost of shipping from Montreal to Winnipeg and then on to Regina be no more than the $2.27 charge for direct shipping.

In June 1886 a Winnipeg delegation, including some Board members, went to Ottawa. They met with Canada's Minister of Public Works Hector Langevin about the issue of building locks at the St. Andrew's rapids and were told the Department would study the matter. They also went to talk to William Van Horne, vice president of the CPR, who told them that a 15% reduction in freight rates would begin on June 1, 1886. The same reduction would apply to Brandon, Regina, and Calgary. The Winnipeg Board, while complaining that 15% fell considerably short of "what was due to the wholesale trade of this city," made sure to take credit, mailing a "circular" to traders west of Winnipeg reminding them that the reduction was the result of the Winnipeg Board of Trade's efforts.

A Second Era of Growth

In 1896, for a number of reasons, Winnipeg began a period of growth that continued with short interruptions until 1913 and 1914 when the approach of war created a depression. The immigration policy of Clifford Sifton welcomed eastern European peasant farmers who were experienced agriculturalists. The last of the homestead land in the US was taken, and the stream of people wanting to claim a homestead was diverted to western Canada. Large numbers of English immigrants were encouraged to come and settle in the West. As a result, the numbers of new immigrants passing through Winnipeg began to increase. In 1897, a total of 21,716 immigrants arrived in Canada from the United Kingdom, Europe and the United States. In 1910-1911 the figure was 311,084, and the total number of new immigrants who arrived and stayed in Manitoba during the 1901 to 1911 decade was 111,000. Winnipeg grew enormously in this period, from a population of 25,529 in 1891, to 42,540 in 1901 (a 60% increase), 90,153 in 1906, and 136,035 (a 219% increase) in 1911.

New immigrants travelling to the western part of Manitoba and to the northeast bought equipment and supplies in Winnipeg. The produce of the West, principally wheat, cattle, and hogs, was processed in Winnipeg flour mills or slaughterhouses or passed through the city on its way to markets farther east.

Existing businesses prospered, but many new businessmen arrived in Winnipeg attracted by the city's reputation as a booming community. On December 16, 1905, the *Winnipeg Tribune* printed one of the year-end special sections that were common at the time. The paper stated that 1905 had been a "Record Year in Building." The total expenditure on construction having been in the neighbourhood of $11 million, a figure that, the paper was sure, was within a few thousands of the Toronto figure.

The special section contained a good deal of boosterish talk. An introductory article, featuring a picture of James H. Ashdown, called the greatest of the city's wholesale men, asked the rhetorical question: why does Winnipeg have the tracks of every major railway running through it? One word, wheat, was the answer. The exploding wheat boom had created the impetus that changed the city from a remote Hudson's Bay Company fort to a modern metropolis, the "bull's eye of the Dominion." No less a business tycoon than James J. Hill of St. Paul, was quoted as saying "the future of Winnipeg should be almost without limit. It is the country makes the city and you have the country back of you here to support more people than presently live in all the Dominion. All you have to do is sit tight and grow."[51]

Winnipeggers, however, were not simply sitting tight. They were working day and night to ensure the growth happened. For example, several large projects were built in the area of Notre Dame and McPhillips on the western edge of the city in 1905. The Canada Malting plant with its massive grain silos was completed west of McPhillips, where it still stands near the junction with Notre Dame. The project cost $85,000 and had a capacity of over 250,000 bushels of barley. The facility was fitted with the latest equipment for cleaning the barley and collecting the grain dust that could be a cause of explosions in big elevators. Malt for the brewing industry was produced in the plant's malting plant for many years. More recently, the grain elevator has been used to store and move grain by a number of companies, and the malting plant tanks were used as a fish farm.

Nearby on Notre Dame, the Metallic Roofing Company had built a new plant that would employ 45 workers making metal grain silos and roofs. Also in the area was the Winnipeg Oil Company property, two and half acres with storage for 200,000 gallons of gas, a fuel in ever greater demand as the numbers of automobiles and trucks increased. C.W. Fillmore had started the business in 1903 with a capital of $50,000 and served as its president. He came to Winnipeg from Iowa, where he had owned a bank, in 1902. Andrew Wright was the vice president; G.E. Cooper, the secretary-treasurer; and L.A. Warner, the plant manager. Winnipeg Oil made gasoline, linseed, and other oil. They manufactured a line of products under the REGA trademark. The business employed 25 workers until it closed in 1916. In 1920 Fillmore was back in business as president of North Star Oil, located close to the Winnipeg Oil site on Notre Dame, with a refinery and warehouse on Archibald Street in St. Boniface. North Star manufactured gasolines and greases, and marketed William Penn Motor Oil in western Canada. They supplied customers across the prairies and operated five filling stations in Winnipeg.

South of Notre Dame, Peter Lyall and Sons, Contractors, had established a stone yard. There were two large sheds where stone was being cut by hand or with large diamond circular saws to supply the demands of the booming local construction industry. Two travelling cranes, one for loads of thirty tons and one for ten tons had been installed to move the stone blocks. The yard was new although the company had been in operation for some time. It was expected that 60 to 100 hands would work there. Peter Lyall and Sons was still in operation in 1915 under the name Lyall Mitchell Contractors with Peter Lyall as president and treasurer. In 1925 the business was no longer in existence.

On December 21, 1907, the *Tribune* published another special section on the growth of the Winnipeg business community. They spotlighted over two dozen mostly smaller businesses, many established since 1900.

Several warehouses, storage for the city's huge wholesale sector, were described. The Moline Plow Company had an expanded warehouse at Logan and Chambers next to the CPR tracks. It was four stories high and accommodated agricultural machinery waiting for orders to come in from farther west. Nearby, the brick warehouse of the H.P. Anderson Company at Logan and Owena was also full of agricultural machinery, gleaming with new paint. Neither of these companies were still in business in Winnipeg in 1915 or 1925.

Clare and Brockest had a three-storey warehouse at McPhillips and Ross Avenue that accommodated their inventory of furnaces, stoves, ranges and building material. In 1915 Clare and Brockest was still open under the management of H.J. Clare. By 1925 two sons of the Clare family were operating Northwest Metal Ware Ltd., selling stoves.

The National Supply Company yard near McPhillips and Notre Dame had its own spur track, stables for 30 delivery horses, and stockpiles of lumber, sashes and doors, lime, sand and stone, brick, and all kinds of structural hardware. As the building boom continued in the city, these companies were busy filling contractors' orders. This company was still in business in 1915, a year in which there was very little construction in the city, but not in 1925. There were many businesses like this during the great building boom that ended around 1913. Some lumber companies had yards in smaller communities around the province. The managers of these lumberyards provided many services, including building plans for houses and barns and the lumber needed to complete the structures.

Carter, Halls and Aldinger, another large contractor, began in 1907, having taken over the business of William Grace and Company. W.H. Carter was the president and general manager, and his partners were vice president A.H. Aldinger, an engineer; and Frank Halls, the secretary-treasurer. At the end of 1906 they were working on the train

CPR station, c. 1920   CITY OF WINNIPEG ARCHIVES

shed at the new CPR Station on Higgins. Carter Halls would, over the next decades, be involved in most of the large projects in the city, including the University of Manitoba buildings during the Great War, the Peck Building, and the Hudson's Bay store in the 1920s. W.H. Carter came to play a central role in the affairs of the city, serving as president of the Board of Trade and acting on the executive of the Committee of 1000 during the General Strike. At the end of his career, he was president of the Street Railway and was in charge when it was finally sold to the City in the 1950s.

A much smaller contractor was C. Schack and Company, a cabinetmaker with a shop at 221 Higgins, at the corner of Main Street. Schack's business was building high-quality fittings for hotels, bars, and stores. His staff of carpenters and cabinetmakers worked in cherry, oak, walnut and mahogany building showcases, furniture, shelving, and special fittings for bars. He had operated a similar business in Toronto before moving to Winnipeg. In 1915 he was no longer running his own business but worked as a cabinetmaker for Winnipeg Paint and Glass. In 1925 he was working as a clerk at Eaton's. In the great building boom of 1900 to 1912 there was plenty of work for cabinet-makers, but Schack went to work for other people in later years. At Eaton's he was likely in the furniture department.

A.B. Stewart was in business in 1907 at 642 Main making shoes and boots to order. He had been in business for three years. He did repairs and sold factory-made shoes and boots. He was a Scot who had learned his trade in the old country, which explained the name of his store—The Old Country Shoe Store. In 1915 he was listed as a shoemaker and his store was at 193 Pacific. He was not listed in 1925.

Not far west of Main on Logan was the Swedish Importing and Grocery Company, A. Hallonquist, president, and P.B. Anderson, manager. They carried wholesale and retail groceries imported from Scandinavia, offering stock fish, salt herring, spiced herring, anchovies, and hardware and household equipment like spinning wheels. With a large Icelandic population on the shore of Lake Winnipeg and a growing Scandinavian community in Winnipeg, the store did well.

In 1915 and 1925 the Hallonquist Grocery was still open at the same address and 402 Logan was a revenue property called the Hallonquist Block. In both years Ernest Hallonquist was in charge at the Swedish Canadian Publishing Company at 406 Logan.

Nearby at 325 Logan was J. Gustafson's Swedish grocery store, billed as the leading Swedish grocer in Winnipeg. It had been founded in 1900 and sold Swedish and Norwegian specialties like herring, anchovies, sardines, and fish balls. The store was still open for business in 1915 and 1925 with the name Swedish Canadian Sales.

Other important retail stores included John McKerchar's grocery store at 600 Main Street: the Maple Leaf Store, founded in 1881. The store was located between Logan and Alexander, four blocks north of the City Hall. In the beginning, McKerchar had had a partner called Pickworth, but he bought him out in 1882 and became the sole owner. McKerchar was a fairly typical Ontario immigrant, coming from St. Elmo in 1879. He was a member of the school board for 21 years and served as an alderman from 1921 to 1934, when he was narrowly defeated in the election for mayor by John Queen. As a civic politician, McKerchar was the voice of small businessmen like himself. He consistently spoke out against initiatives that might result in higher taxes. When, for example, the Council was debating the construction of a civic auditorium in the late 1920s, he suggested such projects should be funded by donations from the public.

By 1907 McKerchar's store had grown. There were 15 employees selling groceries and fine teas and coffees. McKerchar offered free delivery to any part of the city, probably because he was by then remote from many of the new residential neighbourhoods in 1907 Winnipeg. In 1915 he was still in business, but in 1925 the store appears to have closed. Instead, there was a McKerchar Block at 602 Main Street, which rented space to a dentist, among others and housed Alderman McKerchar's own office. In this McKerchar was like others of the small businessmen of Winnipeg, choosing to move to managing a revenue property on the site of their former retail business. By 1925 McKerchar lived at 21 Middle Gate, far from Main Street.

Another grocery store, farther north on Main at 1028, was in operation in 1907. It belonged to Robert Templeton and its stock may have been a little broader than McKerchar's. At the time of writing, 1028 Main Street is still occupied by a small grocery store. Templeton sold fancy groceries, provisions, flour, feed, patent medicines and household appliances. The *Tribune* noted that he was known for his accommodating disposition and his fair dealing with all his patrons and had "built up a splendid trade." He was no longer operating the store in 1915 and in 1925 he is listed as living at 244 Magnus Avenue, just around the corner from his store. He was presumably retired.

The Ackerman brothers operated a meat market at 219 Pacific Avenue starting in 1904. This would have been a downtown location in 1907. In 1915 the meat market had moved to Pritchard Avenue. By 1925 there were three Ackerman meat markets, one on Pritchard, one on Derby and one on Salter. The brothers had spread out to serve a larger area in the north end.

G.A. Clarke operated a meat market at 1425 Main Street. A butcher trained in England, Clarke cured his own bacon and ham and sold all types of meat and sausages as well as poultry and fresh eggs. Clarke was not in business in 1915 and in 1925 he is listed in the Henderson Directory as a meat cutter, probably working for someone else.

T.D. Cavanagh operated a liquor store on Higgins Avenue across from the CPR station, where he might have done a good trade with thirsty rail travelers. He had only been in business for a year and a half in 1907 but he was still there some years later.

M. Ruckle was the proprietor of a drug store at 962 Main at the corner of Selkirk Avenue. Ruckle was a trained pharmacist and he also sold chocolates, fancy soaps, patent medicines, perfumes, and cigars. Nearby, E.L. Gowdy had a confectionary store at 1487 Main and he sold candies, cigars, tobacco, fruits, and ice cream.

One of the oldest businesses listed in the 1907 feature was the T.W. Taylor Bindery at 177 McDermot. Taylor had come to Winnipeg in 1877 and opened a book bindery. By 1907 he was operating the largest Canadian bindery of account books, ledgers, receipt books and other business items as well as a regular book bindery. They received orders from across the country. The company was still in business in 1915 and 1925.

The Crown Paper Box Factory had been operating for 10 years in 1907 at 288 King Street. It was owned by G. Phippen and W.J. Milford, employed 60 people and made all types of boxes for Winnipeg firms. A big customer was the Royal Crown Soap company, which was shipping boxed soaps across Canada at this time. In 1915 the company still existed, but by 1925 it seems to have closed.

Hotels were listed among the businesses in 1907 and the Gould Hotel on Jarvis and Derby was one that was still operating in 1915. In 1907 it had the Eagle Turkish Bath House in its basement. Mondays, Wednesdays, and Fridays were ladies' days, and the other days were for men. The owner, K.W. Stanley, was an experienced masseur and he offered Turkish, Russian, medicated, and plain baths. He employed only "skilled technicians." By 1915 this exotic attraction was no longer open.

The *Tribune* listed a number of real estate agents, likely only a small sample of the agents, speculators and developers who were buying and selling city property at the time. The city was in the midst of a boom similar to that of 1880-1882. The papers were full of maps of the suburban districts being laid out beyond the city boundaries. Lots were for sale from Tuxedo to Transcona and in many areas within the city as well.

There were some businesses listed that were survivors from the earlier years of the city. Several livery stables were still in business in 1907, boarding and renting horses and rigs for special occasions and operating cab services, a business that many of the livery stable owners eventually turned to. W.J. Hinman ran one of the city's oldest livery stables at 215 James Street. His brick stable went up in 1880. Hinman was a veterinarian, so people could be sure the horses he rented were well taken care of. He had just invested $8,000 in a renovation and it now had room for 100 animals with 80 open stalls and 20 boxes. There was a waiting room for ladies and a new wash rack with hot water for the animals. It was, the *Tribune* said "one of the most up to date stables in Winnipeg."

Hinman still operated a livery stable in 1915, but by 1925 he was practising as a veterinarian at 172 King Street, falling back on his medical abilities as the livery stable business declined.

James Lightfoot had a dray business at his two-storey office and stables at 339 and 341 Bannatyne. He was able to move baggage or furniture and his staff could pack goods for storage. His warehouse at 119 Charlotte was available for long-term storage. He also kept a tally ho wagon and horses for rental winter and summer.

By 1915 Lightfoot was working as the manager of Winnipeg Taxi. In 1925 there was a Lightfoot Transport Company in Winnipeg operated by George Lightfoot, who may have been James's son. The New Dominion Livery at 333 Bannatyne was operated by Frank Bailey. He had space in his stable to board horses and he also had horses for rent. He had several wagons that could be hired to move freight. In a city where a large amount of merchandise was moved from the railyards to the various warehouses and then moved back again when it was shipped out by rail, there was work for a transfer business. Horses were being slowly replaced as trucks became available. During the First World War, horses were again in use because of the shortage of parts for trucks and the cost of gasoline and tires. Bailey was not in business in 1915 or 1925.

Imperial Luggage Transfer was started by Robert Vincent in 1899 at 186 Rupert Avenue. By 1907 he had a fleet of wagons for moving furniture as well as baggage from the train stations to or from hotels or homes. Pianos could be lifted up to 70 feet for delivery to apartments. He had a reliable staff who would also unload boxcars and deliver any sort of freight. He also had a livery stable. In 1915 the company was still in business, but in 1925 Vincent was listed as a chauffeur at Central Dray, 330 Carlton Street.

The Canadian Baggage Transfer and Express Company had premises opposite the CPR Station in 1907. It had been in business for some time under the name Brooks and Morris. Alan Ramsay was the manager in 1907. They offered a parcel check room and trunk storage service for tourists and travellers. They owned several trucks and different types of horse-drawn wagons for moving furniture and had equipment for heavy loads like pianos and safes. They employed several men. In 1915 Ramsay was operating a livery stable at 322 Elgin and in 1925 he was the manager of the Royal Transfer Company at 143 Lombard.

The Enright Livery Stable had been in business for 25 years at 328 William. It was a boarding and sale stable and was managed by S. Bisonnette. It was not listed in Henderson in 1915 or 1925. Like many livery stables, it had likely gone out of business. The same seems to be true of F.G. Hogle, who operated a livery business at 300 Fort Street next to the Vendome Hotel for eight years. He had a two-storey brick stable and he had "prompt, stylish horses" for sale or rental, as well as a boarding service. He could supply vehicles of all types and he sold harness, whips, and blankets. Like Ramsay, he seems to have gone out of business and is not listed in 1915 or 1925.

The British American Loan Office was another business of 1907 located at 637 Main Street on the main floor of the Bon Accord Block. It had a private entrance on Logan Avenue. The owners were S. Zimmerman and A. Black. They loaned money on watches, diamonds, all types of jewellery, musical instruments, field glasses, trunks, valises, guns, and furs. They had new jewellery for sale and at all times had bargains in unredeemed items. The business was not listed in 1915 or 1925 but by the latter year there were four jewellery shops in the city owned by members of the Zimmerman family.

Developing the Agricultural Industry

The early 1880s saw the beginnings of a wheat boom in other parts of the world suited to the cultivation of red spring wheat. The increasing demand for hard wheats resulted in investment in rail lines linking wheat-growing country with the coast. This was true in India where spring wheat grew in the north in the Punjab and states like Uttar Pradesh and Maddya Pradesh. In Russia too, the expansion of the rail network opened the vast red wheat growing area stretching east for 3,000 kilometers from St. Petersburg to Omsk. In the mid 1880s wheat prices fell, as they would fall again and again in years when Canada's competitors—the countries already mentioned and later Argentina and Australia—had good crops to export.

The speed with which the size of the western crop grew required the various entities involved in the grain trade to scramble to build the infrastructure needed. At first farmers shipped their grain in bags, a method still used in many parts of the world. This grain was stored in so called "flat warehouses," sheds by the tracks where grain in bags or in bins could be kept before loading into freight cars. It took a long time to manually load a car with sacks of grain.

The other type of storage facility was the "standard" elevator that became iconic as the "sentinel of the prairie." These buildings were equipped with a number of bins that could be used to sort grain by grade and motorized conveyor belts that could "elevate" the grain from the pit into which the farmer's grain was dumped from his wagon, up to the appropriate storage bin above the level of the railway. When the time came to ship the grain out, it was sent down by gravity through a spout into a boxcar. Compared to the flat warehouses, a standard elevator was vastly more efficient: a whole train could be loaded in a much shorter time.

In 1879 there was only one "standard" elevator in western Canada. By 1890 the number had grown to 90 elevators, as well as 103 flat warehouses at 56 stations in Manitoba and 16 in the area that would be Saskatchewan. By 1900 the number of elevators had reached 454 compared to 126 flat warehouses, along the rail lines in Manitoba and the Northwest. Up to 1896 most of these facilities were owned by Ogilvie Milling or Lake of the Woods Milling, or individual owners who did not usually own more that two or three elevators.

The CPR encouraged the construction of the more efficient standard elevators by refusing to lease land at their stations to anyone who was not going to erect one. Standard elevators required an investment of at least $10,000 for construction and required paid staff to buy grain and operate the facility. Small independent operators in the country could therefore not usually afford to get into the business in a big way. Large grain companies, millers such as Ogilivie and, later, farmer cooperatives were the main builders of standard elevators. Ogilvie erected one of the first elevators at Gretna in 1883. It was able to hold 10 carloads of grain. By 1885 Ogilvie was shipping large amounts of grain from the country between Gretna and Manitou, home to the new Mennonite settlements. In the week ending June 29, 1885, Ogilvie shipped 25 cars of grain east to be milled in Montreal.

After 1897, following the example of companies in the United States, line elevator firms were established and began to build and buy up the country elevators and manage them in groups. This reduced costs per elevator and the elevator companies could afford to hire experienced managers to oversee operations from central offices in Winnipeg. The grain companies claimed the system gave farmers more competent, efficient service in the handling of their grain. Farmers, on the other hand, accused the elevator companies of colluding with one another on prices, cheating on weights and said they were not to be trusted. Government inquiries would establish that the suspicions of producers were, at least in some cases, well founded.

In 1896, the first of the line elevator companies, the Northern, with 42 elevators, was founded. The Farmers Elevator Company with nine elevators was established in the same year. In 1898 two more companies appeared on the scene, Dominion Elevator Company (35 elevators) and Manitoba Elevator Company (35 elevators). The following year Bready, Love and Tryon launched their firm with 38 elevators. In just three years these five companies had become the owners of half the elevators in Manitoba and the Northwest. This ensured that, at many stations, there was no competition between grain buyers and farmers had to accept whatever price was offered.

Terminal elevators, in the early days mostly built at the Lakehead, were also an essential part of the export trade. The first terminals were built by the CPR, but grain companies and farmer cooperatives later constructed terminals. These massive facilities with their rows of concrete grain silos allowed for the sorting of grain into large cargo sized lots that were loaded into lake ships. In 1883 the total capacity of terminal elevators in the West was 250,000 bushels and by 1902 the capacity had grown to 7,750,000 bushels.

Another important part of the infrastructure was branch railway lines. The arrival of a CPR line in a district or the extension of one of the small railways being built by the 1890s literally opened the area up. Farmers would have a means of marketing their crop and new farmers would be attracted to such a district.

Canada's grain industry is distinguished by having a good grading

system which allows the sorting of a crop into wheat of different quali-
ties that fetch different prices. Before the West began to develop as a
wheat exporting area, the Toronto Board of Trade and the Montreal
Board of Trade administered the grading system for the country. As
we have seen, in the 1880s Winnipeg began to play a larger role and
eventually became the center of the western grain industry.

In 1883 the Board of Trade had set up a Grain Exchange to organize
the buying and selling of grain into a system, replacing the haphaz-
ard methods used up to that time. Standardization of prices was a key
objective of the Exchange, replacing the older system of barter or buyers
offering a price they had pulled out of thin air. The 1883 Exchange,
however, did not attract enough support and it was abandoned.

It was in 1887 that the Winnipeg Grain Exchange was permanently established. The Exchange, a marketplace where thousands of
individual shipments of grain could be bought and sold in an orderly,
efficient way, along with the growing railway and elevator network,
the system of line and terminal elevators, the Board of Examiners, and
the Standards Board laid the foundations for an effective marketing
system for the growing volume of wheat flowing out of Manitoba and
the Northwest. Various Winnipeg companies and individuals had
purchased grain in the past. As early as 1862 one of the firms of free
traders in the colony, Ross and Caldwell, advertised that they would
buy white flour and clean dry grain. They advertised their prices and
said they would buy for half cash and half goods, because cash was
scarce in the colony. Once the railway connected Winnipeg to the
outside world in 1878, rail shipments to St. Paul began. Local merchants—A.G.B. Bannatyne, Higgins and Young, R. Gerrie, Davis
and Smith and Ogilvie Milling Company—began to advertise that
they would buy wheat for 60 cents a bushel for No. 1 Northern wheat.
These companies, with the exception of Ogilvies, were general merchants selling supplies and groceries.

The businessmen present at the founding of the Winnipeg Grain
and Produce Exchange in 1887 were D.H. McMillan, a miller and

Grain Exchange Building, 1925 CITY OF WINNIPEG ARCHIVES

the first president of the Exchange; G.G. Galt; J.A. Mitchell; R.P. Roblin, a future premier of Manitoba; K. MacKenzie; G.R. Crowe; A. Atkinson; N. Bawlf; S. Spink; D.G. McBean; George Maulson; S.P. Clark; C.N. Bell, who would serve as the Secretary of the Exchange for many years; and W.A. Hastings and W.W. and John Ogilvie, representing the Lake of the Woods Milling Company and the Ogilvie Milling Company. Many of these people would remain members of the Grain Exchange for years.

Daniel McMillan was born in Whitby, Ontario and came to the West as a captain in the Wolseley expedition. He decided to stay in

Winnipeg, and he maintained his connection with the militia, serving as the commanding officer of the Winnipeg Grenadiers from 1887 to 1892. He was also involved in politics, serving as a Liberal MLA from 1880 to 1890 and as provincial treasurer in the Greenway government in 1889 and 1890. He was Manitoba's lieutenant governor from 1900 to 1911. McMillan had built the first steam-powered flour mill in the West and he built the first grain elevator, with a 65,000-bushel capacity, in Winnipeg in 1885. He was elected as the first president of the Winnipeg Grain Exchange. Successful in the milling business, he branched out by making investments in Great-West Life, of which he was a vice president, and in the Northern Crown Bank, where he served as president.

J.A. Mitchell was born in Ontario and came to Manitoba in 1886. He was a grain buyer in the Brandon area before moving to Winnipeg and entering into a partnership with William Martin in the grain business. Their firm merged with others in the 1890s to become the Northern Elevator Company. Mitchell was the president of the Grain Exchange in 1892. He was involved in other businesses, partnering with Manlius Bull in the Northern Crown Soap Company and investing in elevator and insurance companies.

Sam Spink was born in Ontario and came to Winnipeg in 1881. He established the first grain commission business in the West, buying and selling grain for clients on commission. He was president of the Grain Exchange in 1889 and was for a time was chair of the Western Grain Standards Board, the group that, each year, established the requirements for grain to be included in each of the western grades of grain.

The founders of the Exchange were, therefore, successful businessmen in the city who understood the importance of establishing an orderly market to handle the ever-increasing volume of export grain flowing out of western Canada.

The membership of the Exchange rose to 50 by 1890. Many of these members were the founders and partners in the line elevator companies.

The city was reliably connected by telegraph with the outside world in 1887. This enabled the Exchange to post Chicago and Liverpool prices to guide what was paid for wheat in Manitoba and the Northwest.

All the components of an efficient and profitable grain industry were in place by the 1890s. But an industry as large as the wheat industry was bound to experience conflict between its different components. As we will see later in this account, the situation after the turn of the century would be marked by friction between producers and the Winnipeg grain industry. This would eventually lead to the establishment of farmer-owned grain firms as well as a government regulatory structure of some complexity.

■

Manitoba and Northwestern farmers began to organize in the 1880s. The Grange farmers organization was imported by homesteaders from Ontario and the US. In the 1890s the Patrons of Industry enjoyed a period of growth and success before disappearing again. The different groups attracted support because of the issues they promised to address and solve. Attempts at political action in the '80s and '90s with the Grange and the Patrons were largely unsuccessful.

Many producers continued to feel they were not earning enough for their work and the crops they were producing. Westerners opposed the high tariff National Policy that increased their costs of production by raising the prices of farm machinery. They complained that implement manufacturers, grain dealers, elevator operators, and the CPR had created a grain industry that benefited everyone but producers. They made accusations about being cheated on weights and grades and charged that the Winnipeg elevator companies were colluding to keep grain prices low. The policies of the CPR, they argued, prevented them from reserving box cars and loading their own grain to ship to the head of lakes, where, they maintained, they could secure a better price.

At the end of the 1890s a new group of political activists began to employ some new strategies. The Reverend James Moffat Douglas had been elected to the House of Commons to represent the constituency of Assiniboia in what would soon become Saskatchewan. Douglas had been involved with the Patrons of Industry while they were active in the West. A Presbyterian minister who had lived in India, Douglas left the ministry and became a rancher. Together with other western MPs—men like Robert Lorne Richardson, owner of the *Winnipeg Tribune*—Douglas set out to deal with farmers' problems by introducing private members bills in the House of Commons.

In 1898 James Douglas introduced a bill to amend the Railway Act to overturn the CPR's policy of allowing only standard elevators. The amendment would allow the construction of loading platforms and flat warehouses where there was a demand for them, whether or not there was a standard elevator at the same station. This change would allow producers to bypass a country elevator manager who might be suspected of short-changing farmers on weights, prices per bushel or grain grades.

James Douglas' bill ran into a good deal of opposition in the Commons from MPs and outside the House from lobbyists working for the railway. The consideration of his bill in committee was delayed and it died with the end of the session in May 1898.

In July there was a meeting in the City Hall in Winnipeg where a group of producers discussed solutions like electing independent MPs who would work to defend the farmers' interests. They formed an "Anti-Elevator Monopoly Association" with executive made up of farmers and farm supporters.

In the same month, the CPR announced that they would now allow farmers to load boxcars from loading platforms. This was heralded as "a great point gained" by Douglas. The *Winnipeg Tribune* assumed, wrongly as it turned out, that this would mean that flat warehouses would now be permitted. By December there were stories of farmers like the one who was offered 56 to 57 cents a bushel for his grain at the local elevator until he announced he would send his grain to the Lakehead in his own car. The price offered at the elevator then rose to 63 cents. In at least one location with a loading platform, the elevator closed for lack of business.

During the 1899 session of Parliament, several private members' bills, including another written by Reverend James Douglas, were introduced that would have established the right to build flat warehouses where there was a demand. Douglas' bill also included a provision for the appointment of a chief grain inspector, an official who, while mentioned in the General Inspection Act, had never been hired. This person would, in Douglas' words "when disagreements about grain grades did arise, be the one to whom the parties would refer their difficulties and have them adjusted properly."[52]

If there was a difference of opinion about the grade, the farmer would take payment for the grain at the grade assigned by the elevator operator. Then a sample of the grain agreed upon by buyer and seller would be taken and sent to the Chief Inspector in Winnipeg. He would grade it and if the grade was higher than the original the buyer would pay the farmer the difference. This ability to appeal was new and was welcomed by the producers.

The Liberal government of Wilfrid Laurier took note of the widespread discontent among producers in the West and of the relative sophistication of their political action, compared to earlier farm organizations. Clifford Sifton, the Minister of the Interior, supported Douglas' bill in the Commons and suggested that a Parliamentary Committee be established to look into the problems of western producers. This committee recommended a Royal Commission, and one was duly established in October of 1899.

The Commission was instructed to look into the problem of excessive dockage, the question of unfair weights and whether there was a monopoly operating in grain buying which, because of the refusal to allow flat warehouses, was able to pay lower prices for the farmers' grain. The Commission consisted of Judge Senkler as chair, with members C.C. Castle, W.F. Sirrett, W. Lothian, and F.H. Phippen.

At the end of January 1900, Rodmond Roblin, Conservative politician and president of the Dominion Elevator Company testified before the Commission. The lawyer for the Commission questioned Roblin all afternoon. His answers can be considered to represent the private trade's opinion on things.

Roblin said he had been in the grain business since 1881. He was interested in elevators and had a good knowledge of the business. He said it was not such a profitable business as it was sometimes thought. Many prominent grain men had failed in the past decade. There were 75 or so grain merchants in Winnipeg and the Northwest Territories. There were plenty of elevators—in some places too many. The complaints about excessive dockage—the weed seeds, stones and other foreign material removed from a farmer's grain—were baseless, according to Roblin. As were complaints about unfair weights. Roblin said he had a farm on which he raised from 15,000 to 30,000 bushels of wheat a year. He had always received fair treatment when putting this grain through the elevators. He took precautions to check the weight. He said he had known of collusion between farmers and elevator managers to defraud the elevator companies. He had not heard of dishonesty otherwise. This comment had to be taken with a grain of salt, coming as it did from the president of one of the elevator companies.

He said that the railroad's sometimes gave a "monopoly" to the elevators so as to avoid the long wait involved when farmers loaded cars by hand. The normal charge for shipping grain was 1.5 cents per bushel, set by the Canadian Pacific. Normal elevators charge 1.5 cents per bushel to receive, store, clean and load grain into box cars.

Roblin said that as president of the Dominion Elevator Co. he had always tried to earn 1.5 cents per bushel profit for his company on all grain handled, but due to the fierce competition between companies he had never succeeded. Competition often resulted in grading wheat too high in order to secure the sale and farmers made quite a lot of money this way.

Roblin said he would welcome government supervision of weighing and cleaning. He would also not object to a system of appeals between the farmer and the elevator manager, but he failed to see how it would work if it was put in place. During the decade ahead, an appeals system was put in place and it exists to this day as one of the services of the Canadian Grain Commission.

Roblin gave an account of business at several Dominion Elevator points. All showed a net loss for the company. He said the quantities were in favour of the elevator, but the grades were the other way. Asked about dishonesty of buyers, Roblin gave a number of cases of dishonesty. He said Dominion Elevators did not have a written formal contract for buyers who worked for the company.

In March 1900, the Royal Commission issued their report, which, among other things, established that Ogilvie Flour Mills, Lake of the Woods Milling, Northern Elevator Company, the Dominion Elevator Company, and the Winnipeg Elevator Company controlled 67% of all the standard elevators. The Commission recommended that the farmer be guaranteed the right to load grain himself and that flat warehouses be built where requested. They made other recommendations based on the State of Minnesota's "Act to Regulate Warehouses and Inspection, Weighing and Handling of Grain."

The office of the Warehouse Commissioner was created to investigate all complaints that were made under oath and in writing about unfair practices in country elevators. The Commissioner could examine records, inspect the weigh scales in the elevators and other machinery, and order any necessary redress. If action was not taken, the government could take the company to court.

Problems over dockage cleaned out of grain were addressed by requiring everyone to use the same standard sieve and making space on the Inspection Certificate in which to record the amount of dirt to be removed in order to bring the shipment of grain up to a specific grade.

In 1900 the Manitoba Grain Act, incorporating all these recommendations, was passed, bringing a good deal of much needed regularity to the process of buying grain at country points. It had been weakened on its way through the Commons by supporters of the grain trade and almost immediately complaints arose about the shortcomings of the new Act. While, for example, farmers had the right to a car to ship their grain, they had problems securing one in a timely manner, especially at harvest time.

In 1902 a new organization appeared on the scene: the Territorial Grain Growers. This farm organization grew quickly and, in a few years, amalgamated with other provincial grain growers' organizations to form the United Grain Growers. The Territorial group worked on the car problem, using a number of strategies, including a court case. In the so-called "Sintaluta Case" two members, W.E. Motherwell and Peter Damien, farmers from the Sintaluta area in Saskatchewan, sent a complaint to the warehouse commissioner. They claimed their station agent was not abiding by the Act when assigning cars. The matter was investigated, and the agent was found guilty.

Men like Motherwell and Damien and many other Grain Growers members were well organized and better able to present their cases than leaders of earlier producer organizations. Motherwell had a degree from the Ontario Agricultural College in Guelph, and he would hold executive positions in the Grain Growers organization as well as serving as Minister of Agriculture in both Saskatchewan and the federal cabinet.

Laurier and his ministers saw cooperation with the Grain Growers as a way to win support from the farm population, and during the 1900 to 1910 period the Laurier government enacted many reforms suggested to them. In 1902 Laurier told the House of Commons: "It is only for our friends in the northwest to point out the remedy and the government will be only too glad to give them every assistance to make the Act as effective as it can be made."[53] Generally, the grain trade was not against regularising and regulating the various functions of the industry.

As the farm population and the volume of wheat production

increased, the importance of wheat exports to the Canadian economy was symbolized by moving responsibility for the Manitoba Grain Act to the Department of Trade and Commerce in 1902. In 1904 the General Inspection Act sections concerned with grain were moved to a new, separate Grain Inspection Act.

As the decade progressed the Grain Growers turned their attention to the Winnipeg Grain Exchange and the terminal elevators at the Lakehead. Producers placed their concerns before the federal Agriculture Committee and once more a Royal Commission was formed. The members were all grain producers. The chair was John Miller, one of the founders of the Territorial Grain Growers and in the 1920s the Liberal MP for Qu'Appelle. The other members were W.L. McNair and G.E. Goldie. They were to enquire into "any and all matters connected with the Grain Inspection and Manitoba Grain Acts." They were to investigate conditions in the wheat-growing area, in the markets in Winnipeg, Toronto, Montreal and Liverpool as well as the terminal and transfer elevators.

The Commission's report, released in October 1907, dealt with the key issues. The authority of the Warehouse Commissioner, Charles Castle, was increased. He was, for example, given the power to dismiss elevator managers found guilty of wrongdoing. He was given the power to address the problem of car shortages by directing cars to stations where they were needed. The Warehouse Commissioner would now be appointed for a 10-year term, instead of "at the pleasure of the Minister," giving that official more independence.

The Royal Commission found that in the larger terminal elevators at the head of the Great Lakes, there was tampering with grades, and that lots of grain were not being cleaned to the level specified at the time of inspection. The Royal Commission report recommended closer supervision by government weighing staff and by government grain inspectors and these changes were made in the form of amendments to the Grain Act in 1908. An audit of the quantity of each grade in the terminal elevators would now be done each August. Charles

Castle supervised the first audit, called a "weighover," in 1909 and found that the amount of Number One Northern grain in store exceeded the amount received by one million bushels. This was taken as proof that lower quality grain was being mixed with the top grades to miraculously create more top-grade grain. Two elevator companies were found guilty of mixing and fined. This episode increased the pressure in favor of government-controlled Terminal Elevators.

Now let us return to 1906 to look at the beginning of a bitter fight between the organized wheat farmers and the Winnipeg Grain Exchange. In April 1906 plans for a new Grain Exchange building on Lombard Street were announced. The Exchange members were doing well, and a new larger building was wanted to house the Exchange and the grain companies along with the other businesses and agencies involved in the grain industry. In the same year, the Grain Growers Grain Company was founded by a group of Grain Growers members that included Edward Partridge. The Grain Growers Grain Company purchased a seat on the Grain Exchange and began to buy and sell grain, dealing in wheat they were purchasing from Grain Growers members across the west. The company was organized as a co-op and wanted to pay out dividends to the Grain Grower members as would be done in any cooperative. When this was considered by the Council of the Exchange it was deemed a violation of the Exchange bylaw dealing with commissions. Such payments were regarded as a rebate to a customer and an unfair way to attract business away from other Exchange members. The Grain Exchange maintained that a commission of one cent per bushel was the only fair charge that members could collect for their services. The Grain Growers Grain Company's membership was suspended.

This situation was discussed at the Royal Commission on the Grain Trade, mentioned above. On November 20th Edward Partridge appeared before the commission and the next day Charles Bell, Secretary of the Exchange appeared. The two men presented the different sides of the argument. Bell explained that the Exchange demanded an end to the dividend payments and Partridge refused to guarantee it. The Exchange therefore refused to re-admit the Grain Growers Grain Company to membership. The Manitoba Grain Growers Association laid charges of unlawful conspiracy and combination to restrain or injure trade against three members of the council of the Grain Exchange. On December 13, 1906 there was a preliminary hearing before Judge T.M. Daly, who recommended a trial, which could not proceed until the spring assizes of 1907.

Early in 1907 Manitoba Premier Roblin was pressuring the Exchange to allow the Grain Growers Grain Company to pay the rebates to its members. Even though he was a founder of the Exchange, the premier was facing an election in 1907 and a majority of the seats in the Legislature were in rural farming districts.

The case was heard in April and after a very acrimonious trial, the Exchange was judged to be not guilty of restraining trade and the judge praised the organization for its work in promoting and systematizing the grain trade.

In June, Roblin convened a conference at which a resolution was passed that no bylaw or regulation of the Exchange could be adopted without approval of the Manitoba Legislature. In January 1908, the government's Throne Speech called for changes in the Grain Exchange Charter. The Winnipeg business community protested. George Galt of the Board of Trade insisted that "It will be most unfortunate if the farmers of this country, owing to their numerical strength can force through our Legislature laws that are detrimental to their own interests and consequently injurious to every business-man in the country."

In February, the amendment to the Exchange's charter received royal assent. The price of an Exchange membership dropped from $2650 to $1000 if a buyer could be found.

The Grain and Produce Exchange dealt with this challenge by closing and reopening the following September as a voluntary unincorporated association called the Winnipeg Grain Exchange. As a voluntary association it was not governed by a charter granted by the provincial government and so could not have regulations imposed upon it. It moved into its grand new quarters at Rorie and Lombard.

The new organization enjoyed great success and in 1908 it was the largest cash wheat market in North America. In that year, 188 million bushels were marketed on the Exchange, compared to 81 million in Minneapolis, 56 million in Duluth and 26.9 million in Chicago.

In 1909 Charles Bell, the Exchange Secretary stated: "The members of the Winnipeg Grain Exchange have built up at their own cost, unsubsidized by the Government, the most efficient and well-organized commercial institution in the Dominion of Canada; indeed it is today the largest cash wheat market on the continent."

The Exchange soon allowed the Grain Grower's Grain Company to join their organization, but they continued to insist that no patronage dividend be paid to its farmer shareholders. But the organized farmers were not in a mood to accept defeat. The effect of the continued prohibition on dividends was to increase the animosity felt by the producers toward the Exchange. It is unfortunate that this conflict between two of the key parts of the western grain industry was allowed to reach this point. It weakened the industry and resulted in a good deal of wasted energy carrying on the fight for many more years.

The farmers' companies, the Grain Growers' Grain Company, the Alberta Cooperative Elevator Company, and the Saskatchewan Cooperative Elevator Company amalgamated in 1917 to form United Grain Growers (UGG), a farmer-owned co-op with a large network of grain elevators that marketed over half the prairie wheat crop. The birth of the UGG was the first of a number of events that eventually would greatly diminish the size and influence of the private grain trade and the well-organized commercial institution it had built.

The strong position of the Grain Exchange as the sole market for western grain was further undermined during the Great War. In the fall of 1915, during which the largest wheat crop in Canadian history was harvested in western Canada, food shortages were looming in the allied countries and there was a threat of inflated food prices. The price of wheat rose from $1.09 a bushel in June 1916 to $1.98 in November. The British government established a British Wheat Export Company that would act as the sole purchaser of grain for the allied nations to ensure Britain and her allies would have adequate supplies at reasonable prices. The Grain Exchange closed down and Sir George Foster, the federal Minister of Trade and Commerce, commandeered 15 million bushels of wheat at the Lakehead and eastern points for sale at a fixed price to the British Wheat Export Company. Again in 1917 and 1918 the government intervened in disposing of the wheat crop because of concern over rising prices and speculation. This time a special agency, the Board of Grain Supervisors, was created to take control of the crop, set the prices, and decide on grain allocation between domestic users and the Wheat Export Company. Robert Magill, secretary of the Winnipeg Grain Exchange, served on the board of the company and the members of the Exchange offered their expertise to support its activities, saying it was their patriotic duty to do so. In 1917 the price the Grain Supervisors set for Number 1 Northern, the highest grade of western wheat, was $2.21 a bushel for grain delivered at Fort William. In 1918 the price was $2.24 a bushel. These were excellent prices that ensured farmers would make money and stay in the business of growing wheat. Farmer's sons were exempt from military service and, for a time in 1918, from conscription so that they would stay on the land and produce food for the allies and the military. In the spring of 1918, this exemption was cancelled because of the critical situation at the front. The farm community was outraged when their sons were conscripted after all.

For one more year, in 1919, the government maintained a monopoly in the marketing of the western Canadian wheat crop, this time through an agency called the Canadian Wheat Board.

The Wheat Board purchased grain from farmers at a fixed price. The farmer delivering his grain was also given a certificate entitling him to a second payment, his share of any profits the Board might have made by the end of the year. In 1919 farmers received a total of $2.63 a bushel for Number 1 Northern wheat. The prices were stable and high, and many farmers decided that they much preferred government-controlled marketing to the free market of the Winnipeg Grain Exchange.

Building the Aqueduct

Although Manitoba is a province rich in supplies of fresh water in a multitude of lakes and rivers, Winnipeg, whose name comes from the Cree words for dirty (win) and water (nepe), has access to only two large, muddy, slow-moving prairie rivers. Right from its early years, the city was short of potable water. A contract for supplying water had been given to the Winnipeg Waterworks Company in 1880 and a facility was built on the bank of the Assiniboine river downstream from the Maryland Bridge. The Company, with an exclusive franchise for the City of Winnipeg, pumped water out of the Assiniboine and delivered it to the homes of customers in barrels.

The city's sewers emptied industrial and human waste into the Red and the Assiniboine Rivers. As a result, the muddy water was infected with typhus and other germs. The citizens of Winnipeg were generally not satisfied with the service offered by Winnipeg Waterworks and in 1898 the City bought out the Company's franchise for $237,000.

In 1904 a massive downtown fire destroyed Ashdown's store and other buildings in the neighbourhood. There was not enough pressure in the mains to direct streams of water onto the flames, so the fire departments pumped river water into the water pipes and infected water was pumped into many city homes. As a result, a typhoid fever epidemic broke out and between 1904 and 1906 over 3000 Winnipeggers caught typhus and many died. This was certainly not the only outbreak of typhus in the City, nor was Winnipeg the only city at this time where typhus and cholera outbreaks claimed the lives of inhabitants.

The aqueduct under construction, 1915   CITY OF WINNIPEG ARCHIVES

This disaster focused the citizens' attention on the water problem. The only alternative to the rivers as a water source were the artesian wells under the northwest of the city. By 1908 seven new wells had been dug. They were eight feet in diameter and from 446 to 102 feet deep. But the well water was "hard," that is full of minerals. This made it undesirable for bathing, drinking and laundry and water softeners had to be added to it to make it potable. It was also unsatisfactory for use in industrial boilers where it left deposits, requiring frequent, expensive cleaning. This was a major disincentive to industrial firms wanting to locate in the city. Winnipeg had a water softening plant to remove minerals from the well water but as the population grew it was overwhelmed and unable to keep up with demand. There was concern that pumping water out of the city's aquifer would lower the water level, resulting in contamination by water from the Red and Assiniboine. A solution adopted by many homeowners was to direct their eavestroughs into the basement where large tanks captured and stored rain water for domestic use.

In 1906 the city established a Water Supply Commission to study the problem of finding a clean source of water large enough to service the growing needs of Winnipeg. James Ashdown and Thomas Russ Deacon, who was an engineer and business owner, were among the members of the Commission. They considered a number of possible sources including the Red and Assiniboine, the Winnipeg River, Lake Winnipeg and Lake Manitoba. In 1907 the Commission asked a board of consulting engineers to make a recommendation and they came out in favour of the Winnipeg River.

They were not, however, able to proceed with that idea; 1907 was the year of a stock market crash and that made raising money to finance a large project like the water system impossible. Also, construction of the City Hydro Dam at Pointe du Bois had been started so that had priority over the city water project.

The Commission asked Judge Robson, the Public Utilities Commissioner, to make a recommendation. Robson turned to Professor Charles Slichler, an American expert on municipal water systems who had consulted with a number of American cities. In September 1912 Slichler delivered his report, which recommended Shoal Lake, on the Manitoba-Ontario border, as the best nearby source for city water. Thomas Deacon ran for mayor in the fall of 1912, promising to provide the city with a source of clean, soft water.

Deacon won the election and set to work immediately. In collaboration with Judge Robson, he organized the Greater Winnipeg Water District (GWWD), selling the idea to councils in Winnipeg, St. Boniface, Fort Garry, St. Vital, Assiniboia, Kildonan and the Town of Transcona. The Water District would be a shared corporation that would cooperate to build an aqueduct to bring water from Shoal Lake to supply the participating municipalities with water.

The proposed Water District was embodied in a Provincial Act, passed February 15, 1912. The mayor of Winnipeg would be the chair of the Water District but had only one vote on the Board. On May 1 there was a vote of the ratepayers—owners of property worth at least $500—who were the only people who could vote on creating debt. The plan was given the 3/5 majority needed for approval.

In October 1913, tenders were called for a $13.5 million project. The design envisaged construction of a 55-mile long concrete aqueduct, 10 miles of pipe, 900 feet of tunnel under the Red River, an 85-mile long railway line, a telephone line and all the clearing and ditching work.

The project's permanent staff consisted of a group of experienced engineers. S.H. Reynolds, a civil engineer, came from Vancouver. He had worked in Winnipeg from 1902-1907 as Assistant City Engineer under H.N. Ruttan. W.G. Chace was to be the chief engineer. He had worked as a senior engineer on the Pointe du Bois dam project.

World War I began in August 1914 and the project was presented with the difficulty of arranging $7 million in credits to begin the work when war expenditures were absorbing vast amounts of capital. James Ashdown, because of his experience dealing with large loans, was made the project's treasurer and he was able to secure the amounts needed.

Because Lake of the Woods is controlled under the 1909 Boundary Waters Treaty, permission had to be sought from the International Joint Commission to remove 85 million gallons of water from Shoal Lake per day. In addition, the permission of the federal and provincial governments had to be obtained to remove water from Shoal Lake. If it was found that the operation of the aqueduct reduced the amount of electricity that the hydro dam on the Winnipeg River flowing out of Lake of the Woods could generate, Winnipeg would compensate Kenora.

The Water District purchased land near Shoal Lake belonging to Shoal Lake 40 First Nation. Because the Falcon River emptied into Shoal Lake near the intake for the aqueduct and the river water had a good deal of debris and discoloration, a dam was built across the lake to separate the river water from the water being used by the Greater Winnipeg Water District. In addition, the peninsula on which the reserve community was situated had a channel cut through it to allow the Falcon River water to empty out into the main part of the lake. These modifications had the effect of cutting the reserve off from the mainland and isolating it on an island. Only now, one hundred years later, has a bridge been built to restore the community's connection with the mainland. The alternative, extending the intake structure out into the lake away from the mouth of the Falcon River, was ruled out because it would have added $1 million to the cost of the project.

Actual construction began in 1915. The route of the aqueduct had been surveyed and finalized by City Engineer H.N. Ruttan between 1912 and 1914. The railway and the telephone line were both completed before the construction began. The railway was used to move supplies and construction material and then for maintenance and moving freight to the communities that grew up along the line.

The concrete aqueduct has a dome-shaped top made of steel-reinforced concrete and the bottom is a dished flat slab of concrete that rests on the ground. There are manholes periodically along the top of the structure for maintenance. Shoal Lake is higher than Winnipeg, so the water flows by gravity until a point 27 miles east of the city. From there it proceeds under pressure to the bank of the Red River and drops to a level 6 meters below the riverbed, is piped 24 meters under the Red and pumped up again and on its way to the McPhillips Reservoir.

Three different companies won the tenders to do the project. Winnipeg Aqueduct Construction Company built the most easterly and most difficult section of the project. This company was a partnership between Carter, Hall and Aldinger, a major Winnipeg contractor, and Northern Construction. The remaining two sections were built by Thomas Kelly and by J.H. Tremblay. The GWWD supplied the concrete and gravel, which was tested constantly to ensure the highest quality.

To avoid labour unrest, the Water District made an attempt to ensure the men were well looked after. A day's work was 10 hours, and room and board was supplied by the Water District for $500 a week. Medical practitioners were employed and for 75 cents a month the men received medical care.

The work was complete in 1919 and water began to flow into the McPhillips Reservoir on March 29th. The Prince of Wales officially opened the aqueduct on September 19, 1919. The aqueduct, along with the hydro-electric projects on the Winnipeg and northern rivers, and the floodway built in the 1960s to control flood waters, are impressive engineering projects that make the city, built as it is in an inhospitable place, habitable, as well as a location of great interest to civil engineers.

Winnipeg General Strike, May–June 1919

The spring of 1919 saw the greatest challenge Winnipeg had ever faced, a massive general strike in which upwards of 35,000 workers walked off the job. On May 13, results of the Winnipeg Trades and Labour Congress general strike vote were overwhelmingly supportive: 8,667 for, 645 against. A general Strike Committee was formed with representation from every union.

From May 15 to June 26 this strike committee and a smaller group of representatives who looked after day-to-day matters assumed virtual control of Winnipeg. The *Western Labour News* was published throughout the strike and carried the Strike Committee point of view on events.

The strike was immediately opposed by the Committee of 1000, a group that the Board of Trade had a large role in creating in mid May. It was a secretive organization, and no papers or membership lists seem to have survived. The Committee of 1000 had various spokespeople whose names became known and members were certainly involved in all aspects of the strike. They published a newspaper, *The Citizen*, which put forth their views. Their first objective was to organize volunteers to replace strikers in various organizations around the city.

Who were the Committee of 1000? We can get some idea by looking at a group that came together after the strike, in the fall of 1919. A Citizen's League was formed by the Board of Trade and the papers of this League are still to be found in the Board of Trade Archive

Winnipeg General Strike, June 10, 1919 CITY OF WINNIPEG ARCHIVES

in the Provincial Archives of Manitoba. It was a large organization designed to support Liberal/Conservative candidates in the city election of November 28, 1919. We can assume that there was a great deal of carryover from the membership of the Committee of 1000. The Board of Trade, worried that although the strike had been defeated and key members of the strike committee were about to be tried for sedition, the city election offered Labour an opportunity to continue the struggle. The feeling was that the Labour group must be prevented from taking over the city government. Labour groups ran strong candidates in the election and in both the city and provincial elections were successful in winning a number of seats, although not enough to form majorities. The civic election has been called a continuation of the strike and it was indeed a noisy campaign with crowded, raucous meetings. Charles Gray, the mayor during the strike, was re-elected, but at some election meetings he was shouted down. The first Council meetings of 1920 were lively events. The visitor's gallery packed with Labour supporters who heckled freely. On one occasion the mayor had the gallery cleared of Labour supporters.

The strike saw a number of different groups with differing points of view about just what the strikers wanted and what tactics would be most successful in achieving the goals or thwarting the objectives of the strike. Besides the two large Committees and their supporters, there was a large and growing number of demobilized soldiers in the city. The Great War Veterans Association (GWVA) tried to represent these men but on the issue of the strike the GWVA was divided. A majority of the returned soldiers voted at a meeting in the Board of Trade Auditorium to support the strike, the remainder, including the Association leadership, preferred to remain neutral.

When the Special Police Force was formed to replace the City Police who had voted to strike, many of its members were anti-strike returned soldiers. The soldiers became an important factor in the strike, and they did not necessarily follow the policies of the strike committee. The riot in June called Bloody Saturday, for example, happened because the leadership of the soldiers insisted upon marching in a parade from City Hall to the Royal Alex Hotel. The mayor had read the riot act and issued a ban on parades. The position of the Strike Committee was that strikers should stay off the streets and not get involved in riots. Alarmed by the large crowds around City Hall, the mayor requested the Mounties be sent in to disperse the people. During a number of charges by mounted police, two men among the onlookers were hit by shots fired by the police. One, Mike Sokolowiski, died at the scene and the other, Mike Schezerbanowicz, died later from gangrene which had developed in his wounds. These men were the only ones to die during the strike, although there were many injured from bullet wounds and in the rioting that occurred in the area later. There may have been other deaths later, of people who were afraid to go to a doctor for fear of being questioned about their injuries.

The official position of the Strike Committee was that the strike was a sympathetic strike to support the workers of the contract metal shops and the building trades in their strikes. The issues were wages, which had not kept pace with the inflation that was very bad at the end of the war, and the question of who would bargain on behalf of the workers. The Metal and Building Trades unions had formed committees called Councils and wanted to collectively bargain through those organizations. Their employers were against this idea and wanted to bargain separately with representatives of each union in their own shops. The metal workers and the owners of the contract shops for whom they worked had a long and bitter history of conflict and strike breaking.

A.J. Andrews was a successful lawyer and former mayor who almost from the beginning of the strike seemed to be acting as a spokesperson for the Committee of 1000. He would also be the lead prosecutor of the strike leaders in the trials that took place at the end of 1919 and beginning of 1920.

Andrews took the position that the strike was a cover for a plot by left-wing labour leaders to overthrow the government. There was some evidence to support this idea because there were labour leaders in the Canadian west who were interested in broader changes than the bread-and-butter issues that had started the strike. Men like R.B. Russell and R. Johns were promoters of the One Big Union (O.B.U.), a new union in the west, which challenged the predominance of craft unions affiliated with the Trades and Labour Congress of Canada and the American Federation of Labour. The O.B.U. was an industrial union modeled on unions in Britain and the United States which set out to organize all workers from skilled craftsmen to general laborers under one union. There was potential, if such unions were successful in signing up large numbers, of strikes involving overwhelming numbers of workers, strikes that would be much more successful than those called by individual unions heretofore. The general strike was seen as a powerful tool amongst supporters of the O.B.U. idea. On the employers side, sympathetic strikes and organizations like the O.B.U. were specifically condemned.

In the days leading up to the Winnipeg strike, the Canadian O.B.U. was established at a meeting in Calgary and people like

Winnipeg General Strike, 1919   CITY OF WINNIPEG ARCHIVES

Russell who were involved in the general strike were also leaders in the new organization. At first the O.B.U. attracted many new members both during and immediately after the General Strike. But, because there were many union members who did not support it, and the established unions were successful in competing with it, the O.B.U. did not succeed in replacing the existing craft unions in representing workers in bargaining or day-to-day matters like grievances. Only the staff of the Street Railway were represented by the One Big Union in Winnipeg and R.B. Russell was the secretary for many years.

The O.B.U. was used by Andrews and the Committee of 1000 as an example of the kind of radical political ideas which threatened if the strike were a success. The sedition charges brought against the strike leaders in their trials were supported by things they had said during meetings before the strike about replacing the current system of government, public ownership of industry and so forth. This was the era of the Red Scare, a widespread fear of communism, and in the US the FBI was set up to fight revolutionaries. There were some bombs and other violence and the rhetoric used by Andrews and others was imported from south of the border. In Canada, the RCMP kept a close eye on left-wing politics; the notes of undercover Mounties who attended meetings constituted damning evidence in the strike leaders' trials. Painting the labour politicians as dangerous radicals who threatened the way of life of middle-class Winnipeggers was a tactic that has continued to be used by some up to the present time.

The strike committee fought back against Andrews and the anti-strike group claims that the General Strike was the first step of a revolution as comprehensive as the Russian Revolution of 1917. The Red Scare narrative did, however, take hold and when representatives of the federal government visited the city in late May, they echoed the charges. On May 22, Arthur Meighen, Acting Minister of Justice, and Senator Gideon Robertson, Minster of Labour, arrived in Winnipeg. On their way they were met by Andrews and some other Committee of 1000 members at Thunder Bay and the Winnipeggers rode with the ministers in Robertson's private car. Undoubtedly, during the trip the two Ministers were briefed about the anti-strike position. The effect of this was that Meighen issued an ominous statement that the strike was "a cloak for something far deeper—an effort to 'overturn' the proper authority." Robertson reported back to Ottawa that "the motive behind this strike undoubtedly was the overthrow of Constitutional Government." The two men did not bother to meet with the Strike Committee while they were in Winnipeg. Their statements established the Red Scare point of view. Bargaining on the original issues of the strike was thereafter difficult or impossible. Andrews, during meetings he had with representatives of the Strike Committee, said he was not willing to bargain until the strikers returned to work.

Andrews organized the raids during which a group of strike leaders were arrested in the middle of the night and taken to Stony Mountain Penitentiary. They were charged with sedition and their trials took place after the strike had ended. Several political leaders who were not, like the main group, British immigrants, were rounded up and threatened with deportation. The federal legislation was changed, at Andrews' request, to allow the deportation of the men of British origin as well. The trials were long and argued in front of juries of mostly rural people, who were secretly and illegally vetted by Andrews. Two of the defendants, Abraham Heaps and F.J. Dixon, were acquitted by their juries, after defending themselves. The rest were sent to jail for periods of one to two years. Some were elected to the Legislature or City Council while serving their sentences.

The strike was defeated but it did have a positive effect on labour politics both in the Legislature and City Hall. J.S. Woodsworth and later A.A. Heaps and others were elected to the House of Commons in Ottawa. Because of the strike, Labour politicians were able to attract more support and labour groups began developing into significant political organizations. Two men, Seymour Farmer and John Queen, were elected mayor in the 1920s and 1930s. During Queen's tenure, Labour also managed to elect a majority on City Council. Fred Dixon retained his seat in the Legislature. He was an effective anti-conscription activist during the war and courageous in championing other progressive causes. Unfortunately, he suffered from cancer which forced him to retire from the Legislature and he died in 1931.

Woodsworth and Heaps were effective MPs and could claim credit for the passage of the old-age pension legislation. Heaps' most important issue was unemployment insurance, without which working class families whose breadwinner was out of work might well lose everything. Both prime ministers Bennet and Mackenzie King offered Heaps a place in their cabinets. He refused, but the Unemployment Insurance Act that finally passed in the early 1940s was largely Heaps' work. After the strike groups like the Independent Labour Party and later the C.C.F. enjoyed steady support and would continue to influence political life.

GROWTH OF THE INDUSTRIAL ECONOMY
Winnipeg in the 1920s and 1930s

The city's establishment as a wholesale, distribution, and transportation hub for the region helped drive the phenomenal growth of Winnipeg between 1870 and 1912. The city's business community had worked tirelessly to achieve this status, building a Red River bridge for the CPR and competing successfully to be the railway's administrative and maintenance centre. The Winnipeg Board of Trade worked to attract the key institutions of the grain trade and to create the conditions that made the city dominant in the warehousing and wholesale business in the west. During the 1920s, Winnipeg would establish itself as a hub for many industries, including manufacturing, insurance services, and hydroelectricity. The industries and institutions profiled below highlight Winnipeg's transition into a diversified modern economy.

Portage and Main c. 1930   CITY OF WINNIPEG ARCHIVES

Board of Trade

The year 1929 marked the 50th anniversary of the founding of the Winnipeg Board of Trade. Membership had risen to a healthy 2,200, 1,350 of whom were members of the senior board and 870 of the Young Men's section. A five-year plan of action had been developed to guide the Board. Some of the points were not exactly new. The re-establishment of the Industrial Exhibition was on the list, something that had been discussed throughout the 1920s, and a draft bylaw was to be drawn up. The Hudson Bay Railway was under construction but there were different options as to where it would terminate on the shore of Hudson Bay. A group was studying that. Roads had become a central issue and the Board had made the completion of a highway to Kenora an objective and were looking at other roads that needed upgrading. The Board's Mining Bureau was promoting prospecting for new mineral finds and had developed a display of Manitoba minerals to be used at fairs and conventions.

The Young Men's Section had taken air service as its area of interest. They were promoting the use of air mail and the improvement

of air traffic into and out of Winnipeg. Stevenson Field, the city airport, had officially opened in 1928 on the site of the present Winnipeg
International Airport. But work was needed to help pilots find
the field.

In July of 1929 an American oil man, L.M. Lockhart, and his
party were on a flying vacation and had landed at Stevenson Field in
his Fokker trimotor. It took his pilot an hour of circling the city to
find the airfield and Lockhart suggested its location should be marked
with arrows painted on the roofs of buildings.

The Young Men's Section and the Winnipeg Flying Club applied
early in 1929 to have Stevenson Field made a "fully qualified customs
airport." One result of this change would be that when pilots wanted
to fly directly from Winnipeg to the United States, they would no
longer have to give notice in writing to Ottawa.

The Industrial Development Board, supported in part by the
Board of Trade, had been organized in 1926. The 1929 report was
very encouraging. Industrial plants in the city had seen $1.92 million
in new investment in the previous year and 37 plants had expanded
their operations with 29 new products added to existing lines. Plans
for 1929 included expansion for 31 plants during the year. The total
output of industrial plants was estimated to be $159,252,000, a figure
greater by $12,000,000 than that of 1927.

On April 18, 1931 the Board held its annual meeting at the Fort
Garry Hotel. The outgoing president, Duncan Cameron, Secretary-
Treasurer of the Adams Coal Company, spoke to the meeting.
Addressing the developing Depression, he said that in order to "adjust
the current economic situation" the government would need advice
from industry and that the Dominion Chamber of Commerce would
be the group to represent the business community. He said he was
sure that if political economists, industrial leaders and government
representatives met "much can be done to dispel the depression now
abroad in the world." He said he believed that efficiency and scientific
methods were needed to solve "the problems of wider distribution of

Upgrading cast iron water pipe on Portage Avenue from Kennedy Street to Main Street, 1938 CITY OF WINNIPEG ARCHIVES

wealth so that the masses can buy and enjoy the increasing output of their mass production."[54]

Board Secretary E.C. Gilliat reported on the progress during 1930 on the Board's various issues. The decision to locate the site of the University of Manitoba at the Agricultural College in Fort Garry had been made and construction of new buildings on that campus was beginning. City Hydro's Slave Falls Hydro Plant was nearing completion, and the all-weather road between Winnipeg and Kenora would be finished by the fall. Manitoba now had a national park at Riding Mountain. These were all objectives that the Board had worked on along with other groups.

In the 1930s the Board began to publish lists of meetings for the coming week in the *Winnipeg Tribune*. On October 10, 1931, the week ahead included a meeting at the Carlton Club of the Greater Winnipeg Welfare Committee, a new city group on which the Board had a permanent member. Board member A.L. Crossin was to outline the aims of the committee. There was also to be a lunch meeting of the Publicity Committee at the Carlton Club to look over the latest edition of the *Winnipeg Magazine*, the Board's publication. On Friday the Civics Committee executive was scheduled to meet at the Princess Tea Rooms at lunch and then to go and inspect the proposed locations for subways on Talbot and Nairn.

On October 21, the Young Men's Section had their annual meeting at the Fort Garry Hotel. The guest speaker was Dr. W.W. Swanson of the University of Saskatchewan who was to speak on the topic of the "Railway Problem" with special reference to the enormous debt that the Canadian National was carrying. Dr. Swanson was a respected economist who had chaired the 1930 Royal Commission on Immigration. He was typical of the calibre of speakers that the Young Men's section invited.

At the end of 1931 the Board's Civic Beautification Committee was canvassing merchants on Portage Avenue and Main Street to each donate a small amount for Christmas lighting. The streets were lit from William to Portage Avenue on Main Street and from Main to the Hudson's Bay Store on Portage Avenue. Mayor Webb arranged for the City to supply decorative evergreen trees. The Beautification Committee also sponsored a campaign to beautify filling stations and their lots.

Unemployment was once again a growing problem in Winnipeg in the early 1930s. The Board started various programs to address the plight of unemployed people. The "Man a Block" program assigned an unemployed man to a residential block. At the end of 1932 there were 40 married men working as local handymen for the residents of 40 city blocks. These men were taken off the relief rolls for a saving of $1500 to the city relief department.

The Board had arranged for local movie theatres to provide free tickets to unemployed individuals and their families and 29 free community concerts were provided for unemployed people during the winter of 1931-32. There were Saturday night variety concerts at Isaac

A filling station at Graham and Fort is decorated for the holiday season in 1937.
CITY OF WINNIPEG ARCHIVES

Brock and Earl Grey Schools with local choirs, singers, and musicians performing.

On April 1, 1933, the Board's annual meeting took place. Among other things, Secretary E.C. Gilliat reported on the work of the Board's Shippers Bureau lobbying for the retention of the higher freight rates charged by the railways for shipping through the mountains. This issue of the 1920s was still alive. Winnipeg argued that the higher rates acted to protect their markets in the area.

The Board's Agricultural Bureau had participated in growing test plots of sugar beets and soybeans in Manitoba as part of an effort to find alternative crops to wheat. The Agriculture group also sponsored talks like the one given in December 1934 by Premier Bracken at the Marlborough Hotel on "The Cooperation needed to Solve the Drought Problem."

The Young Men's Traffic and Parking Committee helped encourage safe driving with Safety Week, which ran from May 27 to June 2, 1934. They focussed on auto accidents, noting that of 733 accidents in 1933, 439 involved automobiles. During Safety Week, a Safety Lane was blocked off on Assiniboine Avenue between Osborne and Kennedy streets where car owners could bring their autos for a free safety check.

On April 6, 1934 the Board held its annual meeting in the Royal Alexandra Hotel. W. McCurdy was re-elected as president. In all he served as president from 1933 to 1935. McCurdy was the business manager of the *Winnipeg Tribune* and had been the promoter of the Pine to Palms auto tour in the 1920s. He would later be vice president of the Southam Company and publisher of the *Tribune*.

McCurdy gave a can-do speech at the annual meeting, saying that the prosperity of the area around Winnipeg depended upon the prosperity of the city. He said that the Board had made a comprehensive study of the "business and industrial situation in Winnipeg with a view to eliminating weaknesses through business action." He said that the Board of Trade might well take over complete responsibility for the Industrial Development Board, of which it had been one of the founding organizations. He said this might happen if the business community could not raise the money to keep it in operation.

McCurdy praised the recent Winnipeg Auto Show as an example of the success that could be achieved by determined individuals. The show gave work to carpenters, electricians, and decorators and put $50,000 into circulation in the city. He said he preferred this sort of public work to putting people on relief.

He talked about the program of action the Board had developed the previous fall that included a survey of needs in the city, encouragement of the back to the land movement to get unemployed people to take up farming, the Board's accident and fire prevention campaign, and the "Repair, Renovate and Modernize" campaign to upgrade homes and buildings and give work to tradesmen.

By 1936 the Depression was beginning to lift. The Board of Trade began a membership drive in May, hoping to raise its numbers from about 750 to 1,000. They organized the city into 11 zones with a sales

Portraits of relief works committee members surround photos of projects they had worked on, including the Main Street, Norwood, and Assiniboine Park Bridges, the Winnipeg Auditorium, the Sargent Park Swimming Pool, and the Salter Street Bridge, in 1932. CITY OF WINNIPEG ARCHIVES team in charge of each one. The teams went out to talk to all business people in their zone, emphasizing the advantages of being a Board of Trade member, including the opportunity to make valuable business contacts and learn about opportunities and trends. But the advantages went in the other direction as well. Former President Persse told potential members that the Board wanted to have the "benefit of your knowledge and advice." Since 1879 the Board had been a venue where business people could "discuss contentious issues and learn about matters that militated against the best interests of the city."

The campaign was successful and 94 new members joined, producing a total membership of 1,250. People were once again feeling confident enough to spend the money on a membership: an investment that they saw as beneficial for their business. Another symptom of renewed confidence was the plan to hold an industrial exhibition— the first one since 1934—at Polo Park, complete with a grandstand and agricultural show.

Prospective members were also told about the Board's work to reduce taxes, to secure proper transportation facilities to mining locations, and to review all business-related legislation. The Board's year-round safety education campaign was also mentioned. A program of career talks for students at the University of Manitoba was another Board activity that was mentioned, as well as the encouragement of Winnipeg Electric and City Hydro to cooperate in increasing the available supply of hydro-electric power.

At the annual meeting in March 1936, the president, F.J.C. Cox, a commercial traveller who had been an alderman and a board member of a number of organizations, spoke about reducing the amount of interference in business by government. He also spoke about the reasons for the poor state of western agriculture, attributing it to there being too many wheat miners (farmers who wore the soil out growing wheat year after year) and not enough farmers on the land. He said that homesteaders had been permitted to settle on marginal land in dry areas and this had led to the massive failure of western agriculture.

He added that the economy was slowly improving. Exports were picking up with livestock, lumber, newsprint, nickel, automobile and wheat sales improving.

One result of the Depression in western Canada had been the birth of new political parties with new ideas of what to do about the poor state of the economy. The Co-operative Commonwealth Federation (CCF) was founded at meetings in Regina and Winnipeg and was offering a social democratic program. Many members of the old Independent Labour Party were transferring their allegiance to the CCF. The Social Credit Party was a product of Alberta and its remedies were very different, involving government involvement in banking and other aspects of the economy.

In March 1937 the Board of Trade annual meeting was told that the Board had a role to play in resisting radicalism. J.M. Imrie, the editor of the *Edmonton Journal*, was the guest speaker and he talked about radical political theories. He asked if the members of the Winnipeg Board were ready to give the leadership needed in "realizing the opportunities that lie ahead."

He spoke about the Social Credit policies that had been declared illegal by courts in Alberta. He said that the National Commission just beginning its work—the Rowell-Sirois Commission—provided an opportunity for the west to get some beneficial change, not radicalism. He listed the mistakes that had been made in settling the West—the opening of tracts for homesteading that were far from railway lines, the use of marginal land for grain farming, the conversion of pasture lands to wheat farming in Alberta during the Great War, in an effort to produce more and more wheat. All these things contributed to the drought and depression.

He closed by calling on the Winnipeg Board to lead: "Winnipeg has ever been and still is the great commercial city of the prairies and it is this city above all others that should give leadership in this direction, that should sound the rallying call to the businessmen of its own and the two adjoining provinces. Is the present generation of

Winnipeg businessmen prepared to duplicate in principle the spirit and achievements of their fathers? Are they ready today to make their voices heard and their influence felt...in opening the eyes of the people to the dangers of radicalism and bureaucracy?"[55]

This stirring challenge was delivered to a Board of Trade that had played a role in having two Royal Commissions appointed: The Rowell-Sirois Royal Commission on Dominion-Provincial Relations and the Goldenberg Royal Commission on the Municipal Finances and Administration of the City of Winnipeg. These commissions gave the board the opportunity to make its views known[56] in cooperation with the Manitoba Association of Boards of Trade, the Union of Manitoba Municipalities, the Canadian Chamber of Commerce, and the Manitoba Industrial Development Board.

In March 1938 the Board of Trade held its annual meeting at the Royal Alexandra Hotel. The President, C.E. Stockdill, commented on the submissions made before the two Commissions. He reminded the members that 1939 would be the 60th Anniversary of the Board of Trade and that there would be suitable celebrations. The guest speaker was J.L. Ilsley, the Minister of National Revenue. He commented on the Rowell-Sirois Commission, of which Winnipegger J.W. Dafoe had been a member. He said that national unity had been threatened and that the Commission was intended to adjust the points of difference that had developed between the federal and provincial governments.

March 28, 1939 saw the Board's Jubilee Annual Meeting at the Royal Alex Hotel. The Jubilee celebration had an "air of optimism not uncharacteristic of Winnipeg in its younger days. There was a feeling that things were working out all right after all."

Board President E.C. McKay said he was proud of the Board's efforts to have the two Royal Commissions established and among other things the Board's efforts to stimulate home-building through the National Housing and Home Improvement Acts.

Freight Rates

Freight rate concessions made by the railways had helped establish Winnipeg as a distribution and shipping hub, but by the 1920s these concessions were being withdrawn due to complaints from rival western cities like Regina, Saskatoon, Edmonton, Calgary, and Vancouver. Winnipeg's early development occurred in a vacuum, without competitors. But with the growth of other western cities, Winnipeg was forced to fight to preserve their special advantages. It was a fight the city ultimately lost.

In the 1920s the city of Vancouver became a major rival of Winnipeg. The opening of the Panama Canal enabled Vancouver to develop its port because of the increasing volume of material shipped into and out of the city. As Vancouver built additional storage space for grain, its participation in the grain trade increased dramatically. In 1920-21, 700,000 bushels were shipped through Vancouver; in 1921-22 this increased to 7 million bushels; in 1922-23 19 million bushels were shipped, and in 1923-24 25 million bushels. The grain moved to Vancouver from Alberta and western Saskatchewan, formerly territory serviced by Winnipeg. Vancouver was also becoming a warehousing and distribution center for incoming goods. *Canadian Finance* acknowledged the effect of the Panama Canal on this growth, "though its effect was not noticeable until after the war." Another key factor in the shipment of grain was that the number of ocean-going freighters or tramp steamers available for hire in the port had risen from 82 in 1921 to 200 in 1923.[57]

The Crow's Nest Pass agreement of 1897 contained freight rate concessions important to Winnipeg and its abolition also became an important political issue in the early 1920s. Winnipeg's Board of Trade took a leading role on the prairies during the struggle over the Agreement's abolition. The Crow Rate issue came to a head in 1922 although it was not finally settled until 1925. At the same time, a collection of other special freight-rate agreements favourable to Winnipeg that had been entered into by the railways over the years were challenged and the Board of Trade worked to defend those as well.

Rail freight rates were, of course, a major cost for anyone wanting to export agricultural produce or import goods and raw materials for manufacturing, and in Canada, where vast distances often separate producers and consumers, rail freight rates were a perennial topic for argument and negotiation. Until the establishment of the Board of Railway Commissioners in 1904, the cabinet was the ultimate authority over rates, so politics played a big role. Of course, this did not end with the appointment of the Board, but elected politicians were no longer so directly involved.

The Crow's Nest Pass in the Kootenay region of southeastern BC attracted attention in the 1890s when rich mineral discoveries—silver, gold and copper deposits and the vast Crow's Nest coal field—were being developed in the area. The area was sealed off from the rest of Canada by mountains but there was relatively easy north-south access from American rail centers like Spokane. American railways were beginning take advantage of this easier access and the Canadian Pacific hoped to block them by building a line through the Pass, the only route connecting Nelson, BC with Lethbridge, Alberta and the rest of Canada.

In September 1897, the Crow's Nest Agreement was signed between the federal government and the Canadian Pacific Railway. The government undertook to pay the railway a subsidy of $11,000 per mile up to a maximum of $3.63 million for a 330-mile rail line running from Lethbridge to a point near Nelson.

The CPR promised to adhere to a number of conditions contained in sections 9 to 13 of the agreement. Of most interest to western farmers was the stipulation that from Fort William and all points west of Fort William to all points east of Fort William, rates on grain and flour would be reduced below the standard rate by 3 cents per hundred pounds. The lower rates for grain and flour would, for farmers, become "the Crow Rate" and would be the part of the agreement that would survive in one form or another until 1996, when it was finally abolished under the Western Grain Transportation Act.

In addition to grain rates, other rates were also reduced on a specified list of items called "settler's effects"—building materials, iron for manufacturing and other things of use to homesteaders— shipped from Fort William and all points east of Fort William to all points west of Fort William. The goods on the list were of interest to Winnipeg firms that imported and forwarded merchandise to points on the prairie. During the 1920s, rates for shipping grain as well as the items on this list were the subject of prolonged disagreements between the railways and their customers.

In addition to the Crow Rates, there were other special shipping rates that benefitted Winnipeg. The Winnipeg Board of Trade had played a role in establishing special treatment for the city. Early in 1897 for example, the Board sent James Ashdown, the Chair of the Board's Freight Rates Committee, to Ottawa to lobby the CPR and the federal Cabinet. Winnipeg economic historian Ruben Bellan described Ashdown's accomplishment:

> The CPR introduced a new tariff (tariff 490) that resulted in a 15% reduction in freight rates for Winnipeg wholesalers. The enormous warehouses of Winnipeg's Exchange District owe their existence in part to these favorable rates. One result was to enable Winnipeg wholesale firms to stock larger inventories so that their western customers were able to find more of what they wanted in Winnipeg. Winnipeg companies soon replaced eastern wholesale firms in handling the largest part of the western trade.[58]

In 1901 Manitoba won another concession when Premier Roblin negotiated an agreement, known as the Manitoba Agreement, with the Canadian Northern Railway. Roblin and his colleague Robert Rogers negotiated with the Northern Pacific and signed an agreement under which Manitoba would lease the Northern Pacific lines and equipment in the province. The Canadian Northern Railway—soon to be Canadian National Railway—would then lease the same lines from Manitoba for the same amount. The CNR was just beginning a long period of expansion that included building a line from Winnipeg to Thunder Bay. The Province agreed to guarantee the bonds for this line and in return, the Manitoba Cabinet gained the right to set the rates for shipping grain. The CPR was forced to match the lower rates of the Canadian Northern. Roblin considered this agreement one of his most important accomplishments for farmers.

Beginning in 1907 cities west of Winnipeg like Portage la Prairie, ambitious to establish their own distributing businesses, began appealing to the Board of Railway Commissioners, complaining about rates that discriminated in favour of Winnipeg.

In 1909 the Board of Railway Commissioners ordered the railways to completely eliminate the special advantages Winnipeg enjoyed. The railways objected to this order, but they had to comply. They subsequently introduced a new tariff that established Winnipeg's distance from the Lakehead for the purpose of calculating freight rates as 250 miles instead of the actual 420 miles.

The Board of Trade fought the erosion of Winnipeg's special position by arguing that local businesses had made large investments in warehouses and shipping terminals on the basis of the old tariffs. They also argued that because of the great distance from the West to the potential markets for western goods, fairness demanded some form of subsidy. They complained that rates were lower in the East. The answer to this was that the railways had competition from water transport in the East and therefore needed to charge less. This argument was also made for British Columbia, where the railways faced competition from ocean-going carriers.

The Board of Trade not only worked to protect Winnipeg's interests in competition with other cities in the West, but it also acted to counter the attempts of other cities to gain freight rate advantages. For example, they hired Winnipeg lawyer Isaac Pitblado in November 1921 to argue before the Board of Railway Commissioners, at their sittings in Winnipeg, that the special higher rates for shipping goods through the mountains should be left in place.

Pitblado made all the same arguments that the smaller prairie cities made against Winnipeg. He said that removing the higher rates, or equalizing the rates, would destroy industry in Manitoba. Winnipeg was "no mean manufacturing center" but equalizing rates would allow Vancouver firms to "snatch" customers in the prairie region that were rightfully Winnipeg's. He said that Vancouver merchants only thought of themselves and ignored the result the change would have on other cities. Pitblado said Vancouver used the "development argument" that the rates were standing in the way of their firms growing and opening new markets. And yet their businesses had grown and prospered during the period of higher mountain rates.[59] Pitblado was successful in having the higher rates left in place for the immediate future, but the fight was not over.

The railways made a compelling case in favor of higher rates. Vancouver merchants and manufacturers argued that the rates—based on the railways' claim that it cost more to build and operate rail lines in mountainous country—made it impossible to develop new markets in the prairies and they wanted them lowered. In addition, they had experienced huge cost increases during the inflationary war years. The CPR was still a profitable corporation but increases in the costs of equipment, coal, wages, and every other input meant it was faced with lower profits and lower dividends. The Canadian Northern and the Grand Trunk Railways had both boldly set out to build transcontinental lines in the boom years. Both companies ran into serious financial difficulties during the war because of rising costs and the unavailability of capital to pay interest charges and complete their lines. Both railways were taken over by the government and amalgamated to become the Canadian National Railway.

The Board of Transport Commissioners and the Supreme Court to which the Board's decisions could be appealed both recognized that a crisis faced the railways. As the country's largest corporations, their difficulties had national implications and the Transport Commission generally issued decisions that supported them in rates disputes.[60]

In 1919 the Board of Transport Commissioners suspended, until 1922, special freight rates like those in the Crow's Nest Pass Agreement and Roblin's Manitoba Agreement. In addition, in September 1920, after a long series of hearings, the board granted the railways freight rate increases of 40% in the east and 35% in the west as well as a 20% increase in passenger fares.

In 1922 the matter came to a head as the suspension expired. The Transport Board held hearings across the country. The Crow Rate was a political issue of some importance for W.L. Mackenzie King, whose Liberal government was dependent upon Progressive Party support in the House. The Progressives, the voice of Canadian farmers, wanted the Crow Rate on grain restored. The railways wanted it permanently abolished. The Conservatives favoured placing the rates under the Board of Railway Commissioners, with the freedom to make changes as they saw fit.

Each camp had lawyers to argue their case before the Board. H.J. Symington, KC, of Winnipeg was engaged by the Board of Trade and represented the three prairie provinces in arguing that the Crow's Nest Pass Agreement rates for grain should be restored. Symington was a Liberal and a friend of *Free Press* editor J.W. Dafoe and Progressive Party leader T.A. Crerar. Symington would be named to the board of the CNR in 1936 and served as the president of Trans-Canada Airlines later in his career.

Prime Minister Mackenzie King set up a committee to look at the issue. It recommended restoring the lower Crow Rate for grain and flour but ruled that the other rates in the agreement, covering such things as building materials, should remain in suspension until July 6th, 1924.

As the end of the rates suspension period approached in July 1924, the railways circulated a letter suggesting that they be abolished altogether. The Winnipeg Board of Trade again fought hard on the issue, lobbying, writing letters, and convening protest meetings where the premier, the mayor of Winnipeg and local MPs as well as representatives from other prairie cities passed motions calling for the restoration of the non-grain special rates.

In the end, the King government moved to end the controversy by passing a new Railway Act on June 18, 1925. The new Act left the Crow Rates on grain and flour shipped out of the West alone, establishing them at the 1899 level for all western points. All other freight rates in the old agreement were now the province of the Board of Railway Commissioners. The board proceeded to hold a cross-country series of 59 public hearings on freight rates between January 1926 and August 1927, after which they handed down decisions in 311 cases of alleged discrimination. One of these decisions eliminated the non-grain parts of the Crow's Nest Pass Agreement.

The cancellation of the Manitoba Agreement of Premier Roblin was referred to the Supreme Court and the Court ruled against Manitoba in 1924. In spite of a great deal of effort, the Board of Trade ultimately had failed to protect Winnipeg's advantageous freight rate position. Winnipeg lost its position as the primary warehousing and distributing center in the West, although that business and organizations like Eaton's catalogue operations continued to employ large numbers in the city. The 1920s saw the city turn to the Winnipeg manufacturing sector as a replacement for the wholesale business. This particular change was symbolized by a number of large warehouses being taken over by garment factories.

The Garment Industry

For thousands of years, Indigenous people had used the natural materials of the country—furs, skins of bison, deer, caribou, and other animals—to sew comfortable and durable clothing perfectly suited to the climate of what became Manitoba. Europeans who came to trade furs and the children of their marriages with local women dressed in a combination of Indigenous clothing, made for the most part by Indigenous women, and European clothes imported by the trading companies.

By the 1870s the local manufacture of clothing in Winnipeg was in the hands of tailors and dressmakers. In 1874 there were two tailors in the village of Winnipeg, according to Alexander Begg. Ready-made clothes imported from the east or from Britain became more and more common as connections to the outside world improved.

By 1870 an important Canadian supplier of ready-made garments and one of the largest manufacturers was William Sanford, a Hamilton businessman who we have already met. Born in New York City, Sanford had been orphaned at a young age and went to live in Hamilton with his aunt. His firm, Sanford and McInnes, was founded in 1861, its first location a large Hamilton warehouse where fabric for patterns was cut and finished clothes were stored. The actual work of sewing was done in their own homes by farm women who contracted with Sanford through his agents, a group of skilled German tailors who had immigrated to the Hamilton area. Distributing work in this fashion was very common at the time in the garment industry in North America, Britain, Europe and other parts of the world.

Just as Sanford's firm came on the scene, the development of equipment like the treadle sewing machine and the band knife contributed to the industrialization and mass production of clothing. The band knife is a portable power saw that can cut through many layers of cloth, producing large numbers of identical pieces that are then assembled into finished garments.

Sanford's main contribution to the success of his firm was as a salesman. He opened new stores, all with the distinctive name "Oak Hall," in the major Ontario towns and the company had stores and warehouses in the Maritimes, Winnipeg, and Victoria. In 1861 Sanford and McInnis had sales of $32,000. Ten years later they were employing 455 people to produce clothes worth $350,000. They were the largest ready-made clothing company in Ontario.

When John A. Macdonald's government introduced the National

Policy in 1878, protecting Canadian manufacturers with tariff walls
that kept out foreign competitors, Sanford's firm was one of the beneficiaries. His factories shipped between $12,000 and $15,000 worth of
clothes every day at peak times of the year. In his factory, band knives
enabled workers to cut the cloth for 100 pairs of pants an hour and
produce 350 suits and 50 overcoats in a day. In the 1880s Sanford and
a few other large manufacturers produced all the uniforms required
by the Canadian militia.

A wealthy man, Sanford was involved in large-scale land investments in Manitoba along with local and Ontario based partners.
He employed Robert Riley, who would later become a leader in the
Winnipeg business community, to manage these investments, as we
have seen earlier in this account.

Sanford had a warehouse in Winnipeg for distribution to smaller
communities in the west. His building was on the northeast corner
of Princess and Bannatyne; the ground floor is still standing.

Other eastern firms were also active in the West. An example is
the Empire Importing and Jobbing Company, a wholesale firm dealing in "gents clothing and furnishings." The owners were S.H. and
M.H. Narovslovski, President and Secretary Treasurer. The company headquarters was in Montreal and they opened their Winnipeg
warehouse in 1900 at 166 Princess Street. They imported clothing
from Europe and the United States and operated a garment factory
in Montreal.

Western Commission was an agency that was founded at the
end of the 1890s. The owner was B. Schachter and in his offices in
the Bon Accord Block at 645 Main Street, he carried a wide range of
the products of eastern manufacturers. His sample room included
boots, shoes, gloves, socks, Maple Leaf Rubbers, hats, caps, and other
men's furnishings. The Bon Accord Block was a five-storey building on Main Street of which only the ground floor survives today.
Western Commission sold to jobbers in all parts of western Canada.
Schachter's salesmen went out to sell to other wholesalers or retail

stores. Later, three members of the Schachter family were involved in the garment business as wholesalers or manufacturers. In 1925 Ben Schachter was the director of Wholesale Distributors Ltd. at 528 Alexander. Harry Schachter managed Lady's Craft Manufacturing at 100 Dagmar, and Reuben was the proprietor of Bon Accord Clothing.

Canadian Dry Goods was a clothing wholesale at 209 to 213 Logan Avenue that imported clothing and did some manufacturing. Max Steinburg had established the company, which also handled foreign and domestic dry goods and grocers' specialities. In 1915 Steinburg was managing Golden Rule Clothing. This company is not listed in 1925, but Steinburg was managing Leadlay Manufacturing in that year.

Actual manufacturing began in Winnipeg during the 1890s on a small scale. The influx of homesteaders, all in need of overalls, gloves and sturdy boots, as well as the growing number of men employed in railway and other kinds of construction and lumbering created a market for work clothes. Although handmade clothes were still important—there were 31 dressmakers and milliners and 25 tailors in the city at the time of the 1891 census—mass production of work clothes began in the 1890s. In 1893 the partnership of Emerson and Hague, a Brandon company, purchased the manufacturing business of Hope and Company that had been making tents, awnings and mattresses. Emerson and Hague added shirts and overalls, probably as a sideline.[61] They bought the Hope and Company machinery and intended to expand the operation to handle an increased workload. They hired more staff to work in their two-storey building on Portage Avenue east, then called Thistle Street. The basement and the second floor were used for manufacturing and the main floor was a showroom.

Some firms began as the expansion of a merchant tailor's facility. The tailor might only have a handful of sewing machines but would contract work out when there were enough orders to make this necessary. He might begin by spending his savings on a supply of fabric and then make a range of clothing, perhaps employing his children and his wife in the business. If he was successful in selling the garments, he would re-invest the money in more cloth, more sewing machines and more staff.

The large stone and brick warehouses in the Exchange District are a product of Winnipeg's favourable position as a distribution point for the whole of western Canada. Winnipeg had been able to arrange special freight rates that made it possible to carry larger inventories of goods. While it lasted, the freight rate regime encouraged the construction of ever larger warehouses. The Whitla dry goods warehouse on the corner of King and McDermot, for example, was expanded three times in the decade after 1900.

In the 1890s and the 1900 to 1910 period, some of the large dry goods wholesalers began producing their own clothes, converting areas in their warehouses to garment factories. Most specialized in overalls, work shirts and other items of use to labourers. They would simply turn over some of their floor space to garment manufacturing, either bringing in manufacturers, selling them denim and buying everything they made, or establishing a factory of their own. The favourable freight rates did not last and many of the large warehouses were completely converted into garment factories. They were ideal with their large open floors, loading docks, freight elevators and proximity to the rail yards.

Garment Industry, 1900–1929

The first three decades of the twentieth century saw a remarkable growth in Winnipeg. The centre of the city developed as a wholesale, retail, banking, garment and grain industry district. The large warehouses proved to be ideal for the small factories that now began to locate in the area. The manufacturers of candy, biscuits, cigars and clothing found homes in the warehouses. But the most important tenants in the big warehouses were the garment industry firms that became increasingly common in the district. The garment trade flourished in Winnipeg because workers skilled in the clothing business were available. After 1911 electricity rates fell when City Hydro came online and offered competition to Winnipeg Electric. This meant a reduction in one of the main costs for garment factories, where sewing machines and other equipment were all powered by electricity. The area was also close to the CPR yards for receiving cloth and other supplies from eastern Canada and shipping the finished products to customers.

In his excellent *Winnipeg Garment Industry 1900–1955,* historian Gerry Berkowski traces the growth of the business in central Winnipeg.[62] Between 1900 and 1920 over 70 factories were established along Notre Dame Avenue and the streets running into it, as well as, to a lesser extent, east of Main Street along Higgins Avenue and Market Avenue. During this period, it was common for garment factories to rent part of the space in one of the large warehouse buildings in the area. After 1920 many wholesale firms ceased to operate and warehouses were completely taken over by factories. In 1928, for example, the former warehouse of the G. and J. Galt grocery wholesaler on the corner of Bannatyne and Princess was for sale and was purchased by a garment manufacturer. The Bedford Building that had been originally built by F.W. Stobart's wholesale firm was eventually completely occupied by garment factories.

Berkowski describes a typical factory located in a large former warehouse. In addition to a sample room and offices there would be a cutting room where cloth was cut by skilled cutters, key members of a factory staff. Their skill in using patterns to produce the component parts of garments had a great deal to do with the profitability of the company. A basting room was set aside for the assembly of the garment pieces and a sewing room would accommodate the many sewing machine operators who finished the clothes. There would also be a room for pressers and storage and shipping areas.

In some cases, wholesale dry goods merchants like R.J. Whitla and D.K. Elliot, used space in their warehouses to begin manufacturing clothing. Whitla had built two warehouses before 1899 when he erected his largest building on McDermot and Arthur. This building was enlarged twice and in addition to being used for dry goods wholesale it was also the site of some manufacturing. Whitla also owned the Imperial Dry Goods store on Albert Street and in 1901 he began using space on the upper floors as a garment factory.

In 1903 the firm of Whitla and Elliott built a two-storey brick factory on Hargrave and Ellice to make overalls. This facility had 150 sewing machines and 100 employees. In 1906 the company built a three-storey building at McDermot and Kate at a cost of $75,000. The factory made women's ready-to-wear clothing. The top floor housed 140 machines. These were grouped into five rows of 28 machines, each row powered by a single electric motor. Buttonholes and riveting were also done by machine.

The second floor had the cutting department, cloakrooms, bathrooms and a lunchroom for staff. There were offices on the ground floor and storage in the basement. This building is still in use as a factory by the Raber Glove Company.

The F.W. Stobart and Sons dry goods wholesale company began manufacturing smocks, overalls and underwear in their warehouse at the corner of King and McDermot. This building, which still stands, came to be used extensively for garment manufacturing and fur processing over the years. The Stobart firm founded Faultless Garment Company in 1912. Stobart imported management experts from Boston, New York, and Montreal. There were three floors of the Stobart building occupied with the production of ladies' garments. The managers of these firms began to earn good wages. A Mr. Waldman, who had moved to Winnipeg from Montreal to manage Faultless, earned an unheard of salary of $500 a month.[63]

In 1916 Stobart closed his Winnipeg factory. This resulted in

Many of his managers, cutters and pressers—Morris Stall, Shia Feldman and Morris Neaman among them—who had managed to save enough money, opened their own plants. Ben Jacob and

John Crawley, both of whom had been working for Faultless, put up $1,000 each and hired an Eaton's presser, Mr. Geller, to form Jacob-Crawley Cloakmakers.[64]

■

In the pre-1910 period other larger factories opened. Union Overall, Winnipeg Shirt and Overall and Winnipeg Clothing, Harris Manufacturing, and Bromley and Hague were examples. Work clothes for farmers, railway crews and men involved in lumbering continued to be the most important products.

During the Great War some Winnipeg manufacturers were able to bid on producing uniforms for the British and Canadian armed forces. This was facilitated by F.W. Stobart of Faultless Clothing, who had returned to England after 25 years in Winnipeg managing his wholesale business. He was appointed by the British government to manage procurement for the military, a fact that was advantageous for his and other Winnipeg firms that were large enough to take on the government orders. In 1919 Stobart received the Order of the British Empire for his work during the war.

In the 1920s new firms opened for business in Winnipeg and their product lines were more diversified. Hats, caps, gloves, women's and men's everyday clothing, and men's suits and overcoats joined the basic overalls and work clothes being made in the city. During the decade, many improvements were made. Railway spurs were built through the warehouse district, and showrooms and sample rooms and offices were added to the factories. Architects like J.H.G. Russell designed renovations to make the buildings more useful.

Many of the early firms were owned by people born in Ontario or Great Britain. R.J. Whitla was Irish and his partner D.K. Eliott was born in Ontario. Frederick Stobart was English. The firm of Jacob and Crawley was in business for many years and was a partnership between Benjamin Jacob, who was Jewish, and John H. Crawley, who was not.

During the 1920s Jewish owners and workers became more promi-nent. The industry employed around 3,000 people 60% of whom were Jewish. As many as 25 to 30% of all Jewish people in Winnipeg were employed in the garment trade.[65]

By 1929 there were over 200 firms in operation. About 45 new firms had been established and capital invested rose from $470,000 to $902,000. The number of people employed rose from 498 in 1925 to 694 in 1931. Most were concentrated in the area bounded by Notre Dame, William, Main Street, Portage and Hargrave. The area far-ther west, along McDermot as far as Dagmar, Ellen, and Lydia was home to fewer businesses. East of Main Street the area bounded by Main and the Red River along Market, Higgins and Pioneer had only about 20 factories. During the 1920s the local industry survived and grew in spite of eastern factories in Montreal and Toronto dumping their surplus production here. The market for work clothes declined somewhat and Winnipeg factories turned to men's and ladies' ready-to-wear clothing, although Winnipeg-made overalls were still sold all across the West.

Garment Industry, 1929–1939

During the 1930s, the garment industry was one of the few areas that saw growth in Winnipeg. In fact, it doubled in size in terms of number of workers, wages paid and production. There were many more firms belonging to Jewish owners in the 1930s. Many factories were located close to one another in the area between Main and Hargrave, Portage and Higgins so the managers tended to meet often over lunch. Although they were competitors, they worked together in the Garment Manufacturers Association (GMA) to discourage unionization and to cooperate in areas like cloth purchases. Because they had a common background, Jewish business owners tended to support each other and they worked together to support institutions in the Jewish community.

The Jewish firms were often family operations and many owners had a history in the craft of tailoring and a sense of pride in the work they were doing. Some firms that had started earlier were, by the 1930s, large and successful. In 1898 Moses Haid and Harry Steinberg had opened the Winnipeg Shirt and Overall Company with six operators. Mrs. Haid was the forewoman and her husband was the cutter. It was relatively easy to start in the garment business. The cost of a sewing machine and a second-hand cutting knife would have been about $100 and the whole family would work in the factory. By the 1930s Haid's Western Shirt and Overall was well established. Haid spent one term as the president of the North Centre Winnipeg Liberal Association. He was prominent member of Shaarey Zedek Synagogue and supported the Winnipeg Hebrew Free School and the local B'Nai Brith chapter.

Sam Stall started in the business around the turn of the century as well. He spent his savings on cloth and with his brother began manufacturing coats. They sold coats to Eaton's and the Hudson's Bay, employed travelling salesmen to sell to retail stores in small towns, and during the 1920s operated their own clothing store on Selkirk Avenue.

Skilled workers were key to the success of a clothing manufacturer. Ike Glesby was one of many cutters in the Winnipeg industry. He began working for Sam Stall and in 1932 moved to KBB Manufacturing where he developed into an expert cutter. Later he was hired by Jacob and Crawley to work in their factory on Portage Avenue East. The best workers often would be hired away from the firm they worked for by other managers.

In the 1930s many of the Jewish merchants who operated dry goods or grocery stores in rural communities began to move to Winnipeg to ensure their children had a Jewish education. They often invested in garment factories. An example was Harry Silverberg, a store owner in Manitou who moved into Winnipeg in 1936 and bought Canadian Sportswear. He invested in other things—real estate, apartment blocks, a cap factory in Toronto—and hired good managers to look after his investments. He became a wealthy man.

In the 1930s the garment firms were faced with competition from Eaton's garment factory, a large producer of clothes located in the company's Catalogue Department on Graham Avenue. The Hudson's Bay Company also maintained a special clothing shop for railway workers in the basement of their store. Smaller chain stores, like Woolworths, came to dominate clothing retail in the 1930s and their buyers had the power to push down prices, forcing some of the smaller factories out of business by demanding lower prices.

Retailers in the 1930s preferred to make small orders to lower the amount of money tied up in merchandise at any one time. They tended to deal with local Winnipeg manufacturers who could provide them with small shipments and who were knowledgeable about their needs. Eastern firms, struggling because of the Depression, dumped their products in the west at low prices but this threat was met by the GMA firms cooperating on prices.

Unionization became an important issue for the industry. In the early 1930s many of the garment workers belonged to the Industrial Union of Needle Trades Workers (IUNTW). This union was affiliated with the Communist party and tried to address problems like layoffs, poor working conditions and wage cuts, which were used by the garment industry to cut costs. There was a sense of comradery in the union and, as historian Jodi Giesbrecht has shown, union activities were a way for immigrant women to join forces with fellow workers and become more integrated into the community.[66]

Many manufacturers did not want unions in their factories. Jacob and Crawley said they preferred to negotiate with a committee of their workers and not with the union organizers. A story told by Jacob Weinberg, a Jacob and Crawley employee, illustrates why the workers wanted unions. Weinberg checked his pay envelope one payday and found that instead of $29, his usual wage, he was paid $24. He went to see Ben Jacob who told him he could leave if he did not like the pay. Weinberg found another job that paid $32. When he got back to Jacob and Crawley, Jacob asked why he wanted to go and told him he could not leave. He said the managers had an agreement that they would not hire staff away from each other. This was confirmed by his new boss who told him he could not hire him because of the agreement. So he stayed on at Jacob and Crawley.[67] The partners had been negative about unionization. When tailors working for Jacob had earlier tried to unionize he simply locked them out.

In February 1931 there was a strike at the Jacob and Crawley factory in the Keewayden Building on Portage Avenue East. The issues were wage cuts the management had imposed as well as the firing of several employees. The cloak makers went on strike first and then were followed by dressmakers. The strike was organized by I. Minster of the IUNTW. After three weeks, on February 20th, there was a meeting of the two sides. Ben Jacob and J.H. Crawley came with S. Hart Green, a lawyer who often represented the garment manufacturers.

The meeting was not a success. On February 17th, City Council had set up a committee to help with negotiations. It consisted of Mayor Webb, Councillors John Blumberg, Gray and Andrews.

Two days later the union held a mass meeting in the Queen's Theatre on Selkirk Avenue. Minster hinted about having approval for a general strike in the industry. In the end the union decided conditions were not right for such a strike. The next day J.H. Crawley announced that as far as he was concerned the strike was over. New workers had been hired to replace the strikers and production was in "full swing." He said he did not see any point in wasting more time meeting with delegates who were just "stalling." He informed the mayor that the company was withdrawing from further attempts to settle the dispute. Webb expressed regret at the abrupt end of negotiations.

Some of the striking workers had not returned to work, but Crawley said that with 30% to 40% of positions filled the company could resume work without them. He told strikers that they would be taken back as jobs became available but people hired during the strike would be kept on.

In 1934 there was another strike involving a number of the local garment factories and a total of 450 workers. Once again the issues were working conditions, the union demands being wage increases of 15% for workers earning more than $20 a week and 20% for those earning less than $20. They were asking for time and a half pay for overtime and for work on legal holidays. And they wanted the firms to formally recognize the workers' shop committees and their right to organize with a union of their choice. The strike lasted over a month and tempers became frayed. Several strikers were charged for attempting to prevent workers from entering the various factories to go to work.

The fact that the IUNTW had connections to the Communist Party was again used to attack the organization. Mayor Webb said he was happy to work for fair wages for garment workers but he warned the strikers not to listen to the "poisonous schemes of the communists."

The strike failed and was called off after six weeks and once again, no gains were made by the workers and employees hired as replacements during the strike were kept on. Wages continued to be among the lowest in Canada. Workers were expected to work overtime without additional pay.

At the end of 1934 an organizer for the International Ladies Garment Workers' Union (ILGWU) arrived in Winnipeg. One account claims that he was invited to come by leaders of the workers and by some of the owners of firms. The ILGWU was affiliated with the American Federation of Labour, and was less radical in its approach than the Communist unions. The Winnipeg Trades and Labour Congress supported their campaign to sign up members and they were eventually successful in replacing the IUNTW in Winnipeg.

Sam Herbst, the local organizer for the international union, met with factory owners and held out the prospect of there being no more strikes if all the workers were represented by his union. Herbst's less militant style was criticized for being too friendly with the bosses. He was, however, successful in organizing most of the Winnipeg workforce. One of the first contracts he negotiated was with Jacob and

Crawley and it included a $1 raise for all workers, a 44-hour week, dropping to 42 hours in the second year, plus time and a quarter payments for overtime. Other owners were soon happily leaving labour relations to Herbst so the endless labour strife would end. Herbst often worked with former Communist union executives, using their organizational skills to get the locals set up.

The firms that managed to survive the Depression profited during the Second World War. The larger firms like Jacob and Crawley won contracts for uniforms and battle dress from the armed forces. Their factory produced a total of 75,000 great coats in the Keewaydin Building on Portage Avenue East. Firms began to use assembly line methods in order to handle large orders and subcontracted work to other garment manufacturers. They were paid well and used their profits to modernize their factories and buy new equipment. The industry continued to flourish and by the 1960s the Winnipeg garment sector was the third largest in Canada after Toronto and Montreal.

The Changing Wheat Market

In August 1920 government subsidies ended and the Grain Exchange began to operate once more. Prices fell from $2.74 a bushel in August to below $2.00 in December. The general downward trend continued until December 1923 when the price reached 93 cents a bushel and then began to slowly recover. Canadian farmers had to pay shipping and storage and marketing costs out of these declining prices before they deposited their dollars in the bank and made their loan payments.

Canadian wheat prices were hit hard by a complex of factors including the postwar re-emergence of Australia, Argentina, and other wheat exporters. Because of the danger of submarines and high cost of insuring shipping during the war, these countries had been virtually eliminated as competitors. The inability of Canada's former customers in Europe to afford wheat imports was another factor. After the war Europe was burdened with massive debts and, in the case of Germany, reparation payments imposed by the peace treaty.

Canada's customers began to move toward self-sufficiency in food production. Tariff barriers were erected, and subsidies were paid to farmers in former customer countries. This had the combined effect of reducing food imports and strengthening the politically conservative rural populations of these countries so they could act as a bulwark against the radical politics of the urban working class. In 1932 even the United Kingdom introduced a tariff to protect farmers, partially closing the door to what had always been one of Canada's most important markets.

In some parts of the prairies, natural disasters like the dreaded leaf stem rust disease and drought were added to farmers' problems in the 1920s.

Wheat prices fell but farm costs and farm debts remained the same or rose. Some farmers simply gave up and walked away from their land. The fall in prices was seen by farmers as proof that the Exchange did not work to their benefit and that the traders were once more busy stealing their profits. The earnings of grain traders and elevator companies did not depend on wheat prices but on commissions for selling and storing wheat. A large crop meant more profits for them, no matter the price of wheat.

The government in Ottawa responded, predictably, with yet another Royal Commission, this time on grain marketing. It reported in early 1925.[68] While the commissioners made numerous suggestions for revisions to the Canada Grain Act, they found no proof of wrongdoing on the part of the grain trade. Futures trading, considered by many farmers as a form of gambling, was found to be a legitimate way of protecting grain marketers from an unexpected drop in prices. The findings of the Commission had little influence on farmers' opinions and agitation to re-establish the wartime Wheat Board on a permanent basis continued.

When attempts to do so failed, a new strategy emerged. As H.S. Paton wrote:

In 1923, when the futility of the campaign for the re-establishment of government marketing became conclusive, the western farmer's organizations turned their efforts from the direction of government compulsion and monopoly to voluntary and cooperative action.[69]

This voluntary and cooperative action took the form of the Wheat Pool movement and the first Pool was established in Alberta in 1923, followed by Saskatchewan and Manitoba. In a wheat pool the members contracted to sell their wheat through a Central Selling Agency. The agency had seats on the Grain Exchange and used the Exchange's facilities to sell their grain, although the Central Selling Agency also sold increasing quantities directly to customers.

From 1924 to 1928 western farmers enjoyed stronger prices and a period of good crops, culminating in the record 1928 wheat harvest, which was large but of low quality. The prices paid by the Pools between 1925 and 1928 ranged from $1.42 a bushel to $1.45. Wheat exports grew steadily and in the 1928–29 crop year earned $429 million, 40% of all Canadian export earnings. The pools were credited by many farmers with the improved economic situation, and by the end of the decade the three prairie Wheat Pools were selling around half the western Canadian crop. The private grain companies competed for what was left. The Pools and the farmer-owned United Grain Growers between them controlled 38% of the country elevators in western Canada and a good deal of the terminal storage space in Vancouver and at the Lakehead.

A war of words raged between representatives of The Grain Exchange and the Pools through the 1920s and for many years after. The central question was whether or not the prices the Central Selling Agency was able to get for pool members' grain were greater than those obtainable on the Grain Exchange. There never has been a satisfactory conclusion to this debate.[70]

An example of the sorts of arguments made is found in Winnipeg Grain Exchange President James Richardson's address to the

December 22, 1924 annual meeting. He was critical of the Pools, pointing out that the price paid for Alberta wheat was set by managers based in Fort William, whereas a large portion of the Alberta crop went out through Vancouver. He mentioned the administration expenses of the Pool that had to be paid out of the money owed to pool members. Alberta farmers who sold on the open market received as high as $1.50 per bushel while the Pool price could be as low as $1.02:

> We still tend to the belief that the free play of opinion of farmers, merchants, millers and exporters and importers the world over, year in and year out, will record in the future, as it has in the past, a wheat price that has an uncanny way of reflecting true conditions and reflecting them much better than any group of men can possibly forecast them.

The years 1928 and 1929 saw good crops and good prices. These years would turn out to be the last of the wheat booms that had been the motivating force behind the opening of the prairie provinces. The income from wheat sales, especially in the growth years from 1900 to 1913, had attracted homesteaders and investors to the west. The oceans of wheat and the income they produced had been a key part of the prosperity that built the Winnipeg wholesale trade and enriched the members of the Winnipeg Grain Exchange. And after each bust with their falling prices and recessions there had always been a revival building up to another wheat boom. That would not be repeated at the end of the grueling Depression about to settle upon the prairies.

The Canadian wheat industry is an export industry and markets were drying up in the early 1930s. Europe was still recovering from the effects of the Great War. Former customers for Canadian wheat all began to impose tariffs on imported grain at the beginning of the 1930s to encourage the development of their own farm industries. Germany, France, Italy and the United States all erected import barriers that damaged the wheat industry that had produced Canada's most important staple export for decades. At the same time Russia and the United States flooded the international market with their own grain, driving down prices.

The wheat industry was on the threshold of a collapse that would pull the western Canadian economy down with it. Drought and low prices would continue for several years. In the late 1920s the average annual production of wheat in the West had been 220,500,000 bushels. Between 1928 and 1938 the figure declined to 138 million bushels. The average export price dropped by 50%.

Saskatchewan, the hardest hit of the prairie provinces, had earned a net income of $218 million in 1928. By 1933 this figure had declined to $42.3 million and in 1937 net income from wheat stood at only $17.8 million. The drought conditions combined with the decline in prices spelled ruin for many farm families as well as the business men who depended on farm customers. During the decade 250,000 people left the prairies in search of opportunities elsewhere.

The decline of the wheat industry had begun in 1929, the year after a record harvest in western Canada. A smaller crop, about half the size that of 1928, was taken off. The price of wheat rose to $1.56 per bushel and the Pool Central Selling Agency made an initial payment to producers of $1.00 a bushel. Then in October, after the stock market crash, the price began a long slow decline.

This produced a crisis for the Wheat Pools. When prices fell below the $1 level of their initial payment, it seemed they would be bankrupted. Because they refused to use the futures market to provide themselves with a measure of protection, the decline in prices hit the Central Selling Agency very hard. When there was no improvement in 1930, they appealed to the provincial governments to bail them out and guarantee their loans with the banks. On February 27, the Manitoba Legislature responded with a bill that committed Manitoba to guarantee the advances made by the Pool; the Saskatchewan and Alberta governments had already done the same. The entry of the provincial and then the federal government into the wheat marketing business marked the end of the Pools as sellers of wheat, although they continued to operate their extensive elevator systems in order to purchase grain. Western grain producers took the first steps away from being autonomous growers and sellers of their crop to become participants in a state subsidized industry. In 1930 the federal government of R.B. Bennet guaranteed a basic price of 70 cents a bushel. This was done as much to support the banks as it was to help farmers. Other measures including a direct payment of 5 cents a bushel to producers, were used by the Bennet government to support producers.

Grain man John McFarland was appointed by the federal government to be general manager of the Pool Central Selling Agency. He was to sell the huge surplus of grain that had been delivered to the Pools.

The bailouts of the Pools were not popular with the private trade that had been making important changes to deal with the decline in their share of the business. To quote one historian of the grain trade: "to the private firms the answer to this new threat seemed clear; if they were to survive and prosper then they must look for ways to combine together to match the efficiencies of large-scale, centralized management and administration then being realized by the cooperatives."[71]

There had already been a number of mergers of smaller companies. For example, in 1928 six companies with a total of 223 licensed elevators amalgamated to form the Western Grain Company. It was incorporated in 1929 as a public company with issues of bonds and preferred shares. It became the fourth largest private company after Alberta Pacific, Federal Grain and Searle Grain. The Pools said this was a plot to build public support for the private trade—an editorial in the February 1929 *Scoop Shovel*, the newspaper of the Pools, warned Pool members not to invest in the company's bonds and once again accused the private trade of making profits on the backs of farmers.

Federal Grain, another new entity incorporated in 1929, resulted from the amalgamation of eight smaller companies. Three men, James Stewart, J.C. Gage and H.E. Sellars owned a majority of the shares in the constituent companies and they filled the offices of president and vice presidents.

In 1929 James Stewart, President of Federal Grain and one of the wealthiest of the Winnipeg grain merchants, had made the same mistake as the Central Selling Agency of the Pools and assumed that the price of grain would rise. He bought a good deal of grain but did not follow the normal practice of hedging it in the futures market. As a result, when the price began to fall, he suffered enormous losses. H.E. Sellars' son George later remembered the incident:

> The market went down instead of up, and, like the guy going to the races Stewart kept doubling up to make up. Ultimately, on a Sunday, he asked Gage and my father if they would come over to his house, and they went over and he told them they were virtually bankrupt. This was quite a shock of course. Stewart was about the biggest grain man in Canada…but despite that, out of all this debacle he didn't get any money personally. There was no intended fraud on his part; on the other hand, he had no business doing what he did without the directors' or his partners' knowledge.[72]

Stewart sold everything, including his house, to cover his losses. Gage died soon after leaving H.E. Sellars in charge of Federal Grain, in financial difficulties at the opening of the Depression. Thanks to careful management he survived and so did the company. It was also in 1929 that Augustus Searle amalgamated his family firm with a number of smaller firms like the Liberty and Home grain companies to form Searle Grain Ltd., a company owned privately by the family.

The other large organization in the private grain trade, the companies belonging to the Richardson family, took a slightly different course in the 1920s. James A. Richardson diversified his business enterprises, establishing Western Canada Airways in 1926. He had a great deal of success with the airline, winning the first airmail contracts and playing a strong supporting role in the opening of the North. Piloted by ex-military fliers, his planes carried the mail, transported prospectors and anyone else who had business in the North. By the end of the 1920s Richardson's airline was one of the largest in the British Empire.

James Richardson himself was by then on the boards of a wide range of national companies including the Bank of Commerce and the CPR as well as being a generous donor and the chancellor of his alma mater, Queen's University. He and his wife had become leading figures in the world of Winnipeg charities and the city's social life.

In the late 1920s Richardson was also heavily involved in the investment and securities business through the stock brokerage organization he established for James Richardson and Sons. Richardson did not escape the damage inflicted by the stock market crash. In 1929 work had begun on the basement of a new headquarters skyscraper for the Richardson companies at Portage and Main but when it became clear that he was faced with heavy losses, Richardson ordered the basement filled in and put his new building on hold. Richardson continued to develop Western Canada Airlines, aiming to make his company central to a successful Canadian airline industry. His plans were, however, defeated by C.D. Howe, a government partner of Richardson in the airline planning, who decided to take a different course.

Richardson had always been involved in building communications networks using telegraph and radio stations connected to the grain trade. He had a line of radio stations which broadcast news and entertainment and information on the grain trade for farmers. James Richardson died in 1939 and his widow, Muriel, carried on in charge of the family businesses for 30 years.

Some other private grain companies weathered the changes of the 1920s very well. Parrish and Heimbecker, a company that is still in operation, is a partnership established in 1909. In that year it was a line elevator company that was one of the smaller organisations. But the two founders, William Parrish and Norman Heimbecker, both came from Ontario families that had been involved with milling as well as grain buying. They maintained offices in Toronto and Montreal and sold grain for clients on the Grain Exchange. In the 1920s they built a line of country elevators and a terminal elevator at the Lakehead. They did not, as many other private companies did, participate in mergers except to acquire one small elevator company but they continued to add to their line of elevators through the 1920s and 1930s.

N.M. Patterson and Sons also survived the era of amalgamations in the 1920s. After working for railways, including a period as secretary to David Hannah, Vice President of the Canadian Northern, N.M. Patterson established a business in Fort William that developed into a terminal elevator and line elevator company in 1912. He began to purchase lake steamers which sailed between the Lakehead and eastern ports. The company survived the 1930s by becoming a chartering firm in order to make maximum use of its fleet of lake ships.

As the 1930s went on, the federal government became more and more involved in providing relief payments in the cities and rural areas. In Saskatchewan alone $140 million was distributed through the Farm Relief Program.

The situation in the 1930s led to important changes in the marketing of wheat. We have seen how the Wheat Pools' Central Selling Agency was damaged by the drop in the wheat price. They were left with a huge carryover of unsold wheat. After this fiasco the federal government took on the job of selling the wheat that had accumulated. The Pools continued to operate as elevator companies and each provincial organization developed its own marketing department but the farmer-owned cooperatives were no longer in control of the actual selling of the Canadian crop. The federal government established basic prices and supplied money to make up the difference between their artificial prices and the actual market prices of wheat.

In 1935 the Bennet government established a Wheat Board as an interim organization to sell the still enormous surpluses of wheat. The Board did succeed in significantly reducing the amounts in storage. Farmers could sell their wheat to the Board although they still had the option of selling to the private grain trade if the price was better. The Wheat Board would pay a minimum price upon delivery and give farmers a certificate entitling them to a share in the profits from the final sale of the grain if there were any.

The private grain trade in Winnipeg lobbied against the Wheat Board model. But government marketing persisted and when they were re-elected in 1935, the Mackenzie King government continued to operate the Wheat Board to market wheat as part of an array of subsidies designed to help producers stay on the land.

In 1943 the federal government closed the futures market, making the Wheat Board the sole marketing agency for western grain. Establishing prices and making trades no longer took place in the Grain Exchange for most grains. Sales were made from government to government and prices were set by officials. The handling of grain did not change. It was delivered to country elevators, purchased and given a grade and then shipped to the Lakehead or Vancouver for export.

The private trade continued the process of merging into larger and larger firms through the 1930s. As the Wheat Board began to take over the role of marketing western grain, the private trade was limited to operating lines of elevators and terminal elevators, acting as agents for the Wheat Board in assembling the western crop. The total number of line elevators declined from 3,167 in 1932-1933 to 2,438 in 1947-1948. Companies sometimes swapped elevators giving up a facility in an area of less interest to them in return for one in a district where they did more business. The companies left after the series of mergers were better able to compete with the Pools and United Grain Growers.

At the end of the 1930s the problem of overproduction continued. The world was simply growing too much wheat and Canada again had large surpluses. The federal government and the Wheat Board began to develop a quota system in order to control the amount of wheat that could be brought to market as well as programs to limit the amount of acreage devoted to wheat. The era of the great wheat booms was over.

The New Fur Trade

In 1905, when the massive new Eaton's Store rose on Portage Avenue, the local Canadian administration made the case to the London board of the HBC for a new store to face the competition in a more central location. All the London board would approve were some renovations to the Main Street building. While Eaton's put one or two local dry goods stores out of business, the Bay survived, although the store's retail sales fell disastrously.

In 1911 Hudson's Bay House was erected across Main Street from the former location of Upper Fort Garry. In it were located the fur trade department, the land department, the wholesale department, and the administrative offices.

In the same year, the Company embarked on a new building program in response to the huge population increase in western Canada. Elegant new stores were planned for Winnipeg, Calgary, Edmonton as well as Vancouver and Victoria. In Winnipeg, the land was acquired for the new building at the corner of Portage Avenue and Colony Street. Unfortunately, the economy slowed in 1913 and a recession set in. Then the war put a stop to all expansion and building plans.

It was not until 1926 that the Portage Avenue property saw the construction of a new Hudson's Bay store. The Board of Trade and the City Council saw the store as key to the success of the city's new Memorial Boulevard development. It was the first grand limestone building of several that would eventually line the Boulevard. Winnipeg's leaders were sure that the store would trigger more development at the western end of the Portage Avenue business district. Some new growth did take place before the onset of the Great Depression. The Winnipeg Electric Company's new Power Building, the new Bank of Montreal, and some other business buildings, all faced in limestone to match the Hudson's Bay store, went up on Portage Avenue in the first block east of Vaughan Street.

Around 1911 the London board of the Company had decided it needed Canadian businessmen to advise them and a Canadian

Committee Advisory Board was established. In 1923 the name was changed to simply Canadian Committee. In 1930 the Committee was given the power to make all the senior administrative appointments for Canada. Winnipeggers played a prominent role on this body and Augustus Nanton, George Galt and George Allan all served as chair in the 1920s and 1930s.

Winnipeg had started as a fur trade center and there are still fur businesses in the city. The fur trade prospered during the years 1895 to 1911, a time of economic growth when fur sales boomed. London continued to be the site of the major fur auctions and the HBC continued to play a leading role in the London fur industry. Once the west joined Confederation and railways began to link western Canada to the outside world, however, the Hudson's Bay Company faced increasing competition from fur buyers based in Montreal, Toronto, and Minneapolis as well as Winnipeg. In 1907, for example, B. Levinson was in business at 281-3 Alexander Avenue. He bought furs direct from trappers and sold locally as well as exporting to all parts of the world. He had come to Winnipeg in 1904 but had been in the fur business for many years before that. In 1915 and 1925 he was still operating at the same Alexander Avenue address.

Then, with the outbreak of World War I, the Company's situation changed drastically when the British Board of Trade suspended fur auctions, opting to put any available money into war material instead. The Company decided to direct its employees in Canada to stop both buying furs from their Indigenous suppliers and extending credit to them. This situation continued until 1923, and the bonds of loyalty between the HBC and Indigenous trappers were weakened. Other individuals and firms moved quickly to fill the gap left by the HBC. Auction houses in Montreal and companies like the New York Fur Auction Sales Ltd and the International Fur Exchange in St. Louis threatened to replace European fur centres like Leipzig and London. In Montreal, the Canadian Fur Auctions Company began to handle large amounts of fur. It was financed by businessmen like Herbert

Holt, who as the owner of Holt Renfrew began to do an expanded business in furs.

Other firms now began to buy furs in the North. Lampson and Hubbard, Revillon Frères and the Alberta-based Northern Trading Company were three of the biggest firms competing in areas where the Hudson's Bay Company had previously been dominant.

During the 1914–1918 period, as the United States began to feel the effects of war prosperity, the demand for luxury items like furs grew. Then when the war ended there was a period of inflation that raised the value of furs and the newcomers to the industry prospered. In the middle of 1920 prices began to drop as the post-war recession began. The large fur auction houses were facing difficulties and the Hudson's Bay was soon in a position to buy out its rivals.

Hyman Yewdall, a Winnipeg fur dealer, took a lead role in organizing the Winnipeg Fur Auction Sales Ltd. in 1921 to take advantage of the difficulties facing the St. Louis and Montreal auction houses. Yewdall won the backing of many of the Winnipeg dry goods and wholesale companies in like R.J. Whitla, John W. Peck, Robinson Little and Co., Greenshields Ltd., and Western Grocers, who took furs in payment for their merchandise. Whitla and Peck had been taking considerable quantities of pelts in payment since the late 1800s.

The Winnipeg Fur Auctions tried to attract business by saying they wanted to make sure Canadian trappers got fair prices. It was argued, with some justification, that the St. Louis and New York auctions mixed Canadian furs with American furs from farther south to increase the overall value of the lots for sale. This meant northern Canadian trappers had their higher quality furs devalued. The Winnipeg organization attracted a large volume of furs from Saskatchewan and Manitoba.

The Winnipeg auction house advertised that it would hold frequent sales—one per month during the trapping season—and this meant that losses that shippers and their creditors experienced would be reduced, and trappers, because they would receive more frequent payments, would need less credit to operate.

During their first year Winnipeg Fur Auctions grossed over $1 million. Nearly all the furs sold were high quality and so the prices received were on average 10% higher than Montreal and New York.

In 1922 Yewdall was able to convince some of the larger fur-buying companies to sell their furs in Winnipeg. Although Winnipeg did not replace Montreal, sales volumes increased yearly. Max Finkelstein, "the dean of the Winnipeg fur trade" estimated that $45 million in furs changed hands in the City in 1929.

As the Depression set in, however, it became clear Winnipeg Fur Auction Sales Co. was in trouble. They had extended credit to smaller fur dealers who could not now pay. This situation and the long struggle they had had with the Hudson's Bay Company over control of the Northern Trading Company, resulted in the failure of the company.[73]

A local fur broker, C.G. Wilson, took over the assets of Winnipeg Fur Auction and combined it with his own brokerage firm to form the Dominion Fur Auction Company Ltd. In 1931 he did quite well and declared a dividend of 50% that he held back as a reserve. Also in 1930 another local broker, George Soudack, who had branches in Fort William, Edmonton, Regina and Vancouver, formed the Soudack Fur Auctions Ltd. and began holding regular sales. The two auction houses competed for northwestern furs. They extended liberal credit and placed advertisements and fur market reviews on commercial radio.

Following World War II, the Winnipeg auction houses continued to be successful, handling furs equal to 2/3 of the volume of the Montreal Canadian Fur Auctions Ltd. A sizeable portion of the Winnipeg houses' furs came from Saskatchewan, Alberta, the Northwest Territories and northwest Ontario, areas where Winnipeg dealers were very active.

Great-West Life

Dr. Richard Bennet, the historian of the Great-West Life Company, said that "if the new company was individually inspired, it was collectively supported and directed in its formation by Winnipeg's commercial leaders."[74] In fact, Great-West is one of the best examples of the city's early business community working together to build the Winnipeg's economy.

The formation of the company came about first because Jeffry Hall Brock proposed it, but also because his colleagues on the Winnipeg Board of Trade supported the idea, bought stock in the new company and served as board members, presidents and vice presidents.

Jeffry Brock was born in Guelph, Ontario, in 1850. He went to school in Guelph and in Montreal but at 15 he was already working as a salesman in a stationery shop. He went to St. Louis, Missouri and worked for five years in a dry goods store, returning to Canada in 1872 to work for his older brother, William Rees Brock. William was already on his way to a successful career in business, as a partner in the W.R. Brock and Brother wholesale dry goods firm.

The younger Brock wanted to make his own way in the world and in 1879 he and his young family joined many other Ontarians in Winnipeg, where he became the partner of George Carruthers in a growing general insurance agency with offices on Main Street. Brock was a good salesman and was soon the western agent for the Canada Permanent Loan and Savings Company, the same firm of which Robert Riley would be a board member.

Carruthers was a native of Toronto, where he was educated at Upper Canada College and at the University of Toronto. He served with the militia during the Fenian Raids, 1866-1870, and held the Fenian Raid medal. After four years with the Grand Trunk Railway, he came to Manitoba in 1871. He was first associated with journalist Alexander Begg and later became joint editor and proprietor of the *Manitoba Gazette*. In 1874 he entered the fire insurance business and became managing director of the Canada West Fire Insurance

Company, in partnership with J.H. Brock. He was both a city councillor and an MLA, a president of the Board of Trade and a founder of the Winnipeg Real Estate Board and the Parks Board. He died in 1918.

Richard Bennett describes the aftereffects of the speculative boom that crashed in spring 1882. At first, Western real estate was unsaleable at any price. The value of land, driven up by speculation, dropped and many speculators could not raise money to pay off their loans by selling. Brock and Carruthers survived the collapse of the boom, although they lost a great deal of money foreclosing on mortgages and because potential customers were leaving the city in large numbers. The partners survived because they had a solid base of faithful customers who escaped the effects of the crash.

Both men were active Board of Trade members. Brock opposed the National Policy of John A. Macdonald, introduced in 1879. The high tariffs on manufactured goods were intended to protect Canadian industry, but for western farmers and the West in general it meant that essentials like farm machinery were more expensive when imported from the United States. He also worked to end the monopoly of the CPR and supported the construction of branch lines into new farming areas. Brock also joined others in Winnipeg in arguing for a Hudson Bay Railway that could compete with the CPR and ship grain to Britain faster than by the Thunder Bay/St. Lawrence River route.

The Winnipeg business community was upset about interest rates and insurance premiums that were much higher than in the East. These were effects of the real estate crash after which Eastern banks were leery of investing in the West. The insurance underwriters were accused of colluding with insurance companies in setting rates that were called extortionate.

In March 1890 there was a meeting of retail merchants who passed a motion calling on the Board of Trade to protest the rates to the insurance industry and warn them that unless the rates came down, Winnipeg would invite more insurance companies to set up offices in the city and establish some local insurance firms to enter the competition for customers.

The next month, on April 5, the *Winnipeg Tribune* printed an editorial complaining that no intelligent man who knew both communities would be able to explain why Vancouver commercial customers were charged 60 cents per $100 of insurance coverage while in Winnipeg the rate was $1. The *Tribune* added that when the Board of Trade considered "the enormous amount of money that is annually taken out of this city in excess of a fair charge for the insurance given, we believe they will join us in thinking that it is time some steps were taken to stop the unnecessary and unfair drain."[75]

It was noted at the time that at least one million dollars was being sent to eastern Canada, the US and Britain to insurance companies that invested it at 5% and made loans to Winnipeggers at 8%.

At this time Brock was offered the opportunity of going back to Ontario to join his brother William in business but he decided to instead stay and found his own insurance firm. On May 15, 1891 Hugh John Macdonald, an MP for Winnipeg and the son of the former prime minister, introduced a petition on behalf of James Ashdown in the House of Commons for an act to incorporate the Great-West Life Company.

Before the new company could begin selling policies, $400,000 worth of stock, 25% paid up, had to be sold; a provisional board, consisting of the original petitioners, must be appointed; and the firm would have to make a $50,000 deposit with the government. A permanent board of directors could be appointed once $250,000 in stock was sold. The new company was allowed to sell insurance anywhere in Canada and abroad and to raise money it could invest in debentures, stocks or other securities of Canada or its provinces, make mortgage or other loans, and carry on the business of life insurance.[76] Brock thought that lending money in the form of mortgages to Westerners would earn better returns for the new insurance company than the investments in stocks and bonds favoured by most other insurers.

Secure investments in mortgages would allow the company to charge lower policy premiums. He also calculated that selling life insurance to young, fit homesteaders meant the company would be faced with lower mortality rates.

Brock set out to sell the required $400,000 of company stock in 1891 and 1892. He had great difficulty in finding buyers. The economies of Canada and the US were in a depression at this time and the company did not grow rapidly in the early part of the decade. In western Canada wheat prices were low and there had been three bad harvests in a row. Brock took six months to sell $75,000 worth of shares in 1891. There were 89 shareholders in Winnipeg, 59 in rural Manitoba, 29 in British Columbia and a few in the other parts of the west.

But as the decade progressed, a growing stream of homesteaders flowed through Winnipeg on their way to establishing farms where they would grow the wheat that became the basis of western wealth and prosperity.

The $50,000 deposit was paid in the form of City of Winnipeg debentures. At the first shareholder's meeting Brock accepted the job of general manager and withdrew from his partnership with George Carruthers. The provisional board consisted of Alex Macdonald, President, a position he would hold for 34 years, and the members Stephen Nairn, owner of an oatmeal mill; R.T. Riley; George Galt, grocery wholesaler; P.C. McIntyre, a printer; A. Kelly, a Brandon merchant; D.H. McMillan, a miller and grain trader; T.J. McBride; James McLenahan and the Quebec-born S.A.D. Bertrand.

In 1894 Brock made his first foray into expanding Great-West Life. He acquired a New Brunswick insurance company called The Dominion Safety Fund Association to gain a foothold in the Maritimes. The next year the company opened a branch in Montreal and began selling insurance there.

Various attempts were made, especially in Ontario, to put a stop to the success of Great-West. One man literally gave his life in this cause. In 1893 J.A. Taylor, a Hamilton publisher, took out a $10,000 life insurance policy, making his brother-in-law, David Blackley, the beneficiary. Taylor lied about his health, not informing the company that he was actually dying and was a heavy drinker. When he passed away, Great-West declared the policy void because of his deception. Blackley sued the company for $10,000. Such a large payout might well have been the end of the young insurance firm, and it was decided to fight the lawsuit. The issue went to trial in Ontario and Great West won.

This incident moved the company's actuary to advise more caution, Great-West being a relatively small company. They built a larger, 4% reserve fund, mandated careful medical examinations for prospective policy holders, and based their premium rates on British Mortality Tables. There was higher mortality in Britain because of the generally older population, and using these tables resulted in higher premiums to help build the surplus.

Great-West Life agents were given rate books that listed prohibited conditions: those with poor health, dangerous occupations, vicious or intemperate habits were not to be sold insurance. No one under 18 or over 65, no one in the liquor business, no one manufacturing or handling explosives, miners, men working in railway yards, brakemen on freight trains, ordinary seamen were all on the list of bad risks. Soldiers on active service during World War I would be insured but would have to pay a higher premium than other customers.

Great-West Life, 1900–1929

Beginning around 1896, western Canada began its long boom period that only came to an end in 1913. Great-West Life was in an ideal position to grow with the western provinces and the rest of the country as well. The company made an important contribution to the development of agriculture in the west by investing $13 million of its premium income in farm mortgages and mortgages on rental producing properties. Across the West, the wheat boom was creating previously undreamt of prosperity, making farm mortgages seem more stable than the stocks and bonds that were the usual investment choices of the insurance industry. Mortgages did not earn anything beyond the interest and there was a cost to administering them but Brock wanted to invest in western Canada.

In the boom years mortgages did earn more than stocks and interest rates were higher in the West than in eastern Canada. No mortgages were granted without a unanimous vote of the Board of Directors and Brock and other directors inspected the properties personally. Mortgages were given for five or seven years and did not exceed 60% of the property's value. The company's mortgages made a checkerboard pattern on a map of farms, showing where Great-West Life had ensured that soil quality, rainfall, and agricultural potential were all good enough to result in low risk.

By 1906, Great-West had invested $1.6 million in farm loans and $1.2 million in the debentures of small towns and rural school districts. By 1913 they were carrying a massive $15 million in mortgages, a third of the $47 million total investment of all the various mortgage companies. The company had never had a foreclosure, and in 1914, with 6,000 mortgages in force, there were fewer than 50 in arrears.

Policy sales grew during the period from 1896 to 1914 because the popularity of life insurance grew. Overall, life insurance sales rose from $45 million in 1892 to $221 million in 1915. The share of the Canadian market belonging to Canadian firms rose from 55% in 1892 to 63% in 1915. The share of US companies stayed the same and that of British firms dropped from 12% to 8%.

Great-West benefited from this growth and its assets increased faster than any other company except Sun Life. In 1892 the company had a 5% share of Canadian insurance company assets and in 1915 the figure was 13.8%. It was selling more life insurance on the prairies than any other company in 1912, and in that same year it sold 50% of the insurance in force in eastern Canada. Great-West was able to declare a 6% dividend in 1899 and by 1911 the dividend paid was 15%.

The increasing volume of business required the company to open full branch offices in Calgary, Edmonton, Vancouver, Halifax and Ottawa.

The expansion of the industry led to a Royal Commission in 1910, assigned to look into certain questionable investment practices, payments to company officers without a vote of the Board and giving rebates as an inducement to buy a company's products. A federal Insurance Act was passed and it dealt with these and other issues and increased the power of the federal Superintendent of Insurance to regulate the industry.

Entry into the American market was a way some large Canadian firms sought to expand. Sun Life and Canada Life had done so in 1899. Canadian firms found that US nationalism, higher costs, taxes and competition made foreign sales less profitable and many abandoned their foreign branches.

In 1906 Great-West ventured into North Dakota, a state that was enjoying the same wheat boom as prairie Canada. North Dakota law required that insurance agents had to live in the state so the company hired the three Hatcher brothers, established local insurance agents, to represent them in the state.

By the end of the long period of growth, Brock's health was failing. His personal life was marred by the death of four children including his favourite son. He was depressed and he became seriously ill. He travelled to several places, including Egypt, in search of a climate that would help him regain his health but nothing worked and he died in March 1915 in Long Beach, California. R.T. Riley, long-time colleague, vice president and board member was with him when he died.

Brock's vision and untiring salesmanship had been the most important factors in building Great-West Life. In addition, the group that worked beside him for over 20 years gave their time and energy to make the company a success. Arbuckle Jardine was the manager of the company from the days when it literally consisted of him and Brock. Jardine was one of an army of managers and accountants who worked in the offices of the many enterprises clustered around Portage and Main without whom the business of Winnipeg could not have been successfully conducted.

William McQuaker was another such person and he worked for the company as treasurer for 36 years. R.T. Riley was a board member for 50 years, Alexander Mcdonald was president for 33 years, Andrew Kelly was on the board for 38 years, George Galt for 36 years, George Crowe for 28 years and Augustus Nanton for 26 years. J.A.M. Aikins was the Company solicitor for 37 years and Dr. Robert Blanchard was the medical officer until his death in 1928.

The death of Brock ended the long period of explosive growth. The outbreak of the war put paid to the conditions that had allowed that growth and a new kind of management was required to bring about "cautious consolidation" of the company. The next general manager, Colin Campbell Ferguson, was an internal choice. Ferguson was from Prince Edward Island and he was described as determined and deliberate; "Too Fast a Pace is Dangerous" might have been the company motto under Ferguson.[77] After decades of growth, the focus of the company now was to ensure continued success. The Board was divided between those who favoured caution and those who wanted to continue expanding. When their search for a younger, better-trained general manager was made difficult by so many men being away at the war, the Board settled for Ferguson as general manager and actuary. A mathematician and classics scholar, he had no experience in sales, which had been Brock's great strength. Nevertheless, he announced upon being hired that he had no intention of departing from the successful practices of the past.　.

The war presented the insurance industry with a massive new challenge. One in every three Canadians who volunteered to fight in the Great War was either killed or wounded. Many possessed insurance policies. The first soldier insured by Great-West Life to be killed was Captain John Geddes of the Cameron Highlanders, a Winnipeg man who had worked as a grain trader and the manager of a real estate company. He was killed in the second Battle of Ypres in spring 1915. He left behind a wife, living out the war in her native Ireland with her two children. They were paid $5,000.

Dr. H.H. Chown, one of Great-West's medical consultants, gave his opinion about what the war would mean for the company. He said the life expectancy of soldiers at the front would be greatly reduced. The trench fighting "the multiplicity in number and severity and character of wounds received, the almost inevitable infections due to the character of the fertilizers used for ages in the fields of conflict will militate against the recovery of a large number of the wounded."[78]

Chown's grim predictions proved accurate. At first, Canadian insurance companies did not charge higher premiums for soldiers but after the slaughter of 1915 they began to add an extra $100 for each $1,000 of coverage. During the duration of the war, insurance companies paid $18 million for war-related death and disability of which $1.45 million was paid by Great-West Life. They also paid out $22,000 to the beneficiaries of three civilian customers who died when the Cunard liner *Lusitania* was sunk by a German U-boat.

The Company encouraged its employees to volunteer and agreed to pay the difference between their peacetime salaries and their military wages. Of sixty-nine employees who volunteered, many served in the 78th Battalion, the unit raised and reinforced by the Winnipeg Grenadiers Militia regiment.

During the war the company reduced its investment in mortgages and put money into Victory Bonds. By the end of the conflict, Great-West owned $13 million in mortgages and some $6 million in war bonds. For many investors and companies Victory Bonds were their first non-mortgage investment. With the 1913 recession and the post-war depression in the early 1920s farm prices fell and it was difficult for borrowers to keep up with interest and principal payments on farm loans and mortgages.

At the end of the war, the devastating flu epidemic spread through the combatant armies and was carried home with the returning troops. Worldwide, some 22 million people died from the flu. In Canada

50,000 died and by January 1919, 824 people in Winnipeg had died out of a total of 12,863 cases. A total of $1.23 million was paid out as a result of influenza deaths of policy holders.

Great-West lost two staff to the flu. A sad effect of the war and the influenza epidemic was to increase the demand for life insurance. The value of policies in effect doubled between 1918 and 1920 from $30 million to $60 million. The rising cost of living encouraged people to purchase insurance and many women became life insurance customers.

During the post-war depression in Canada, from 1920 to 1924, life insurance was one of the few industries that remained profitable. A full 50% of Great-West Life sales were being made in Toronto, a very competitive market. By 1920 it was outselling most other large companies, with the exception of Metropolitan and Sun Life. Great-West Life became an international company, but the headquarters remained in Winnipeg. The Lombard Avenue building was renovated and four new floors were added.

The Company branched out into new kinds of insurance such as accident, unemployment, and illness. Group insurance became a major new product although it was not popular with sales staff because it meant fewer commissions. The first company to buy group insurance was Great-West itself followed by Manitoba Bridge and Iron Works and Winnipeg Street Railway.

By the late 1920s most of the original founders of the company had retired or passed away. Only R.T. Riley and D.H. McMillan remained on the board. George W. Allen became president after the death of Alexander Mcdonald. Arbuckle Jardine, the longest-serving employee, retired and was replaced.

When the depression of the early 1920s set in, Great-West Life's historic reliance on mortgages as an investment proved to be a serious liability. Many farmers were unable to make interest or principal payments. In many cases in Saskatchewan, families simply walked away from farms on which they could no longer make a living. The company was as lenient as possible with mortgagees, allowing farmers who had grain to pay their obligations with wheat. For investment, the company began to migrate to the government bonds of Ontario, British Columbia and Nova Scotia.

Great-West Life, 1929–1939

Great-West Life emerged from the 1920s full of confidence. At the 1928 Annual Meeting, General Manager C.C. Ferguson reported that the company had sold $2,668,226 in new policies in 1927. For the first time in its history, the total insurance in force had risen above half a billion dollars. The company had purchased land next to its Lombard Avenue headquarters because they were planning to expand and could not add more floors above. The company had continued to invest in mortgages with excellent security. In 1928 and part of 1929 wheat prices were still high so farm mortgages seemed like solid investments.

This was in spite of the fact that the post-war depression which lasted from 1921 to 1924 should have been a warning to the company. During that period wheat prices fell and many farmers had difficulty making payments on debts.

But the investment in mortgages continued. In fact, mortgage loans were made in the dry prairies in southwestern Saskatchewan and southeastern Alberta, a riskier, less productive area than the country farther north because of the arid climate.

At the February 1929 annual meeting the situation continued to be favourable. Once again there had been a large increase in new policies during the previous year, even though the company had decided not to open up any new territory. The company's assets were valued at over $100 million.

C.C. Ferguson reported that "our organization is confident of its ability to advance to new records in business production" and he reminded shareholders of the company's unbroken record of success over the 36 years of its existence. Ferguson said that there was a plan to increase mortgage lending as part of an expansion into new territory in Ontario and Montreal.

The end of the 1920s saw the death of long-time board members Alexander Macdonald and George F. Galt, both of whom had been among the founders. New directors elected to the board were grain men James Richardson and J.C. Gage as well as federal cabinet minister Thomas Crerar.

By the time of the February 1931 Annual Meeting the tone was less optimistic. President George Allan assured the meeting that Great West Life had not been tempted to participate in the rush to buy stocks in the late 1920s. He emphasized that the company held over 50% of its assets in the form of government bonds and mortgages. He said they had made large purchases of high-class Canadian and US utility bonds. They were required to hold a percentage of US investments in order to do business in their American branches.

Prairie wheat farmers had seen the collapse of their industry as wheat prices fell from $1.24 a bushel in early 1929 to 59 cents in 1931. There was overproduction of wheat as Canada's rivals in the wheat export trade all harvested large crops and the traditional customers in Europe turned to a policy of encouraging their own wheat farmers to produce what they needed. The Canadian Pools faced ruin after making an initial payment to members that turned out to be more than the final price earned. They were saved from bankruptcy by the provincial governments.

All across the prairies, farmers were unable to make their mortgage payments. In 1928 the net cash income per Saskatchewan farm had been $1,614; by 1933 it had fallen to $66. Of 7,027 farm mortgages held by Great-West Life, 607 had been in arrears for several years by 1939. Only a small percentage of farmers had been able to keep all their payments up to date throughout the 1930s.

In some areas, governments passed legislation making it impossible to foreclose on mortgages so the company simply carried many people. The loss to the company from mortgages during the Depression was estimated to be $30 million.

There were serious discussions about simply closing Great-West

Life down. In 1934 President George Allan reported that the company was continuing its practice of decreasing mortgage investments and increasing its holdings of bonds. Company assets were 40% bonds and debentures, 21% city mortgages, 17% farm mortgages, 20% loans to policy holders, 0.4% stocks and 8% cash.

In 1931 a new assistant general manager had been hired. H.W. Manning was Canadian by birth and had worked in New York for large American life insurance firms as superintendent of agencies. He encouraged a more aggressive sales program in the United States and improved the training and morale of the sales staff. As the Depression wore on, Great-West Life continued to sell insurance. In 1933 the sales of new policies were up 18% over 1932. Manning opened new agencies in Washington State in 1931 and in Wisconsin in 1936. He also emphasized the group life insurance area, doubling Great-West Life's market share from 4.69% in 1930 to 9.16% in 1939.

In 1935, however, $141 million in municipal bonds and debentures were in default. In 1938, with the death of C.C. Ferguson, new managers assumed control of the company. H.W. Manning became general manager, and the company's fortunes began to improve. In 1938 the practice of investing in bonds and debentures continued and President Allan declared that the company was in a "strong liquid position with unquestionable security."

Manning's aggressive sales program saved the company and during and after World War II it recovered from the damage done by the Depression and once again took its place as one of the major life insurance companies.

Winnipeg Electric

Winnipeg was developing into a city just at the beginning of what we might call the electric age. Electric lights were first turned on in Winnipeg in 1882, the same year Edison began to sell power for lighting from his Pearl Street power plant in New York. At the time, Winnipeg was widely known as a boom town where people were making fortunes speculating in western lands. As a result, promoters with something to sell made their way to the city. P.V. Carroll came all the way from New York and set up four arc lamps for the city councillors to see. The lights ran off a generator and he borrowed the steam engine at the Patterson and McComb planing mill near the CPR station to provide the power.

Carroll was soon calling himself the manager of the Manitoba Electric Light and Power Co. He installed arc lamps on Main street and rented the rather elderly steam engine in the HBC's mill near the forks of the rivers. The power provided was unreliable and the arc lamps' carbons froze in winter. Winnipeggers were not overly impressed by the intermittent light provided.

Carroll soon had a competitor in Fergis Muncie, another American who organized a second company, the North West Electric Light and Power Company. He was more successful, having better equipment, and he contracted with the City in April 1883 to provide streetlights. He was soon serving a number of private customers as well.

Both companies survived into the 1890s. The Northwest Electric Company, as Muncie's outfit was then called, was providing a patented Edison system to Winnipeggers and paying a yearly royalty of $16,000 to Edison for the right to do so. Customers paid $2 for Edison incandescent lamps and 9 cents an hour for current.

The rival Manitoba Electric Company used the Westinghouse system, the main competitor of Edison. They had their own version of the incandescent lamp that they rented to customers and they also charged for power. Both companies had their own steam-driven power plants.

Edison had first developed his system with direct current (DC), that is current which travels from the generator directly to the electric device. The source of power and the device using it have to be close together because a lot of energy is lost during transmission of DC power over wires. Edison's system required the construction of many small generating stations that supplied power customers. The brilliant

Serbian engineer Nikola Tesla had developed alternating current (AC) to solve this problem and industrialist George Westinghouse became his partner. With alternating current, the voltage of electricity could be controlled and changed. Electricity could be generated a long way from the end user, in, for example, a hydro dam, and stepped up to a very high voltage for transmission so that less power would be lost. Then, close to the end user, transformers are used to step the power down to levels that are useable in household appliances and factory machinery. Therefore, AC current could be delivered to customers without having to have generating stations dotted all over the city landscape.

There was a great struggle between the two forms of power in the early days, but at the Chicago World's Fair of 1893 the issue was more or less resolved when Tesla and Westinghouse won the contract to provide electrical power for the entire exhibition. They did so efficiently and with great success. Of course, Edison continued in business and DC power is still used for many purposes, but he did not achieve the complete monopoly he had been hoping for.

Neither Winnipeg company supplied the biggest consumer of electricity in town, the Street Railway Company. Since 1891 Winnipeg had had electric trams and the street railway had its own power plant, also driven by steam, which stood on the bank of the Assiniboine where Bonnycastle Park is now.

Horse-drawn streetcars first appeared on Winnipeg's streets in 1882. A.W. Austin, one of the bright young men from Toronto who came to the city in the 1880s, founded the Winnipeg Street Railway Company with the help of his father, the founder of the Dominion Bank, and Edmund Osler, the Toronto financier who raised the money.

Austin wanted to introduce electric cars in 1888 but City Council refused to approve the plan, nervous about the imagined dangers of electric wires and electric cars. In 1891 Austin did build an electric railway line along River Avenue in the Fort Rouge suburb. This line was the first electric streetcar service to operate in Canada.

In 1892 William Mackenzie, a tough railway contractor who had helped to build the CPR, arrived in Winnipeg and was granted a franchise to operate an electric street railway. Austin sued in an attempt to protect his own franchise. The case dragged on for two years until the Privy Council in London, Canada's last court of appeal at the time, decided in favour of Mackenzie. For two years both companies had operated their lines in Winnipeg and Main Street had two rail lines. When Mackenzie won his case, Austin sold out to him for $175,000 and went back to Toronto where he would have a successful career and eventually become president of the Dominion Bank.

Mackenzie began a period of growth and consolidation. He acquired the two competitor companies, Manitoba Electric and the Northwest Electric Company, which would eventually become part of Winnipeg Electric. He also bought the Suburban Rapid Transit Company and the Winnipeg, Selkirk and Lake Winnipeg Railway, the other electric railway companies operating in the Winnipeg area. These companies gave the Winnipeg Electric Street Railway a monopoly of streetcar service west of the city as far as Headingley and north to Selkirk and eventually Stonewall. Mackenzie's 1904 acquisition of the Manitoba Electric and Gas Light Company meant that his organization was the only source of gas for light, cooking and heating in Winnipeg.

Mackenzie's company supplied electric power for his streetcars and sold current to homes and businesses. Starting with a coal-fired generating plant on Assiniboine Avenue, Mackenzie moved on to build hydro-electric generating stations. As early as 1888 there had been interest in developing hydro power in the city, with plans to use the waters of the Assiniboine river.

But before the Assiniboine could be harnessed, interest turned to the much more promising Winnipeg River. The Winnipeg River is a fast-moving Canadian Shield river that drops 106 meters over its 235-kilometer route from Lake of the Woods to Lake Winnipeg, creating the water speed necessary to turn hydro turbines. Between

1906 and the early 1930s several hydro dams, located at spots where the river dropped over falls or rapids, were built to harness its power. The City would also build two publicly owned power stations, providing competition and forcing Winnipeg Electric to lower its rates.

Winnipeg Electric, 1900–1929

The first power dam that tapped the power of the Winnipeg River was built by the Winnipeg Street Railway Company. In 1902 they established a subsidiary, the Winnipeg General Power Company, which successfully bid on a license from the federal government to build a hydroelectric power dam at Pinawa. This first dam was not actually on the Winnipeg River but on the Pinawa Channel, a stream that cuts across one of the great bows of the river. It was felt that a dam on the main channel of the river would not be able to survive the battering it would get from the ice when the river broke up in the spring. A system of weirs was constructed to increase the flow of water from the main river down the channel.

The Pinawa Dam was completed in 1906 and opened on May 30 of that year. It was a massive $3 million project built by local engineer Donald Ross. It was an impressive accomplishment at a time when such dams were a very new phenomenon. Some of the methods used to build the dam were, however, almost medieval. The dam site was not served by rail or even proper roads and the end of the railway at Pinawa was on the opposite side of the Winnipeg River. Everything, including the massive turbines, had to be manhandled and dragged on skids by teams of horses.

The first electrical power was delivered to Winnipeg on June 9, 1906. Sir Daniel McMillan, the lieutenant governor at the time, was present at the opening and said that it had been 40 years since he first stood on the banks of the Winnipeg River and heard "the roar of its falls." He said the harnessing of the great river was a moment as important as the arrival of the first locomotive in Winnipeg in 1877.

Winnipeggers were no doubt moved by Sir Daniel's words but

what they really wanted to know was how much cheaper power would be than electricity generated in the company's coal-fired power plant on Assiniboine Avenue. The 20 cents per kilowatt hour rate being charged was approximately double the average rate in eastern Canada. They were disappointed to find there would be no immediate reduction in the rate.

Company officials like Sir William Whyte, the western vice president of the CPR and a member of the board of the Street Railway, and Augustus Nanton, the Street Railway Company president, repeated that they did not yet know what prices would be charged but that they would try to keep them low enough that the city would give the company a fair trial. But the *Free Press* felt that the main question "about which citizens are concerned is whether the price will be brought down to a level that will attract industries."

Alderman J.W. Cockburn was a member of a local business group that felt that the construction of a competing City-owned hydro dam was the only way to drive down the Winnipeg Electric rates. In his remarks at the 1906 opening at Pinawa he said that he hoped "at the end of about three years to invite the Directors of the Street Railway to the opening of the city's own power plant." It would actually be five years before the publicly owned dam at Pointe du Bois was in production.

Many businesspeople supported the idea of municipal power as a way to attract manufacturers to Winnipeg. In 1905 three local business leaders were asked their opinion about whether the city should build a municipal power dam. John Stovel, owner of a large printing business, said he favoured a municipal plant. He argued that rates would then be lower. "We in Winnipeg must get lower rents and cheaper power if Winnipeg is to become a manufacturing centre."[79] Stovel said that the Winnipeg Electric company was accommodating toward its customers, but its rates were "much too high," somewhere around $85 per horsepower. The current rate in Toronto was $10 per horsepower and he did not see why Winnipeg could not have power at $15. The extra $5 would cover the cost of bringing power to the city from the Winnipeg River, of higher wages and the higher cost of materials in the west. Large profits would not be necessary if there were no share-holders expecting dividends. He pointed to the success of the City's municipal waterworks as a publicly owned utility.

David Wilson, a partner in the real estate firm of Oldfield, Kirby and Gardner, agreed with the idea of municipal power but thought that it would be wise to import some experts from Britain to share their knowledge and experience. He said that cheap power was a necessity "if Winnipeg is to continue to prosper and be in a position to compete with all comers in manufacturing."

T.J. Bulman, secretary of the Winnipeg Manufacturers Association, told the *Tribune* that "cheap power will be of more importance each coming year." He added, prophetically, that there would be a rude awakening "if the present building boom drops off and there is nothing or very little in the way of manufacturing plants to employ our workmen."

The movement to build a publicly owned hydro utility had begun in 1900 when the City Council had engaged Cecil B. Smith, an Ontario Hydro engineer, to survey the Winnipeg River to look for potential power sites. The City named a Power Committee led by E.D. Martin, a wealthy local pharmaceutical wholesaler, in March 1905. It was chaired by Alderman Cockburn, who had worked for 10 years as an engineer in Ontario and gained some experience during the early development of hydroelectric power there.

Cockburn and Martin both served terms as alderman and from 1907 to 1918 Cockburn was on the city's Board of Control. Thomas Sharpe was another advocate of publicly owned power. Sharpe was a paving contractor and in 1904, mayor of the city.

In 1905 the City once again engaged C.B. Smith to survey pos-sible sites for a hydro dam. Working with city engineer H.N. Ruttan, Smith concluded that the stretch of river at Pointe du Bois, about 27 kilometers upstream from Pinawa, was the best location and issued his report in August. There was, however, a major problem facing the advocates of publicly owned power: the City Charter as it existed did not give Winnipeg City Council the authority to build a dam and sell power.

This problem was partially addressed in August 1905 when the Power Committee met with a number of local businessmen. A Power Association was formed composed of James Ashdown, the hardware magnate; R.T. Riley, President of Canadian Indemnity Insurance; E.L. Drewery, owner of the Redwood Brewery; D.W. Bole, an alderman and partner of D.W. Martin; and Alex Macdonald, a grocery wholesaler. The Association was to take on the task of building a dam and power station for the city in the event that the province failed to amend the City of Winnipeg Act to give the city government the right to do so. The Association would turn over its assets to the city "whenever called upon" to do so if and when the City was given that right.

The proposed amendments to the city charter resulted in a month-long fight during the 1906 session of the Legislature as the Street Railway Company marshaled its supporters to speak against the concept of publicly owned power before the Law Amendments Committee. In the end the necessary changes were passed but victory was not easily won. Prominent people like former premier Hugh John Macdonald supported the company's case and William McKenzie's son Roderick organized an Anti-Public Power League. The company was always a formidable opponent and many Winnipeggers owned stock so it could count on support in the city. But there was also widespread support for cheaper electricity, and this was one battle the company lost. The necessary changes to the City Charter were passed.

Very soon after the amendments became law, in April 1906, Alderman Cockburn proposed a bylaw to create a debt to proceed with the construction of the Pointe du Bois dam. Because it was a money bylaw it needed the approval by the ratepayers—the taxpayers who would pay off the debt. The project was approved in May with overwhelming support—2,000 votes out of 2,300 cast.

Unfortunately, in 1906 there was a panic on the New York stock exchange and banks everywhere grew more cautious in their lending. This was also true in London, where Winnipeg had been selling municipal bonds year after year to finance the growth of the city. In October 1907 James Ashdown, who was mayor that year, visited London and met some of that city's financial leaders to discuss the general situation. He decided that it would be better to wait until spring before placing the Winnipeg bonds on the market. At present, he said, the interest rate was "unnaturally high"[80] and market might well be easier in the spring. Asked what he would do if rates went higher, he answered that Winnipeg might well have to pay the present high rates, although this did not happen.

In spite of the delay in borrowing, work at Pointe du Bois began in the fall of 1906. By 1911 the dam and generating station were completed, along with the infrastructure of railway spur, transmission lines, and substations within the city.

In June 1911, the city established the City Light and Power Department with a general manager who reported directly to Council. John Girdlestone Glassco, an electrical engineer who had worked for power utilities in Montreal, Hamilton and Southern California, was appointed to this post, which he occupied until the 1940s.

At 5 p.m. on October 16, 1911 there was a small ceremony at the Rover Street Substation. Mayor Sanford Evans and members of the City Council were standing in front of the control board with the City Hydro engineers watching the dials as power flowed in from the two big generators 120 kilometers away at Pointe du Bois. The *Free Press* described the scene as Charles Gray, the chief engineer from Canadian Westinghouse read out the voltage—45,000, 50,000, 55,000 volts:

> "That's a full load; the power is all on" he said. Construction engineer Chace said, "now for the lights" and threw a switch that lit six electric globes in the station. "That's your own current" announced Chace. "There you are, gentlemen" exclaimed Mayor

Sanford Evans with a characteristic wave of his arms to show his excitement. The group broke out into three cheers and hats were thrown in the air as Chace, Controller Cockburn and Alderman Cass had their hands shaken by everyone present.

When it opened, Pointe du Bois had five generating turbines producing 20,000 horsepower. In 1917 work was started on the foundations for an extension and by 1921 three new generating units were added to the operation. Demand increased rapidly during the 1920s and by 1926 the dam was fully developed, with 16 turbines producing 105,000 horsepower.

Most importantly, the Street Railway Company had, when construction on Pointe du Bois began, dropped their price from 20 cents to 7.5 cents a kilowatt hour. When the publicly owned dam began to generate power in 1911, City Hydro set their kilowatt hour rate at 3.5 cents and the Company was forced to follow suit. Winnipeg would now enjoy some of the cheapest hydro rates in the country.

Winnipeg houses, apartments and businesses began to wire their premises and connect to the City Hydro. Electric light and appliances like stoves and irons, which had been luxury items, were suddenly within reach of most people in the city.

The Winnipeg Electric Company continued to be profitable in spite of the reduction in the rates it charged. In 1913, for example, it had $9 million in paid up capital stock and $5 million in bonds coming due in 1927 and 1935. In 1913 gross earnings were $4,078,694 compared to $3,765,384 in 1912. After expenses and the payment of over $1 million in dividends, the company had a surplus of $185,461.62 at the end of the year.

In 1913 the board of the company was probably the most powerful group to head up any Winnipeg company. The president was Sir William Mackenzie, one of the owners of the Canadian Northern Railway. William Van Horne, the builder of the CPR was on the board, as was Donald Mann, Mackenzie's partner. Sir Augustus

Nanton, Hugh Sutherland and R.J. Mackenzie, William Mackenzie's son, all of Winnipeg, sat on the board. F. Morton Morse, a Winnipeg hardware wholesaler was the secretary-treasurer of the company. D.B. Hannah was also a board member. He was the third vice president of the Canadian Northern and played a central role in building the railway. For a brief time, he was president of the Canadian National Railway when that company was formed out of the ruins of the Canadian Northern and Grand Trunk lines. Board members also served on the boards of the company's subsidiaries, the Winnipeg, Selkirk and Lake Winnipeg Railway and the Suburban Rapid Transit Company.

The Street Railway owned over 100 miles of track in the city as well as 263 street cars and 27 trailers. The rail system saw a lot of growth in 1913, with 18 miles of new track laid. A third of this was heavy track on concrete foundation laid in asphalt, another nine miles was laid on the surface with gravel ballast. The new track included a line to the new Manitoba Agricultural College in St. Vital. At this time, the company was still building its own cars in its extensive car shops and 1913 saw 40 new, up-to-date streetcars built and put into service.

The company operated a coal gas plant on Palmerston Avenue and delivered gas for heating and cooking to customers through 100 miles of gas mains. In 1913 the gas department laid 86,000 feet of new gas mains under streets and lanes and connected 1,263 new customers to the gas service.

Among other buildings, 1913 saw the construction of a brick battery storage house next to the Mill Street substation. It was equipped with a 6,000-ampere storage battery to store excess electricity for use in emergencies. A new substation was built at the Canada Cement Plant in Fort Whyte with transformers so that power transmitted from the Pinawa hydro dam could be used in the plant. This substation was also connected to the new Agricultural College in Fort Garry so that facility could be provided with power. Contracts were also signed for electric lighting and power in the new CPR shops and roundhouse in North Transcona, and for street railway service in St. Vital and Fort Garry.

The company's subsidiaries were smaller organizations. The Winnipeg, Selkirk and Lake Winnipeg line ended the year with a surplus of $11,296 and a balance in its profit and loss account of $48,205. The Suburban Rapid Transit Company with a line that ran along Portage Road to Headingly and on the south side of the Assiniboine to the city park, ended the year with a deficit of $23,801 and an overall deficit of $67,171.

In 1913 the company began to plan for the construction of a second hydro dam, this time on the Winnipeg River at Great Bonnet Falls, later called Great Falls. In 1913 it was stated that the Pinawa Dam and the power plant on Mill Street were nearing the point where their total output would be needed for the company's operations. They expected the dam at Great Falls would be completed in two years but the coming of the war delayed the project until the early 1920s.

The following year, 1914, the final surplus in the profit and loss account of the Winnipeg Electric Railway Company was $816,309. During the year, seven new miles of track were laid in the city and 20 new streetcars were constructed. Almost all the company's cars had been converted to accommodate the company's new pay-as-you-enter system, which replaced the older method of having a conductor sell tickets to people once they were on the car.

A new line was built to connect the Selkirk line with Stonewall and contracts for providing street lighting in St. Boniface, Stonewall, and the municipalities of Rockwood and Assiniboia were signed.

As usual the company paid the City of Winnipeg 5% of its gross earnings in the city and a $20 tax on each car. The company's exclusive right to provide service in the city would remain in force until at least 1927 when the franchise agreement would either be renewed, or the City would purchase the system.

In 1915 earnings dropped from $1,769,114 to $1,331,737. The Annual Report explained the decline in this way:

The decrease in earnings was due to the general depression following the first winter of the war, coupled with the advent of the jitneys in the spring. The duration of the depression from both causes was thought to be temporary. The excellent crop prospects of the West, followed by an enormous yield, had a stimulating effect upon the business of the company and caused a gradual advance toward normal conditions.

But normal conditions did not return, and the inflation caused by the war began to have a negative effect both on the cost of supplies and demands from staff for wage increases. In 1916 "the serious competition of the jitneys" was blamed for a further decline of $35,742 in net income. The company announced that the best way to deal with its financial situation was to announce that no dividend would be paid for 1916. In 1917 the net income suffered a further decline of $151,621. The Annual Report identified rising prices and wage demands from staff as well as the fact that the "jitney question remains unsettled" as the reasons for the decline. The Board of Directors, however, "believe that the sentiment of the citizens of Winnipeg is favorable to a permanent settlement of the vexed question, and it will be the duty of your Board to endeavor during the present year to so adjust any outstanding differences between the City and the Company that the jitney and other matters may be speedily and satisfactorily arranged to all interests concerned."

The Annual Report ended with a proposition: "if a satisfactory adjustment of the jitney question is reached at an early date, arrangements will be made to carry out certain improvements in the physical properties which have engaged your directors' attention for some time."

Jitneys had first appeared on Winnipeg streets in early 1915 and they were a common sight in many Canadian and American cities. A jitney, explained the *Winnipeg Telegram*: "from a circus term for a 5-cent show, is nothing more nor less than an auto operated by a private owner and carrying passengers for a 5-cent fare in active competition with the street railway."[81]

Many people assumed that the jitney was the next big thing in urban transportation and that they would soon take the place of the streetcar. There was a lot of unemployment in 1915 and going into the jitney business seemed like a good option for men who were out of work. In Winnipeg there were plenty of recent immigrants who decided to buy a car and a $20 license and take to the streets. Model T Fords could be had for $850 and there was beginning to be a second-hand market for more expensive cars.

Taxi companies soon got into the act and A.M. McLeod of the Exchange Taxi Company had a 14-passenger bus built on a Packard chassis and by March 1915 was running on a regular schedule beginning at 8 a.m. from the Maryland Bridge downtown to Portage and Main and back.

Most of the cars were on the streets at rush hours when impatient streetcar customers were most likely to choose a ride home in an automobile, sitting down inside instead of strap hanging on a crowded and poorly heated streetcar. Street Railway manager Wilford Phillips complained that the jitneys worked "the centre of the City to death without going out far into the suburbs the same as the cars of the street railway are obliged to do."

The company tried to fight back with advertising campaigns portraying themselves as a pillar of the community, proof of Winnipeg's solidity and its desirability as a place to live and do business. Its employees were portrayed as exemplary citizens. As the losses continued, the company threatened to claim $1 million in lost revenues from the City, arguing that the licensing of jitneys violated their agreement under their bylaw.

Jitneys did increase the volume of automobile traffic on the streets and there were accidents causing death or injuries to pedestrians. Generally, the political left supported jitneys, saying they provided the competition needed to force the street railway to ensure better service. But the business community began to ask for more regulation of the over 500 jitneys operating in Winnipeg. In 1917 the City passed new regulations requiring, among other things, that those applying for licenses would have to be bonded so that any accidental injuries would be covered by insurance.

In 1918 the company made an offer to the City saying that they would agree to a number of long-standing demands if the jitney business was abolished in Winnipeg. Augustus Nanton, now president of Winnipeg Electric, went to a meeting of the Board of Trade Council to ask for support for this proposal. The Board gave its support and so did City Council. Councillors passed two bylaws: number 9750 to abolish jitneys and number 9757 to embody the promises the company had made. The second bylaw came to be known as the Jitney Agreement by which the company agreed to make a number of improvements and changes to their system that had been asked for by the City Council for some years.

One long-standing issue was the damage caused by electrolysis. Because the street railway tracks were not properly bonded with copper connectors, electric current, instead of flowing in a circuit from the company's power plant to the car and back again often jumped from the rails into the soil. The current then travelled along any metal objects in the ground under the street and caused damage to such things as the city's iron water pipes. Many water pipe breaks resulted in flooded streets. Part of the jitney agreement called for the rails to be bonded and for the company to pay the city a sum of money to repair damage. The matter dragged on for years and in October 1926 council accepted an offer from the company to pay $38,000 by way of settlement.

Another issue was the decrepit state of many streetcars after several years of little or no maintenance. To demonstrate its willingness to upgrade its fleet one of its cars, number 314, was taken out of service and rebuilt at the Fort Rouge car barns. Smaller wheels were fitted to bring the entrances closer to the street level, and new folding steps were installed. The car was parked for four weeks on William Avenue beside City Hall and 50,000 people came to have a look.

■

The renewal of the Winnipeg Electric Company's franchise to oper-ate the street railway system became a major issue in the 1920s. The street railway operated under an agreement signed with the City in 1893 and embodied in Bylaw 543 passed in that year. The agreement stipulated that the City had the option to buy the streetcar company in 35 years, in 1927, if it so chose and an agreement could be reached. If the City did not purchase the system, the franchise would continue with a review every five years.

In 1922 a special committee of Council had been formed to handle the matter of the franchise. The position of the company, as put for-ward by Vice President and General Manager Andrew McLimont in April, was that they wanted a 10-year renewal of the franchise to give the company time to carry out all the repairs and upgrades they had undertaken to complete in various agreements with the city. The Liberal/Conservative majority on Council accepted this proposal but the Independent Labor Party councillors wanted a publicly owned system like the one in Toronto.

The issue was the main one in the 1922 civic election and although the Labor aldermen failed to take over the street railway, their leader, Seymour Farmer, was elected to two terms as mayor.

In the later 1920s, with the economy improving, the need for more hydroelectric power was identified. Winnipeg Hydro was already buying extra power from Winnipeg Electric and had won approval from voters for the construction of a new dam at Slave Falls to supply the expanding demand for electricity. One last power site remained to be developed on the Winnipeg River—Seven Sisters. This was potentially the best of all hydro sites. Passing over seven rapids, the river fell 18 meters, the biggest drop on its entire course. By consoli-dating the rapids into one waterfall, the dam was provided with a flow of water capable of driving turbines that would produce more power than any of the other Winnipeg River dams.

The provincial government had made an application to develop the site but there was controversy over whether the dam should be built by the Province or the Winnipeg Electric Company. Premier Bracken kept his options open, refusing to withdraw the Province's application. He called in J.T. Hogg, an Ontario Hydro Engineer, to write a report with recommendations about the best option for the government. In March 1928 Hogg delivered his report. It concluded that it would not be economically feasible for Manitoba to build the dam.[82] It would be preferable to allow Winnipeg Electric to do the work on the condition that they guarantee a supply of electricity to the province for 30 years at a certain price. Also, the agreement should stipulate that after 30 years the province would have the option of assuming ownership of the facility.

Bracken did not let Winnipeg Electric know that this was what was contained in the report but negotiated with McLimont and the Winnipeg Electric lawyer, Edward Anderson, for the best possible price for the 30-year contract. Bracken, a skilled negotiator, was able to secure a price lower than the best price that had been achieved anywhere in Canada up to that time—$13.80 per horsepower for a 30,000-horsepower contract.

Construction began in 1929 and the first half of the power plant with three turbines was completed in 1931. In 1932 it closed down because of the lack of customers. The rest of the plant was not completed until 1952, when the sixth turbine was installed.

Premier Bracken said the Hogg report had only come to him the day after the Legislature rose in 1928 so it could not be discussed or debated. There was a huge uproar from the opposition parties when he announced his decision to contract with Winnipeg Electric. In the fall of 1928, there was a by-election in Lansdowne constituency and the opposition parties made the Seven Sisters agreement the central election issue.

During the campaign Colonel Taylor, the Conservative leader, charged that Bracken's party had received a donation of $50,000 from Winnipeg Electric in return for letting them build the dam. Taylor got this figure from a Conservative Party supporter who claimed the information came from his brother-in-law, James Coyne, a member of the Winnipeg Electric Board. Coyne denied telling him anything of the sort and the informant confessed to making up the $50,000 figure. Bracken denied the charges and campaigned solely on the favorable deal he had negotiated, carefully laying out its merits at meeting after meeting. On election day the Bracken candidate, Donald McKenzie, won by a slim majority of 200 votes.

Taylor kept calling for a Royal Commission and finally Bracken set one up. The commissioners did not find any wrongdoing. The company refused to have its books audited but testified that Winnipeg Electric had made donations of $3,000 to the Progressives, $3,500 to the Conservatives and $500 to the Liberals.

At the same time, it came to light that William Major, Bracken's Attorney General and William Clubb, his Minister of Public Works, had purchased Winnipeg Electric stock because they were privy to the upcoming deal and expected its value to rise. Major had actually told Conservative member J.T. Haig about the deal before it was made public and Haig offered to get him some stock. Several others bought stock at the time, including the Speaker of the House and even John Queen, who invested $75. Everyone who bought stock claimed to have lost money.

Although Clubb and Major were obliged to resign from Cabinet, there was no long-term damage to the government. After the end of sitting, Bracken re-appointed them.

In January 1929, an article published in *Canadian Finance* traced the extraordinary development of the hydroelectric industry in Canada. In 1901 the whole country produced only 150,000 horsepower. By 1928 the total had risen to 5.1 million hp. The investment paying for all this development was 66.9% Canadian. Of the other

33%, 15% was US, 6.3% was British and 11.8% from a number of other countries, making the industry unusual, given the penetration of American capital into virtually all of Canada's economy.

As the country entered the years of the Great Depression, Winnipeg quickly found itself oversupplied with electrical power. Bonds had been sold and work had commenced on the Seven Sisters power station, but the list of potential customers had begun to shrink.

Winnipeg Electric, 1929–1939

On August 4, 1934, the *Winnipeg Tribune* carried an article by Edward Anderson, now president and general manager of the Winnipeg Electric Company, reviewing the history of the corporation. He wrote that in 1891 an initial investment of $300,000 was made by the partners William Mackenzie and Mann and they began to run electric streetcars on the streets. Since 1892 the company had had an exclusive franchise to operate a street railway. The initial 35-year agreement under city bylaw 543 had expired in 1927 but the City had not exercised its option to buy the system.

He listed all the subsidiaries of the company and the services they provided. He noted the new and modern gasification plant that was providing all the heating and lighting gas used by their customers. He claimed that altogether the company was worth $60 million.

Winnipeg Electric had its own industrial development department dedicated to attracting new enterprise to Winnipeg, using the lure of cheap power. Anderson said that the transportation part of the company employed over 1,000 people who operated 300 streetcars and 50 motor buses.

Anderson then made the arguments for change that he had been talking about for years. He said that the franchise agreement embodied in the bylaw was out of date. In 1892 the company had very little competition, now there were over 20,000 automobiles in Winnipeg. The jitney issue had been solved satisfactorily for Winnipeg Electric, but no one could deny Winnipeggers the right to drive their private cars instead of taking the street railway. In 1893 the street railway had carried 1,111,938 fare-paying passengers. In 1929 the number had risen to 61,238,734 but by 1933 the number had fallen to 57,868,761. A lot of the decrease could likely be attributed to the use of private cars, but in the worst years of the Depression not as many people were going to work or travelling downtown to shop.

Anderson reminded his readers that the company publicly traded, and 244,772 common shares were owned by investors along with $5 million in preferred shares. The company had not paid any dividends until 1900 because the money was needed to invest in building the system. Then from 1900 to 1915 dividends were paid regularly. From 1915 to 1924 there were no dividends, largely because of the damage done to the company by the jitney phenomenon. From 1924 to 1930 there were dividends but since 1931 the company was once again unable to afford it.

The Pinawa Dam, completed in 1906, made the use of the coal-fired steam generation plant on Assiniboine Avenue unnecessary and it was used only as a standby facility in case of interruption of current from Pinawa. A few years later a more efficient steam-powered generating plant was built on Mill Street. Before the outbreak of World War One, work was started on a modern hydroelectric dam at Great Falls on the Winnipeg River. The war caused this project to be shut down, but it was restarted and completed in 1920–1921 and began producing power in 1922. In 1928 the company was contracted to build the dam at Seven Sisters.

The gas subsidiary of the company was described by Anderson. He traced the beginning of the gas business to the company's acquisition of the Manitoba Electric and Gas Light Company and its franchise in 1898. In 1905 the company's facility on Sutherland Avenue had a capacity of 500,000 cubic feet per day. The technology involved burning coal in a vacuum and separating coal gas to use for lighting and fuel. In 1906 there were 45 miles of gas mains carrying gas from the company's plants to individual homes and businesses. A new plant was constructed in 1924 with a capacity of 2.5 million cubic feet per day of water gas, a more efficient heating fuel than the regular coal gas produced by the company's plants. In 1933 the company was producing millions of cubic feet of gas for home heating and refrigeration and commercial and industrial uses.

Anderson summarized the company's situation in 1934. The Pinawa dam was still operating with a capacity of 30,000 horsepower. Great Falls was also generating power with a total capacity of 90,000 horsepower. The Seven Sisters dam would have a capacity of 225,000 horsepower when it was complete. This would not happen until the 1950s. Also, the total capacity of the company's dams would be reduced because in order to produce a flow on the river powerful enough to produce 225,000 horsepower, the original Pinawa dam would have to be taken out of service, reducing the total by 30,000. The City-owned Pointe du Bois dam (105,000 horsepower) and Slave Falls dam (90,000 horsepower) were also functioning by 1934.

During the Depression, relations between the City of Winnipeg and Winnipeg Electric were, as usual, not the best. People wishing to complain about poor streetcar service chose to write irate letters in the newspaper. Anderson was trying to make the case that Winnipeg Electric was in serious financial trouble and needed concessions from the city. In 1930 Anderson argued that the company should not be expected to pay charges like the 5% of gross earnings charge that had been part of the original 1892 agreement between the company and the City. He wanted to be able to raise fares from 5 to 7 cents to cover the costs of operation and to enable the company to survive the effects of falling ridership. City council was always suspicious of these sorts of requests from Winnipeg Electric. They had asked for a complete audit of the company's books to make sure that declining income from the streetcars was not being compensated by other business such as the production of gas.

By spring of 1933 Council gave their response—there was no evidence that the company was in financial difficulties and if that became the case, they would take action. At the company's annual meeting on April 4, 1933, 75 worried shareholders attended, crowding into the boardroom of the Street Railway Chambers on Notre Dame. Anderson tried to calm their fears, saying the City Council had been asked for relief from payments to the city. Expenses had been cut and wages reduced.

Anderson had been trying to make the point that the company was in real financial difficulties since January and on January 28 he said that he was going to ask the Legislature to pass a bill that would serve to relieve the company of some of the obligations it had to the city. In 1931 the company's 5% payment amounted to $136,657.

Rulings of the Public Utilities Board (PUB) added to Anderson's worries. The Manitoba Appeal Court had upheld the PUB decision to make the company pay the whole cost of paving beside the track on the new St. Norbert and Main Street bridges. Paving overall had cost $30,133 in 1931 and the company also paid for snow removal costing $210,000.

The City's response to these points was a request for improved service on the Park Line and other lines. Anderson referred to the schedule to show that cars left on that particular line every three minutes in rush hour. He claimed no improvements were possible because of the heavy burden of taxation.

This is the sort of circular arguments that often went on between the company and the City. In February, the perennial question of selling the company to the city came up. In February 1933 A.J. Nesbitt of Nesbitt Thomson Investment in Montreal, one of the larger shareholders in the company, visited Winnipeg and met with J.G. Glassco, Manager of City Hydro and J.B. Coyne, a member of the Winnipeg Electric board. This led to speculation that the sale of the company was imminent.

It became known at this time that the City Hydro expected to have a deficit of $421,000 for the 1932-33 year. This was in part due to the agreement the city utility had signed with Winnipeg Electric to sell extra power to the city for a period of 10 years to satisfy increasing demand until the Slave Falls dam was complete. Conditions had now changed, and demand for electricity had fallen so Slave Falls, although it was completed, was sitting idle.

A few days later, Anderson appeared before a committee of the legislature asking for a board of arbitration to settle the differences between the company and City Council. He said that the company's creditors were considering receivership for Winnipeg Electric. It was suggested at the meeting that the problem should be referred to the Public Utilities Board.

City Solicitor Jules Prudhomme expressed his suspicion that PUB would simply hand down a decision that "let the company off the hook." Anderson attributed the intense feelings over the issues to the company having been a "political football" in city politics for many years.

The PUB's rulings could be appealed in court, making it an ineffective place to find permanent solutions. When the PUB ordered the company to pay the whole cost of laying streetcar track on the new Main Street and St. Norbert bridges, Winnipeg Electric took the matter to court and this order was upheld. On the other hand, when the city appealed an order of the PUB allowing Winnipeg Electric to discontinue bus service on Manitoba Avenue, the court decided in favour of the company.

Late in February, Mayor Webb told the Board of Trade that he was asking the City Council and Winnipeg Electric to sit down and talk about their problems and find a solution. He summed up the situation, saying that: "The situation today is that both the city and the company are confronted with serious problems. The City is trying to find ways and means of carrying on essential civic services...the company is trying to get relief from its difficulties by having certain civic taxes cancelled."

Instead of negotiating, Council criticized Webb for his Board of Trade speech and created a committee whose assignment was

to counter Winnipeg Electric propaganda. Meanwhile, a Greater
Winnipeg Car Riders Association had been formed to find ways to
improve the streetcar service without additional expenses. After sitting down with Edward Anderson and Winnipeg Electric officials,
they said they would be meeting with the City Council.

Relations between the company and the City Council continued to be bad. Anderson spoke to the Board of Trade at a meeting
at the Marlborough and quoted Alderman Honeyman as saying the
city should begin operating its own buses in order to drive Winnipeg
Electric into bankruptcy, making the company cheaper for the city
to buy. Council carried on the controversy with newspaper ads. On
March 7, an ad placed in the papers asked what Winnipeg Electric
intended to do with money they would save by not having to pay the
5% levy on income. Would they use it to improve service? Or would
they pay dividends and interest payments to their shareholders and
bondholders?

At the beginning of March, the bill that Anderson had asked
for came before the Legislature. It was decided that second reading
would wait until the Public Utilities Board issued its report on the
situation. This report presented two options. First that a Transport
Commission should be formed to take over Winnipeg Electric and its
various subsidiaries and run the new organization. The second option
was to set up a new operating company supervised by the PUB that
would include the Winnipeg Electric Company and its subsidiaries.
The report recommended that no matter which option was chosen,
the 5% payment on gross income should be dropped, paving should
be paid for by the company, and snow removal should be done by
the city, except for sweeping the tracks.

A meeting was called for March 9 at the Civic Auditorium where
four aldermen would present and discuss the options. Anderson liked
the report but all of the aldermen—Gray, McKerchar, Simpson, Flye,
Honeyman—rejected it, no doubt preferring that the city buy and
operate the utility.

The *Tribune* printed an editorial the next day agreeing with the commission model. The whole thing had dragged on too long said the editorial and the city needed a functioning streetcar system. Several meetings then took place in the PUB offices between the two sides, but they were unproductive, with representatives of the city objecting to various proposals. They finally ended in a failure to agree. Mayor Webb remained optimistic and called for the meetings to continue.

The bill was given a six-month hoist in the Legislature on a motion introduced by Ralph Maybank, a former alderman, now an MLA. The Council went on record as being opposed to the Winnipeg Electric bill. The bill to amend the Winnipeg Charter, legislation that was updated each year, included a clause giving the city the power to operate its own public transit system, a provision that was not in the end passed.

In January of 1935, the issue was described as being "still up in the air." It was at this point that local journalist Vernon Thomas report-ed that a reorganization of the company would likely be announced soon. He had learned that the company would seek to reduce its interest payments for a period of years while leaving its capital intact. Winnipeg Electric also hoped to have arrears of interest cancelled. He said that as compensation bondholders were to be offered a number of common shares in the company. In 1935 $5 million worth of Winnipeg Electric bonds were due to mature.

While the City Council was still talking about buying Winnipeg Electric and Aldermen Honeyman and Simpkin went to Toronto and Montreal to talk to the bondholders of the company about a pos-sible sale, Anderson began moving forward with the reorganization. On February 1, 1935 he made a statement about Winnipeg Electric's results for 1934. In response to a report that the company's net income had improved, Anderson explained that what had improved was the income from the sale of gas and electricity. The Street Railway results did not improve, in fact the number of passengers carried dropped once again from 1933 to 1934. He said that the company showed a deficit of $605,444 in 1934, after deducting operating expenses, depreciation, taxes, bond interest and other fixed charges. Anderson said "This is why we are trying to bring about a reorganization so our fixed charges may be reduced to a point where our revenues will be sufficient to pay them.[83]

In essence the plan was to ask bondholders to exchange their investments for new common stock. Holders of existing preferred and common stock would also be offered new stock in exchange for their investments. The company would then be relieved of the obligation of paying the interest charges on close to $40 million in bonds and $6 million in preferred shares. Anderson said that these changes would enable the company to survive the current depression until business conditions improved.

In March, the bill to enable the readjustment of the company's finances passed in the Legislature and then there were a series of meetings with the bond and shareholders of the company and its subsidiaries. By the end of the year the different shareholders groups had all approved the plan. The Public Utilities Board gave its approval in February 1936, the final step in the process. In June it was announced that all the preliminary work for the reorganization was complete and the actual transfers to the new securities would take place in August.

In 1927 the city had made a 10-year contract to buy power from Manitoba Power, a subsidiary of Winnipeg Electric. At the time Slave Falls had not yet been built and the city was not able to meet the growing demand of its customers. In 1935 the city decided to cancel the contract and add capacity to the Slave Falls dam. Anderson and Winnipeg Electric argued it would be cheaper to continue buying power from them. The City Council, however, decided to expand Slave Falls.

The Company's franchise agreement was up for renewal on June 4, 1937—it was now being renewed every five years. Anderson asked for a renegotiation of the agreement with the city and said that the company had plans to spend close to $3 million upgrading the system. There would be more purchases of both gasoline buses and electric trolley buses.

City Council responded by asking Anderson for a detailed plan. By 1939 some changes had been made. Fifteen new trolley buses were operating, and the number of gasoline buses had doubled since 1929, from 40 to 99. Streetcars were not being added—in 1929 there were 314 streetcars in the fleet and by 1939 the number was 250. In 1938 the company paid taxes of $585,764 and employed over 2000 people with a payroll of $2.5 million. In 1938 the company's gross income was $6,584,148, up slightly from the previous year's $6,401,799. The most remarkable change, however, was in the number of passengers carried. In 1929 61,238,734 individual fares were paid and in 1939 the number was 42,000,000.

The gas utility continued to be profitable and demand for cooking, heating and industrial uses continued to rise. There was capacity to produce 2.2 million cubic feet of gas every day. In 1938 the gas production plant at Gladstone and Sutherland was completely overhauled. Many of the gas mains and pipes were dug up and received maintenance. The sale of electricity was also holding its own and the company had considerable potential for new sales with its three underutilized hydro dams.

The war years saw increased ridership because of the presence in the city of large numbers of military personnel. Further additions of new buses and other improvements were impossible because of lack of funds and some retired streetcars were actually brought back into service. With the passage of each year more and more employees volunteered or, later in the war, were conscripted. As a result, a total of 53 women were hired to operate streetcars and around 30 worked in the maintenance shops. In the post-war years, these numbers declined as men came back from the forces. In 1940 Edward Anderson retired as president and W.H. Carter took his place. Carter was a successful builder whose company, Carter, Halls and Aldinger, had managed many large building projects in Winnipeg and across the west in the previous 40 years.

When the war ended, Winnipeg Electric returned to its program of modernization. They put a great deal more money into trolley buses and by the early 1950s 25 had been added to the fleet along with 25 new gas buses. Many of these were manufactured in the 1940s at the new Motor Coach Industries plant at Wellington and Erin at a cost of $13,000 to $16,000. These figures are equivalent to $243,000 to $295,000 in current buying power. Streetcars, the newest of which had been in service for 25 years, the oldest for 39 years, would have cost about $16,000 to replace but there was also the additional cost of repairing and renewing the long-neglected track, an estimated $3 million investment. So more and more older cars were taken out of service and tracks were pulled up.

Toward the end of the war, City Council once again began to press for the purchase of the streetcar and bus system and once again they wanted a bargain. President Carter said that the bondholders and shareholders had to be compensated after taking heavy losses in the 1930s in order to preserve the company. Altogether the company stock was worth $85 million. The City Council said they could not afford that much and asked for a fare reduction.

Carter said that the company could not pay its 5% tax on gross income. The city was also asking for a new license fee of $300 for each trolley bus to repair any damage the big vehicles did to the streets. Carter said the company needed a fare increase in order to pay these charges.

In 1948 the company board of directors approved a $10 million spending program to both complete the Seven Sisters dam by adding two final turbines and to further modernize the transit system. There would be no new borrowing. Instead, funds in the depreciation and deferred maintenance accounts were used. New bonds were, however, issued in order to pay for a refinancing project approved by shareholders. Once again existing securities would be exchanged for others carrying a lower interest rate, thus decreasing the company's annual charges.

The late 1940s was a time of streetcar retirements as route after route was converted to trolley or motor buses. The company struggled on until in October 1952, the Manitoba Hydro Electric Board, later Manitoba Hydro, offered to purchase the electric utility part of Winnipeg Electric, including its hydro dams, on condition that the gas and transit parts of the company were separated and taken over by a new company that could be sold to the city.

This offer was accepted, and the Greater Winnipeg Transit Company was incorporated in February 1953. It operated the transit system until April when the Greater Winnipeg Transit Commission was formed and set out to buy the shares and debentures of Winnipeg Electric. A referendum was held in the city in March and this plan was approved. The purchase took place in May and the Winnipeg Electric Company was no more.

North Star Oil

Oil had been produced in Ontario since 1858 when James Miller Williams, the owner of an asphalt plant in Petrolia, hand dug a well and discovered free-flowing oil. He built Canada's first oil company, pumping the oil from underground, refining it and selling the various products. But the Ontario deposits were not large and by 1880 Canada was importing much of its oil from the US.

The vast Canadian deposits of oil in western Canada under the Western Canadian Sedimentary Basin were not discovered until 1914 when the Turner Valley oil field was first tapped. For a time, it was the biggest oil field in the British Empire. For many years, until 1938 when the Alberta government stepped in, oil companies wasted vast amounts of natural gas in this field by simply burning it off because there was no market for it. This damaged the field by removing the gas that makes it possible to extract oil from deep underground. In 1947 the enormous Leduc field was discovered south of Edmonton and engineers began to realize for the first time the enormous extent of oil reserves under Alberta and Saskatchewan.

A single well had been drilled in Alberta in 1902 but it did not produce for very long. The Winnipeg Oil Company may have used oil from this well and after 1914 the company brought Turner Valley oil to Winnipeg.

C.W. Fillmore, founder and president of North Star Oil until his death in October 1931, had been in Winnipeg since 1902. He was an American, born in Chicago, who had practised law and been a member of the state legislature in Iowa. He had also been president of a private bank.

He was 52 when he came to Winnipeg and in 1903 he founded Winnipeg Oil with an investment of $50,000. At its refinery on Notre Dame, the company produced gasoline and lubricating oil, products that would be in demand for the thousands of new cars that would soon be on the roads. The company also manufactured its own line of oil products under the Rega trademark—sewing machine oil, grease and linseed oil. The plant and warehouse occupied 25 acres and the company had a staff of travelling salesmen who sold products across the prairies.

Fillmore retired from Winnipeg Oil in 1916 when he was 65. He had three children, William who was a lawyer and partner in a distinguished Winnipeg firm; Charles, who owned a farm near Clandeboye; and John, who lived in New York. None of this generation of Fillmores went into the oil business. But the company continued to operate and grow. In January 1921, BA Oil of Toronto, a company operating in eastern Canada, purchased Winnipeg Oil outright in order to expand into the west.

On July 25, 1919 another oil company, North Star Oil, appeared on the scene in Winnipeg. At the same time, it was announced that North Star had purchased the Continental Oil Company, a ten-year-old firm with service branches in Winnipeg and across the west.

North Star's first president was Samuel Messer of Oil City,

Pennsylvania, the largest shareholder and president of Quaker State. By the end of 1921 Messer resigned his post, citing the distance between Winnipeg and home as his reason. The board of North Star then elected one of their members, C.W. Fillmore, as president. T.N. Clayton was vice president and general manager, F.W. Deer was secretary and general sales manager. Deer was born in England and had worked in Ontario for Imperial Oil and Cataract Refining before coming to Winnipeg in 1920 to work for North Star.

North Star purchased oil from the Turner Valley field in Alberta. After 1920 Imperial Oil controlled production from the field through a subsidiary company.

The 1920s were good years to be in the gas business. Not only did the total number of automobiles in Winnipeg increase but the use of gasoline on farms, where at least 30,000 gas tractors had been purchased by the beginning of the decade, created a vast new market for petroleum. Small stationary gas engines were also in use for many farm jobs that had formerly been done by horses.

■

By 1930 the company had 11 filling stations in Winnipeg and 300 service branches across the prairie.[84] The company was declaring regular dividends on its preferred shares and adding to its list of service stations. Not all the applications for new stations were approved. In 1930 they submitted a plan for a station on the southwest corner of Arlington and Westminster. The site was in the middle of a residential neighbourhood and a good many home and apartment owners objected, citing noise and lights and traffic in the evening as reasons they did not want the gas station on that particular corner. The City public safety committee that had to make the decision was informed that there were already 17 filling stations on Portage Avenue between Maryland Street and the subway at Polo Park and the permit was denied.

The company was less profitable in the years of the Depression as the demand for oil products declined. The Annual Report for 1930 showed a decline in net profits from $455,497 in 1929 to $354,187 in 1930. The working capital increased by $76,000 from $269,000 to $345,000. Some of this amount was added to the company reserves.

In May 1931 there was an explosion and fire at the company's refinery on Archibald Street in St. Boniface. The two-storey concrete pump house was completely destroyed, as were the five motors used to move oil into storage. Something caused a spark that resulted in a blast that shook the neighbourhood, breaking windows and blowing the company's fence across Archibald Street. The St. Boniface Fire Department had just acquired chemicals for fighting oil fires and they were able to contain the flames before they threatened the company's large storage tanks. The damage was only partially covered by insurance.

In the fall of 1931 the company president, Charles W. Fillmore, died at his son's farm near Clandeboye.

The results for the 1931 fiscal year saw a net profit of $70,147, down from $345,187 in 1930. Overall sales had dropped 33%, reflecting the crisis in the agricultural community, but business in Winnipeg was about the same as the previous year. Net profits continued to fall: $36,249 in 1932 and $10,919 in 1933. In 1933 sales dropped another 6%. North Star was feeling the effects of competition from two new refineries in Saskatchewan, at Regina (1935) and Moose Jaw (1934).

In 1933 there were a little over a thousand shareholders owning preferred and common shares. About 30% of shares were owned by individual Winnipeggers or Winnipeg firms. In the case of both the common and preferred shares the majority of Winnipeg shareholders owned 100 or fewer shares. Seventy-five Winnipeggers, or about 12% of the total number of shareholders, owned between 100 and 1,000 preferred shares and only seven owned over 1,000 preferred shares. In the case of common shares 26, or 5% of shareholders owned between 100 and 1,000 shares. Only 14 local people owned more than 1,000 common shares. So there were local shareholders but they were vastly outnumbered by individuals and firms in Toronto and other locations.

In 1934 the company began to claim in its advertising that it had helped to build western Canada. A new filling station was under construction at the corner of River Avenue and Osborne Street. In October another fire broke out at the refinery on Archibald Street. St. Boniface Fire Department put it out quickly with a product called Foamite that smothered the flames.

Through all the years of the firm's existence its name appeared in the sports pages more often than the business pages of the newspapers. There was an extensive system of company sports teams in Winnipeg and North Star staff participated in everything from curling to baseball. They were also prominently listed in reports about charity donations. The company continued paying regular dividends to holders of preferred shares.

In spite of poor business results, the company upgraded the refinery in 1935 by installing a new $10,000 still. A still is where crude oil is heated and different products are boiled off at different temperatures. The company service station at Ellice and Colony was sold to B.F. Goodrich and the building was remodelled to serve as a tire service centre. At the same time, a new service station and other buildings were built in Kenora, and new stations were built in Winnipeg at Nairn and Desalaberry and on Marion Street.

North Star began to advertise oil burners for home heating around this time, for sale at a storefront on Fort Street. Sales may have been affected after October 1937 when an oil burner installed in 187 Harvard exploded, blowing the basement door off its hinges and lifting floorboards on the main floor of the house. The lady of the house was on her way to basement to turn the heater off when the blast occurred. Luckily she was not injured. It turned out that a valve between the boiler and the radiator pipes had been left closed by some maintenance men who had been working in the basement.

In 1937 North Star bought the rival Prairie Cities Oil Company for $300,000. Negotiations between North Star and grain merchant H.E. Sellers, the president of Prairie Cities, were carried on in Toronto.

North Star acquired Prairie City warehouses in Winnipeg and 250 oil distribution facilities in Saskatchewan and Alberta. In the later 1930s new stations were acquired and renovations to old stations occurred in each year.

In 1939 the company faced a threat that did not in the end materialize. The provincial government had introduced a bill that would allow municipalities to sell gasoline. John Queen, Mayor of Winnipeg, was a supporter of this legislation. He said that it should be possible to find sources of gasoline outside what he called the "gasoline trust" and reduce the price of gas by 2 to 4 cents.

Oil company executives, including T.N. Clayton of North Star Oil, said they would wait to see what happened before commenting. Clayton, nevertheless, said that it seemed to him that the proposal had not been given much thought.

Another executive said that if the government wanted to lower the price of gas they should remove the 7 cent per gallon gas tax. Imperial Oil responded by lowering the price of gas by one cent a gallon. Filling station owners argued that the scheme would put a lot of stations out of business, resulting in losses of business tax to the government. Another opponent pointed out that the City would have to move gas from tanker cars and store it before moving it by truck to filling stations. The labour costs would eat up any savings. City Council in Winnipeg voted 11 to 4 in favour of the legislation but the scheme came to nothing.

With the coming of the Second World War the company began to prepare for the new situation. On September 12, North Star purchased six acres of land adjacent to its property on Messier Street to provide room for new storage tanks. In spring 1940 they added a new cracking unit at a cost of $300,000 in order to "permit a further and more complete refining of the Turner Valley oil the Company uses in the plant. One result will be the production of gasoline of a higher octane rating."[85] To support the war effort, North Star provided special fuel services to mines in the province.

In mid-1941 the government announced it wished to reduce by half the consumption of gasoline. Filling stations were open shorter hours. T.N. Clayton was reported as saying there was actually very little reduction in wholesale sales in the first few days. The following day he wrote an angry letter to the editor of the *Tribune* saying the paper's reporter had inferred that he did not support a reduction in gas consumption. He maintained that "my opinion is that the public will cooperate as they have in the past and as they have done on every occasion when the government has asked them to."[86]

In October 1941 G.R. Cottrelle, the Dominion Oil Controller, spoke in Winnipeg to an audience of Young Board of Trade members and oil company executives. He talked about demand for petroleum, saying that normally Canada needed 45 million barrels a year but now, with the added use of war industries and the armed forces, the figure was between 60 million and 63 million. So far, he said, they had been able to cut down consumption by the general public enough to supply war requirements, but it might be necessary at some point to introduce rationing, something which did in fact happen. Canada only produced 15% of the petroleum it needed and the rest had to be brought by tanker (74%), by pipeline (22%) or by rail (4%).

North Star continued to open new filling stations and pay dividends. On September 19, 1942 a new oil field at Tabor, Alberta was in production, pumping 200 barrels a day. Much of this oil came to North Star's refinery in Winnipeg.

As the war went on, North Star profits improved. In 1943, net profits for the year were $598,060, an increase over the $507,463 earned in 1942. Net working capital was three times higher at the end of 1943 than a year earlier. Increased demand from the armed forces and war industries explained the financial recovery.

Two men associated with North Star passed away in 1944. T.W. Gwyn had been a board member for many years. He came from Ontario to Winnipeg in 1902 and worked for the Dominion Bank, and as Osler Hammond and Nanton before, he established his own brokerage firm. President and General Manager T.N. Clayton also passed away in 1944, having worked for the firm since its beginnings. G. Chisolm now took over as president and general manager. W.R. McArthur, a long-time employee, became vice president and assistant general manager.

The company began to go in a very different direction. The refinery was greatly expanded in the 1950s and North Star sold debentures to raise several million dollars. The objective was to be able to double output from 4,000 to 8,000 barrels a day. Before the expansion the company was producing enough petroleum to service central and eastern Manitoba and northwest Ontario and they wanted to supply the west as far as the Rockies. Twelve new filling stations were built in 1952 and fifteen more were planned for 1953.

A new issue of debentures was announced in the *Montreal Gazette* to raise $5 million. When the new refinery came on line in 1955 the company's finances improved. In 1957 earnings were $660,000 in the first quarter. The operating profit was $1,365,649 compared to a figure of $808,869 a year before. The company's expansion program had cost $27 million at this point.

In April 1960 Shell Oil issued an offer to buy North Star, offering $34.10 for North Star common shares and $18.85 for preferred shares. The shareholders voted to go ahead with the sale and by May 1961 North Star was a wholly owned subsidiary of Shell. Shell acquired two refineries and the network of service stations in western Canada, making it a national company.

CONCLUSION

The Winnipeg business community, whose origins can be traced to the trading that was conducted by Indigenous people at the Forks centuries ago, began to take shape during the last decades of the Hudson's Bay Company regime in the area that was to become the present city. As we have seen, some of the pre-Confederation free traders who operated businesses while the Hudson's Bay Company still controlled the northwest became partners with the Canadians who began to come to the area after Confederation. By the turn of the last century, the business community became a powerful force in Winnipeg as the Board of Trade worked in tandem with the City Council to build the city. The General Strike really marked the beginning of Labour influence in the city and provincial governments.

Wheat replaced the fur trade beginning in the 1880s and Winnipeg was the centre of the wheat trade, where the Grain Exchange and the various private and cooperative grain companies had their headquarters. Our exploration of the 1920s and 1930s reveals the efforts made to build an industrial component to the city's economy, something that would only pick up after the war.

Our account of the business community ends in 1939 after a difficult decade when the city's major companies, such as Great-West Life and Winnipeg Electric, had to struggle to survive. Survive they did and as the war began there was a sense that the threats and hard times of the Depression were beginning to lift. The war years, while they brought tragedy and loss to the city also gave birth to new enterprises and new jobs. The postwar city would grow and prosper in a manner that can be called miraculous, developing into a very different place than it had been in the first 70 years. Through it all the business community did their best to lead and guide the development, never giving up its practice of thinking big.

ACKNOWLEDGMENTS

This book was written at the urging of Michael Nesbitt, a Winnipeg businessman. He has been a helpful collaborator through the whole process of putting it together. We have had many meetings during which Michael shared his extensive knowledge of the Winnipeg business community with me. He also kindly always supplied me with a cappucino. His support has made the book more interesting and useful.

I owe a lot to the staff at Great Plains Publications. Editor Catharina de Bakker has been patient with me, made many important additions and corrected many mistakes and I thank her. Marketing Director Sam Mackinnon and Gregg Shilliday have also helped me along the way.

As always the help of the staff at the Provincial Archives, especially the guidance offered by Kris Kotecki, has been invaluable.

I am indebted to these people but I would add that any errors or omissions are my responsibility alone.

ENDNOTES

1   Kroker, Sid and Pam Goundry. *A 3000 Year Old Native Campsite and Trade Centre at the Forks.* Winnipeg: The Forks Public Archaeology Association Inc., 1993.

2   Redekop, Bill. *Lake Agassiz: The Rise and Demise of the World's Greatest Lake.* Winnipeg: Heartland Associates, 2005. (p. 112)

3   Sinclair, Niigaan. "New Name for Historic Space" *Winnipeg Free Press,* September 14, 2018.

4   Bliss, Michael. *Northern Enterprise: Five Centuries of Canadian Business,* Toronto: McClelland and Stewart, 1989. (p. 33)

5   Op. Cit., p. 39

6   Bliss, *Northern Enterprise,* op. cit. p. 92.

7   The term Métis originated in the 1500s and referred to people who had both French and Aboriginal parentage. There were also many Scots/Indigenous people in Red River.

8   Coutts, Robert. *The Forks of the Red and Assiniboine: A Thematic History, 1734-1850.* Ottawa: Environment Canada, Parks Service, 1988.

9   Coutts, Robert and Richard Stuart, eds. The Forks and the Battle of Seven Oaks in Manitoba History, Winnipeg: Manitoba Historical Society, 1994.

10 Begg, Alexander, *Ten Years in Winnipeg: A Narration of the Principal Events in the History of the City of Winnipeg from the Year A.D 1870 to the Year A.D. 1879, Inclusive,* 1879. (p. 83)

11 Begg, Alexander, *Ten Years in Winnipeg: A Narration of the Principal Events in the History of the City of Winnipeg from the Year A.D 1870 to the Year A.D. 1879, Inclusive,* 1879. (p. 10)

12 Bumsted, J.M. *Trials and Tribulations: The Red River Settlement and the Emergence of Manitoba 1811-1870.* Winnipeg: Great Plains Publications, 2003. (p 108-109).

13 Ray, Arthur J., "Hudson's Bay Company," *The Canadian Encyclopedia.* Historica Canada, 2009

14 Quoted in Knox, Olive, "Red River Cart Trains", *Manitoba Pageant,* September 1956.

15   Klassen, Henry. "KITTSON, NORMAN WOLFRED," *Dictionary of Canadian Biography*, vol. 11, University of Toronto/Université Laval, 2003, http://www. biographi.ca/en/bio/kittson_norman_wolfred_11E.html.

16   Bumsted, J. M., *Trials and Tribulations: The Red River Settlement and the Emergence of Manitoba*, 1811-1870. Great Plains Publications, 2003, p. 126.

17   Reynolds, George. "The Man Who Created the Corner of Portage and Main," *Manitoba Historical Society Transactions,* Series 3, No. 26, 1969-70. The information about McKenney's store is taken from this article.

18   Lovell Clark, "SCHULTZ, Sir JOHN CHRISTIAN," *Dictionary of Canadian Biography*, vol. 12, University of Toronto/Université Laval, 2003. p. 953.

19   PAC, MG27 ID10, Laird Papers, Charlie N. Bell to Morris, March 23, 1874. Discussed in *Treaty Research Report—Treaty 6,* Indigenous and Northern Affairs Canada, https://www.adnc.gc.ca/ eng.

20   Library and Archives Canada, accessed July 14, 2019, http://collectionscanada. gc.ca/pam_archives/index.php?fuseaction=genitem.displayItem&lang=eng&rec_ nbr=3304565 accessed July 14, 2019.

21   Hall, Norma J., *Red River Métis Farming,*. E-Book 2015, accessed August 9, 2018, https://casualtyofcolonialism.wordpress.com.

22   *Free Press*, March 9, 1882 p. 6

23   Hall, Norma J., *Red River Métis Farming,*. E-Book 2015, accessed August 9, 2018, https://casualtyofcolonialism.wordpress.com.

24   Ray, Arthur. *The Canadian Fur Trade in the Industrial Age.* Toronto: University of Toronto Press, 1990. (p. 41)

25   Martin, Joseph. *Relentless Change: A Casebook for the Study of Canadian Business History*, Toronto: University of Toronto Press, 2010. (p. 43)

26   Martin, Joseph. *Relentless Change: A Casebook for the Study of Canadian Business History*, Toronto: University of Toronto Press, 2010. p. 46

27   Selwood, John. "A Note on the Destruction of Upper Fort Garry," *Manitoba History*, Number 4, 1982.

28   McLeod, Margaret Arnett. "The Company in Winnipeg," *The Beaver*, Outfit 2271, September 1940. (p. 6-11)

29   Burley, David, "Frontier of Opportunity: The Social Organization of Self-Employment in Winnipeg, Manitoba, 1881-1901". *Social History*, Vol. 31, (61), 1998. (p. 2)

30   Begg, Alexander, *Ten Years in Winnipeg: A Narration of the Principal Events in the History of the City of Winnipeg from the Year A.D 1870 to the Year A.D. 1879, Inclusive*, 1879. (p. 110)

31   Begg, Alexander, *Ten Years in Winnipeg: A Narration of the Principal Events in the History of the City of Winnipeg from the Year A.D 1870 to the Year A.D. 1879, Inclusive*, 1879. (p. 59)

32   Begg, Alexander. *Ten Years in Winnipeg: A Narration of the Principal Events in the History of the City of Winnipeg from the Year A.D 1870 to the Year A.D. 1879, Inclusive,* 1879. (p. 143)

33   Begg, Alexander, op. cit. p. 143.

34   Begg, Alexander. *Ten Years in Winnipeg: A Narration of the Principal Events in the History of the City of Winnipeg from the Year A.D 1870 to the Year A.D. 1879, Inclusive,* 1879. (p. 171)

35   See *Manitoba Organizations: Winnipeg Chamber of Commerce,* Manitoba Historical Society website, http://www.mhs.mb.ca/docs/organization/winnipegchamberofcommerce.shtml for a list of the founders.

36   *Manitoba Free Press,* April 8, 1880 p. 2.

37   Creighton, Donald. *John A. Macdonald: The Old Chieftain,* Toronto: Macmillan Company, 1955. (p 478-9)

38   Rostecki, Randy. *The Growth of Winnipeg, 1870-1886.* Winnipeg: University of Manitoba, M.A. Thesis, 1980. (p. 51)

39   Bell, Charles N., "The Great Winnipeg Boom," *Manitoba History,* No. 53, October 2006.

40   Bell, Charles N., op. cit., p.3.

41   Rostecki, op. cit., p. 53.

42   Riley, Robert, *Memoirs,* Winnipeg, 1950. p. 63

43   Fleming, Howard. *Canada's Arctic Outlet: A History of the Hudson Bay Railway,* Greenwood Publishing Group, 1978. (p. 9)

44   Fleming, Op. Cit. p. 9.

45   Fleming, Op. Cit. p. 15.

46   The *Winnipeg Tribune,* March 19, 1926.

47   See the website dollartimes.com.

48   Riley, Robert, *Memoirs,* Winnipeg, 1950.

49   Gibson, Lee and Dale Gibson, "Sir James Aikins' Seamless Web: Finding Fortune and Fame as a Lawyer in the Adolescent Canadian West. *Manitoba Law Journal,* Volume 21, 1991-2. (p. 161)

50   Levine, Allan. *Coming of Age: A History of the Jewish People of Manitoba,* Winnipeg: Heartland Press, 2009. (p 35)

51   *Winnipeg Tribune,* December 21, 1907, p. 17.

52   House of Commons Debates, April 20, 1899.

53   House of Commons Debates, March 13, 1902, column 926.

54   *Winnipeg Tribune,* April 18, 1931, p. 7.

55   *Winnipeg Tribune,* March 16, 1937.

56   The Rowell–Sirois Commission officially known as the Royal Commission on Dominion–Provincial Relations was appointed in 1937 and reported in 1940. During the Depression it became clear that though the provinces were

responsible for matters that required large expenditures—education, health, and welfare—the provinces did not have income to meet these obligations. The Royal Commission recommended that the federal government take over responsibility for unemployment insurance and begin making annual transfer payments to the provinces to equalize their ability to manage their responsibilities.

57 *Canadian Finance*, 1924, p. 297.

58 Bellan, Ruben *Winnipeg First Century: An Economic History*, Winnipeg: Queenston House Publishing, 1978. (p. 73-74).

59 Winnipeg Community Builder, December 1, 1921, 5(58).

60 Hibbits, Bernard. "A Change of Mind: The Supreme Court and the Board of Railway Commissioners, 1903-1929," *University of Toronto Law Journal*, v 41(1), 1991. (p. 96)

61 Berkowski, Gerry. *The Winnipeg Garment Industry, 1900-1955*, Winnipeg: Historic Resources Branch, December 22, 1987 p. 7.

62 Berkowski, Gerry. *The Winnipeg Garment Industry, 1900-1955*. Winnipeg: Historic Resources Branch, December 22, 1987.

63 Kosatski, Tom. "Jews in the Clothing Industry in Winnipeg," *Jewish Life and Times*. Winnipeg: Jewish Historical Society of Western Canada, 1983. (p. 41)

64 Kosatski, op. cit. p. 41.

65 Kosatski, op. cit., p. 42.

66 Giesbrecht, Jodi, "Accommodating Resistance: Unionization, Gender, and Ethnicity in Winnipeg's Garment Industry, 1928-1945," *Urban History Review*, Vol. 36 (1), 2010.

67 Chapter III: the Urban Experience—the worker—the employer, IN *Jewish Life and Times*, Vol. IV, 1993, p. 51.

68 *Report of the Royal Grain Inquiry Commission*, Ottawa: F.A. Acland, 1925.

69 H. S. Patton, *Grain Growers' Cooperation in Western Canada*, New York: AMS Press. 1969. (p. 210)

70 Levine, Allan. "Open Market or 'Orderly Marketing': The Winnipeg Grain Exchange and the Wheat Pools, 1923-1929" *Agricultural History*, 61(2) 1987, 50-71.

71 Anderson, Charles, *Grain: The Entrepreneurs*. Winnipeg: Watson and Dwyer, 1991. (p. 148)

72 Anderson, *Grain*, op. cit. p. 111

73 Ray, Arthur, *The Canadian Fur Trade in the Industrial Age*, University of Toronto Press, 1990 p. 172.

74 Bennet, Richard, *A House of Quality it has Ever Been: A History of the Great West Life Co.* Great West Life Assurance Co., Winnipeg, 1992. p 16.

75 *Winnipeg Tribune*, April 5, 1890, page 2.

76 Bennett, Richard E. *A House of Quality It Has Ever Been*. Canada: The Great-West Life Assurance Company, 1992. (p . 19)

77 Bennett, R. op. cit. p. 55.

78 Quoted in Bennett, R. p. 57.

79 *Winnipeg Tribune*, June 3, 1905, p. 1.

80 *Winnipeg Tribune*, October 21, p. 11.

81 *Winnipeg Telegram*, February 2, 1915, p. 1.

82 *Winnipeg Tribune*, February 1, 1935, p. 16.

83 *Winnipeg Tribune*, February 1, 1935.

84 *Winnipeg Tribune*, February 26, 1939, p. 69.

85 *Winnipeg Tribune*, March 2, 1940.

86 *Winnipeg Tribune*, July 23, 1941, p. 11